The
Apparition
in the Glass

The Apparition in the Glass

CHARLES BROCKDEN BROWN'S

AMERICAN GOTHIC

※

BILL

CHRISTOPHERSEN

THE UNIVERSITY OF GEORGIA PRESS

ATHENS AND LONDON

© 1993 by the University of Georgia Press

Athens, Georgia 30602

All rights reserved

Designed by Betty Palmer McDaniel

Set in 11.50n 13 Garamond Number Three

by Tseng Information Systems, Inc.

Printed and bound by Thomson-Shore, Inc.

The paper in this book meets the guidelines for
permanence and durability of the Committee on
Production Guidelines for Book Longevity of the
Council on Library Resources.

Printed in the United States of America

97 96 95 94 93   C   5   4   3   2   1

Library of Congress Cataloging in Publication Data

Christophersen, Bill.

The apparition in the glass : Charles Brockden Brown's
American gothic / Bill Christophersen.

p. cm.

Includes bibliographical references and index.

ISBN 0–8203–1530–3 (alk. paper)

1. Brown, Charles Brockden, 1771–1810—Criticism and
interpretation.   2. Horror tales, American—History and
criticism.   3. Gothic revival (Literature)—United States.

I. Title.

PS1137.C48 1993

813'.2—dc20   92–39711

British Library Cataloging in Publication Data available

After the Revolution, the colonists,
having resorted to power to throw off whatever power did not
come from themselves, had now to confront the problem of
their own power, coming face to face with themselves and with
the even more demanding problem of self-control. Power was
not only in conflict with liberty, but liberty was in conflict
with virtue. . . . What was now required was not so much
ideology as insight, a new understanding of human
psychology.

JOHN PATRICK DIGGINS,
The Lost Soul of American Politics

Contents

PREFACE

Late-eighteenth-century America, aspiring and insecure republic that it was, needed to see its own picture and hear its own voice. This need for proofs of, if not clues to, its cultural identity and for a sense of independence from Europe that went beyond matters of sovereignty expressed itself in the call for a native literature that rang from book prefaces and magazine articles toward the turn of the century. But what did it mean to write "an American tale," as several fictions of the 1790s were subtitled? For Hugh Henry Brackenridge (*Modern Chivalry,* 1794) it meant political satire employing American folk characters, a frontier setting, and frontier speech and humor. For Jeremy Belknap (*The Foresters: An American Tale,* 1796) it meant historical allegory: his tongue-in-cheek fable limned the "tenanting" of the colonies, their unneighborly rivalries, and their strife with landlord John Bull. For Royall Tyler (*The Algerine Captive,* 1797) it meant a novel of American rather than British manners. His novel deplored slavery and spoofed such regional foibles as dueling and quackery.

For Charles Brockden Brown, author of *Wieland* (1798), *Ormond* (1799), *Arthur Mervyn* (1799–1800), and *Edgar Huntly* (1799), an American tale was something more. *Arthur Mervyn* and *Edgar Huntly* do, of course, present folk characters (native Americans, blacks, rustics), dialects, American settings (plague-haunted Philadelphia, the Pennsylvania wilderness), and social critique. A poker-faced native humor leavens parts of *Arthur Mervyn.* And *Wieland* and *Ormond,* I hope to show, suggest elements of historical allegory. At their most profound level, however, Brown's fictions are American tales because they revolve psychological, philosophical, moral, and sociopolitical dilemmas central to turn-of-the-century America.

To focus on the Americanness of Brown's tales is perhaps to do them injustice as well as justice. Brown, to be sure, was a self-consciously nationalist writer. As editor of the *Monthly Magazine and American Review* he persistently rued our being "content to listen to the music of strangers, without even venturing to fiddle for ourselves,"[1] and as an author he tried to remedy this failing. Yet Brown's four Gothic romances—the subject of this study—are not merely American tales: they are dramas of the soul and psyche first. The truths they tell and the questions they ask about the human heart, the nature of evil, the reliability of the senses, the dubiousness of appearances and of absolutes such as God, virtue, benevolence, truth, reason, and self-knowledge need no anchor in national concerns or character. Brown's fictions could as justifiably be viewed as bridges between the Enlightenment and the Romantic period, or prefaces to symbolism, or "experimental novels" testing various precepts of Western philosophy (indeed, they have been so viewed). Yet because a cultural-historical lens brings aspects of these several themes into focus, and because the American character of Brown's romances, though emphasized by Brown himself in several prefaces, has only recently begun to be probed, I have organized my study around it.

America, to say the obvious, was archly experimental—the result of a Calvinist heritage and a capitalist ethic fertilized by Enlightenment thought and revolutionary impulses, then grafted onto an undomesticated political form. It was no less an exercise in symbolic imagination, its political system hinging on the principle of representation and the largely symbolic concept of the will of the people. And because the temptations and pitfalls that beset any self-regulating body politic—greed, selfishness, hunger for power—are the same that beset the individual, America was also a wide-screen reflection of the human heart. It stands to reason, then, that a writer bent on rendering America might well write romances of an experimental, symbolist, and psychological cast. In short, to consider Brown's fictions from a nationalist perspective need not be to view them narrowly. I don't wish to focus on Brown's nationalism *as opposed to* his philosophical, moral, literary, or psychological concerns, but rather to peer through these concerns, the better to discern the national landscape—and vice versa.

Reading Brown's romances without preconception or ulterior motive, however, will be my priority; only after arriving at a basic reading of the texts will I look to broader contexts. Because one of my secondary goals is to argue that Brown's works are more structured than many critics concede, I will be scrutinizing textual motifs—though not to the exclusion of other forms of criticism. Since my study seeks to set Brown's works in a historical framework, I have included a chapter highlighting key issues and events of the 1790s and tailored to concerns Brown himself voiced about the Republic. And since I wish to upgrade Brown's place in American literature and, at the same time, to more fully ground his perfunctory (some say questionable[2]) title "father of the American novel," I have concluded by viewing Brown's themes against the larger backdrop of the American romance.

My emphasis on Brown's four Gothic novels at the expense of *Alcuin, Stephen Calvert, Clara Howard,* and *Jane Talbot*—and perhaps even my use of the term *Gothic* to characterize these novels—warrants explanation. Brown's four main works combine and transmute elements not only of the Gothic novel, but of the sentimental-domestic novel of analysis and the "novel of ideas" associated with William Godwin, Robert Bage, et al. *Gothic,* however, has the practical advantage of distinguishing *Wieland, Ormond, Arthur Mervyn,* and *Edgar Huntly* from *Clara Howard* and *Jane Talbot,* whereas *sentimental-domestic* does not. More importantly, those qualities in Brown's romances that seem to me most profound and American are their Gothic qualities. Interest in these qualities rather than a wish to survey the whole of Brown's fiction prompts my efforts. While I will draw on his other writings, then, I will limit my scope to those works that highlight my theme, hoping that depth of discussion will make up for a limited breadth.

I wish to express my gratitude to Drs. Robert Bone, Joseph Ridgely, and Sacvan Bercovitch for their encouragement and editorial suggestions when this manuscript was in its larval stage, and to my family for their moral support. A portion of Chapter 3 appeared in a somewhat different form as "Picking Up the Knife: A Psycho-Historical Reading of *Wieland*" in *American Studies* 27 (Spring 1986), and the epilogue to Chapter 4 was previously published as "Charles Brockden Brown's *Ormond:* The Secret Witness as Ironic Motif" in *Modern Language Studies* 10 (Spring 1980).

The
Apparition
in the Glass

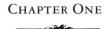

CHAPTER ONE

THE CONDITION
OF OUR COUNTRY

It is the purpose of this work . . . to
exhibit a series of adventures, growing
out of the condition of our country.

CHARLES BROCKDEN BROWN, *Edgar Huntly*

Events of the 1790s shook America's political and social equilibrium as
the booms and busts of the 1830s were to shake her economy. With the
French Revolution seeming, at first, to mirror America's origins, then
turning to lacerate itself, Americans' sympathies were wrenched. As
the decade progressed, political division shaded into faction and grew
with each new British or French provocation, each flexing of Federalist
or Republican muscle. Toussaint L'Ouverture's bloody slave insurrection in nearby St. Domingue added urgency to the already rankling
national debate over slavery. Religious leaders, disturbed by a rising
tide of skepticism, deism, and unchurched college students, called for a
religious awakening, while the president of Yale University went so far
as to conjure the specter of an Illuminist cabal at large in the land.[1] By
midsummer of 1798, with the probability of war with France looming
and John Adams's Alien and Sedition Acts kindling the spark, if not the
fire, of rebellion in Virginia and Kentucky, partisanship and apocalyptic
evangelism must have reflected a range of unspoken doubts: What were
the prospects for the republican City on a Hill we had presumed, against
all political odds, to erect? Would our principles buoy or betray us? Was
our revolutionary heritage a legacy to glory in or guard against? Would
we, like France, self-combust—or, like Britain, consign the fire to the
few for safekeeping?

The country that needed to ask such questions was one whose condition in general, and whose "political system . . . [and] domestic and
social maxims" in particular Charles Brockden Brown engaged to treat
during the last few years of the eighteenth century.[2] Such doubts about

the nation, of course, could scarcely be winnowed from doubts about the broader philosophical premises of the age—America being, as Voltaire among others had suggested, the showcase of the Enlightenment. To question the viability of America was to question the viability of any progressive ideal—was, indeed, to question the sufficiency of reason and the nature of humankind altogether. And if, as Brown seems to have surmised, most people preferred not to ask such questions, then their willful blindness—and, conversely, his own perverse curiosity—demanded scrutiny.

Brown's Gothic fictions undertake these several inquiries. His naive adolescents confronted by evils that are, finally, projections of greater evils within dramatize traumas of self-discovery and denial that make for sophisticated romance. By confounding victim and villain, deconstructing characters' stated motives and employing ironic parallel narratives, these fictions suggest that we are all blind to our inner self—a self that, Brown seems to have feared, may be as depraved as our Calvinist forefathers taught. This vision of self-blindness and universal depravity, expressed most unequivocally in *Edgar Huntly,* heralds lapsarian protagonists from Robert Bird's Nick of the Woods and Hawthorne's Donatello to Melville's Pierre Glendinning and Amasa Delano.

But what gives Brown's fictions epic dimension—and his earliest literary ambitions were epic[3]—are the national dilemmas they mirror: dilemmas involving the ethics of force, the advisability of rigid ideals, the risks of cant and expedience, and the liabilities of ignoring—and likewise of unlocking—the skeletons in our communal closet. Brown saw the young Republic in the same anxious light in which he saw the average man and woman: as a sleepwalking anarchist; a potential psychotic. He recognized the nation's fault-lines: an overconfidence in reason, an inappreciativeness of Enlightenment paradox, an oversusceptibility to dogma (political and philosophical, if not religious), a social system fraught with tensions, and, most pernicious, an unwillingness to scrutinize dark corners of the self. At their most allusive, Brown's fictions about homicidal zealots, Indian-fighting somnambulists, plague carriers, and naive adolescents on the threshold of Gothic experience embody America.

Brown's American avatar Arthur Mervyn twice encounters himself in a mirror. On the first occasion, he beholds a dandy, newly clad in French pantaloons. In the second instance, a "tawny . . . apparition"[4]— a pillaging liveryman whom Arthur has interrupted—leaps, as it were, from the glass to knock him cold. This apparition, a virtual incarnation of plague-ravaged Philadelphia, is both a realistic and surrealistic tour de force. But the "tawny . . . apparition" also suggests an American alter ego, a barbarous counterpart to the gallant, Gallic reflection. Part racial and social nightmare, part revolutionary incubus, part projection of the various violent, self-assertive, and acquisitive impulses that, along with enlightened ideals and rationalist self-constraints, had gone into the making of the nation, it is a stealthy shade, rarely glimpsed, yet denied at peril. At their best, Brown's fictions hold up the glass to this many-layered and parlous cultural self.

America, then, is Brown's subject. His quintessential protagonist, "the Man Unknown to Himself" (as he subtitled the lost *Skywalk,* his first "American tale"), is also the young nation, unaware of its atavistic potential. But Brown's purpose, I believe, in holding up the glass, was less to shock or frighten than to awaken. The image of the sleeper in need of awakening pervades Brown's Gothic fiction (and some of his non-Gothic fiction and nonfiction as well) and becomes the controlling metaphor in *Edgar Huntly.* If the word *awakening* rings with religious overtones, that is not altogether amiss: Brown was writing on the eve of the Second Great Awakening. (I will suggest that *Wieland* reflects, among other things, some of the religious tensions that were straining his society.) But in speaking of Brown in this context, I mean less to invoke the Protestant sense of the word than its broader cultural con-notations. Brown's America needed awakening to the extent it needed to acknowledge various gaps between ideals and experience that had grown too large to ignore.

A society or an individual may sleep, however, precisely to avoid acknowledging such gaps. Brown, at least, suggests as much. Besides identifying a depraved potential in the individual and nation, he also objectifies the ways in which both contrive to hide from their deep selves. Hence a series of related motifs: transformation (of truth into palatable fictions); biloquism (the projection of an altered voice, or ver-sion of self); the writing process—especially forgery (as a metaphor for the mind's self-serving re-creation of reality); blindness (the inability to see our true selves); the "secret witness" (who sees the truth but refuses to acknowledge it); and somnambulism (as a metaphor for func-tioning without self-awareness). Brown's works, in other words, are not only dramas of transformation, of innocence tainted, undone, or unmasked, but studies of the reverse transformation that is the ratio-nalizing process.

In *Wieland* Brown, inverting standard Gothic expectations, articulates a drama of universal depravity and self-discovery with political, historical, and cultural implications. *Ormond* and *Arthur Mervyn* explore alternatives to the verdict of *Wieland*. Neither Constantia Dudley's purblind dedication to principles, however, nor Arthur Mervyn's synthesis of virtue and expedience proves viable. In *Edgar Huntly* Brown deliberately redramatizes the transformation presented in *Wieland*, tracing its source to our most basic instincts—then damns the very act of self-scrutiny as fatal. This final turning aside from inquiry represents not only a general disillusionment but an almost supernatural dread of the artistic process, the tool of inquiry. Brown's self-conscious reflection of the American scene, his skeptical moral vision, his symbolistic approach, and his meditations, within his fiction, on the nature and function of the artistic process make him, I hope to show, a major forerunner of Poe, Hawthorne, and Melville, rather than a minor author.

Charles Brockden Brown was born to Philadelphian Quaker parents in 1771. Classically educated at the Friends Latin School, where he distinguished himself, Brown pursued law, then forsook it for letters. He began writing fiction in the mid-1790s, encouraged (and occasionally chastened) by such friends as Dr. Elihu Hubbard Smith, William Dunlap, and various New York intellectuals in the Friendly Club, and inspired by the radical English novelist and political philosopher William Godwin. A prolific writer, Brown hit full stride toward the turn of the century, but abandoned novel writing in 1801. He went on to edit *The Literary Magazine and American Register* and *The American Register, or General Repository of History, Politics and Science* and, in 1803, authored the first of several anti-Jeffersonian pamphlets. He married in 1804 and remained devoted to letters as an editor, translator, critic, and historian until his death from tuberculosis in 1810.

Brown's life, detailed in several biographies, scarcely requires further recounting. One point, however, may bear reinterpreting. The liberal character of Brown's background has been widely remarked.[5] Brown, whose taste for reading was indulged from childhood by a family who owned books and belonged to Philadelphia's Central Library, familiarized himself while still a youth with the French Encyclopedists and earlier Enlightenment writers. Brown's father was enough of an intellectual to have read the English revolutionary writers William Godwin, Mary Wollstonecraft, and Robert Bage as their works became available, and Brown followed suit. Quakerism, with its ethic of tolerance and its forumlike meetings at which secular and philosophical as well as religious issues of the day were discussed, may well have fostered Brown's developing intellect and curiosity (though he would rebel against Christianity as a young man). Perhaps no other late-eighteenth-century American city could have better encouraged a liberal bent than postrevolutionary Philadelphia, whose French overlay antedated the French and Haitian revolutions of the 1790s that filled its streets with French exiles. How surprising, then, that the young Brown, in a keynote speech to the Belles Lettres Club (1789), should advert, like some seventeenth-century Boston Calvinist, to the "settled depravity of mankind." [6]

The sentiment, of course, may have reflected no more than youthful inconsistency. Or, coming as it did in the midst of an otherwise liberal address, it may have reflected Brown's divided temperament (his letters reveal drastic mood swings, often within the same day). Yet as it happens, the dark allusion comes closer to expressing the spirit of Brown's romances than does any liberal precept or enlightened ethic. Critics of Brown's fiction have only recently begun to confront a similar inconsistency between traditional interpretations of his romances and the evidence of the romances themselves. For generations Brown's fictions were characterized as the works of a radical idealist, an evangelist of Enlightenment thought, a Godwinian disciple who only at last repudiated his radical mentor in *Jane Talbot* (1801).[7] Yet, as scholarship is revealing more and more unanimously, Brown's fictions were far from doctrinaire. From his apprentice piece *Alcuin: A Dialogue* onward, they were dialogues, debates. They tested rather than espoused Godwinism and other ideas of the time.[8] This is as true of *Wieland* and *Ormond* as it is of *Clara Howard* and *Jane Talbot,* Brown's early infatuation with Godwin's *Caleb Williams* notwithstanding. A member of half a dozen societies devoted to enlightened inquiry, Brown (at least until publicly taking up the Federalist banner in 1803)[9] was a quester, not a propagandist.

Brown's liberal Quaker upbringing was, in fact, a two-sided coin. The Friends Latin School that Brown attended until age sixteen was taught by Robert Proud, a Tory who, as Alan Axelrod has suggested, may actually have exerted a conservative influence on Brown. Proud, Axelrod points out, was vehemently opposed to revolutions in general and to the American Revolution in particular, and railed against both in almost biblical terms.[10] Whether or not these diatribes impressed the young Brown, who remained Proud's friend and correspondent for life, the tenets of Quakerism may at least have sensitized him at an early age to the dangers of violence, whether ordained, self-defensive, or politically justified—a theme that pervades his fiction and that haunted Federalist America.

The history of Quaker rule in mid-eighteenth-century Pennsylvania wasn't calculated to magnify the efficacy of liberal ideals in a corrupt world. Daniel J. Boorstin has characterized Pennsylvania's (pacifist) Quaker government as "suicidal," in that it suffered its western settlements to be slaughtered by Indians but refused to fight back or to appropriate money for troops and weapons. He points, furthermore, to trials in which murderers went free because no jury willing to be sworn in could be found among the Quakers, who were conscientiously opposed to oath-taking. The Quakers, Boorstin contends, finally abdicated power (in 1756) because their principles and the practice of politics proved immiscible: "Never has there been a better example of the futility of trying to govern by absolutes, and of the price in self-deception paid by those who try to do so." [11]

Brown, of course, did not personally witness these trials of the previous generation; yet could he have escaped their legacy? His fictions repeatedly concern characters—the fanatic Theodore Wieland, the rationalistic Pleyel, the virtuous Constantia Dudley, the benevolent Edgar Huntly—so wedded to lofty precepts that they are not able to respond appropriately to practical problems. Their dilemmas, indeed, dramatize the dilemmas of Enlightenment philosophy in general. If Quakerism "liberalized" Brown, then perhaps it alerted him as well to the dangers inherent in a liberal ethic.

Even the liberal character of postrevolutionary Philadelphia can be misconstrued. Late-eighteenth-century Philadelphia was a city rich in, but tolerant of, differences: a "meetingplace of divergent and heterogeneous ideas" [12]—not, certainly, a monolithic republican bloc. Politically, it was a city in flux, whose upper-class elite, deposed during the Revolution, jockeyed for a decade or more to regain and consolidate their status. [13] Culturally, it was an ethnic stew—more cosmopolitan and multihued than, for example, Boston. Indeed, the Constitutional Convention, with its diverse constituencies, mirrored in many respects the city that hosted it: More than other cities, Philadelphia was a microcosm of America. Such a milieu, however, must have posed more questions than it provided pat answers.

Brown's progressive milieu, in short, is part fact, part facile fiction; his liberal enthusiasm alternated and, no doubt, coexisted, for the better part of his life, with the skepticism that would finally supplant it. Brown, in other words, was less the incarnation of a liberal zeitgeist than a product of the various tensions—political, religious, philosophical, social—of his time. That may be why we still read him. His romances are anything but tracts. Like the Naturalists' fictions of a century later, they are testing grounds in which characters governed by various imperatives are allowed to develop unhindered. For the Naturalists, the governing imperatives were environmental and biological; for Brown, they were ethical, psychological, historical, and philosophical. Brown was "liberal" in his willingness to entertain the many theories that glittered in the Enlightenment twilight. But he was too much the skeptic to parrot them. His background, like his fiction, suggests a complex, not a simplistic or hortatory, stance toward experience.

Where to begin sketching Brown's America? Ought we to invoke the spirit of the times—a spirit that might tentatively be described as a heady, rationalistic optimism tempered, then traumatized, by a succession of political shocks? Ought we to speak of the industrial and financial revolutions that were transforming the Northeast? of the way cotton was restructuring agriculture in the South? of an ascendant individualism that was making itself felt in everything from the breakdown of the patriarchal family and the relaxation of fornication laws to the burgeoning number of newspapers being published?[14] Ought we to consider the Republic's "peculiar institution"—or the manumissionist sentiment that had begun to surface in public forums? the religious and social tensions that were simmering from New England to the Carolinas, and that were just beginning to find expression under the revival tent? the movement for women's rights and education that crested about the time Brown began writing novels (and whose arguments Brown considered in *Alcuin: A Dialogue*)?

Wherever we begin, what becomes plain is that the nation was undergoing revolutionary changes on all fronts—social, economic, religious, and philosophical as well as political—and that these changes were adding new anxieties to those already nettling the national psyche. Hence, the nation's political vacillation during its first two administrations; hence, the conspiracy fears that surfaced and resurfaced. Brown's America was both a postrevolutionary and a revolutionary society, ionized, as it were, by the changes and uncertainties it was experiencing.

We'll consider some of these changes and uncertainties further as they become relevant to Brown's romances. First, however, it might be worth attending to some of the anxieties that were uppermost in Brown's mind when he surveyed the national landscape in *An Address to the Government . . .* (1803). In this pamphlet, Brown—no longer a novelist but a social commentator—tries to prick the American public and the Jeffersonian administration into seizing Louisiana, which Spain had ceded to France in 1800. To dramatize the threat of a French presence in the West, Brown pretends to have come upon a secret communiqué written by a "French Counsellor of State to the First Consul," advising active deployment of French forces in the Louisiana Territory, because "they whose vicinity to the scene of action puts it most in their power to enact their own safety; whose military force might be most easily assembled and directed to this end, we shall have the least trouble, in dividing, intimidating, and disarming." [15] Brown "publishes" this fictitious document, along with his own tempered ratification of its major points. The device of the French persona permits him to lambaste American manners and morals in the course of his call to arms. (This, indeed, may have been his ulterior motive, considering the extent of his critique.) But more importantly for our purposes, the document sums up what Brown perceived to be America's pressure points:

> This is a nation of pedlars and shopkeepers. Money engrosses all their passions and pursuits. For this they will brave all the dangers of land and water; they will scour the remotest seas and penetrate the rudest nations. Their ruling passion being money, no sense of personal or national dignity must stand in the way of its gratification. These are an easy sacrifice to the lust of gain, and the insults and oppressions of foreigners are cheerfully borne, provided there is a recompense of a pecuniary nature. . . .
>
> They call themselves *free,* yet a fifth of their number are slaves. That proportion of the whole people are ground by a yoke more dreadful and debasing than the predial servitude of Poland and Russia. . . . Devoted to the worst miseries is the nation which harbors in its bosom a foreign race, brought by fraud and rapine from their native land, who are bereaved of all the blessings of humanity; . . . who foster an eternal resentment at oppression, and whose sweetest hour would be that which buried them and their lords in a common and immeasurable ruin. . . .

There is still another rein, however, by which the fury of the States may be held in at pleasure . . . by an enemy placed on their western frontiers. The only aliens and enemies within their borders are not the blacks. They indeed are the most inveterate in their enmity; but the *Indians* are, in many respects, more dangerous inmates. . . .

But the greatest weakness of these States arises from their form of government and condition and habits of the people. Their form of government and the state of the country is a hot-bed for faction and sedition. (37, 39, 42, 44, 45)

Greed, slavery, the Indians, and democratic excess—these are some of the weak spots Brown discerns in America.

Whether the French counsellor has exaggerated or not, he has touched upon several of the Republic's chief paradoxes: the materialistic spirit that underwrote the latter-day City on a Hill; the presence of 700,000 slaves in a land that held it self-evident that all men were created equal; the contrast between a foreign policy of studied neutrality and a domestic policy of de facto genocide toward native Americans; and the extraordinarily self-destructive potential inherent in government by the people. Not that the writer refers to them all as paradoxes: on the contrary, the Indians on the frontier are just so many angry tomahawks to be reckoned with. But for the student of the period—and of Brown—the ironies are essential.

At base, these ironies, like the French counsellor's remarks, suggest a nation more at odds with itself than it realizes, and therefore vulnerable on many fronts. In the pamphlet, the French counsellor—presumably admonishing his native France—says, "It is time to awaken. Should this fatal sleep continue, . . . fortune will have smiled in vain" (18). But the French context, of course, is a fiction. Brown's words are written for and to America, and may be taken as the theme of his pamphlet—and, to a large extent, of his fiction as well. Even a brief glance at the Federalist Era shows the extent to which these paradoxes were foreshortened during the middle and late 1790s.

The rapid growth of the mercantile spirit in late-eighteenth-century America was hardly, as Brown's French counsellor implies, a threat to national security. If anything, the economic strength mercantile capitalism promised was a form of security, however unpleasant the prospect of "a nation of pedlars." Many, though—Brown clearly among them—believed that capitalism was transforming the nation's values, threatening to reduce her conduct to the Old World common denominator of narrow self-interest. In *An Address to the Congress* . . . (1809), Brown, with Jefferson's Embargo Act in mind, chides the nation for "selecting ends with no view but to our profit and aggrandizement": "If a famine rages among [the French or British], we shall hurry, indeed, to their ports, but merely to profit by the high prices which the famine produces. The evil of others is our good. Their sufferings are our enjoyments: gladly do we hear of their calamities, when they can put anything into our purse." [16]

Such protests against the erosion of human values by the money ethic can scarcely be considered apart from Alexander Hamilton's financial programs, the economic agenda that received official expression in 1789–1791. By adopting Hamilton's programs—the federal funding of state war debts, the creation of a National Bank, and the enactment of high tariffs to protect American industry—the federal government radically revised the nation's economic priorities. The colonial economy had derived from agriculture and shipping—in part because England had discouraged, then forbidden, manufacturing. Hamilton's programs, in a sense, brought the industrial revolution to America. His *Report on Manufactures* in particular aligned government with business and financial, rather than agrarian, interests. Historians Rod W. Horton and Herbert W. Edwards stress that, from the moment Hamilton's programs were adopted, the most important battle in American history—that between industrial capitalism and agriculture—had been joined, and its outcome foreshadowed. [17]

This controversy between agriculture and industry involved not just economic, political, and sectional rivalry, but two opposing ways of life and systems of value: one familial, land-oriented, and traditional, the other individualistic, money-oriented, and liberal. Commerce and manufacture, agrarians thought, tended to institute "a world governed by human whim and the fluctuations of the market"; businessmen answered that commerce broke down provincialism, furthered culture and trust, and produced "mutual reciprocal dependencies" that unified national bonds. [18] Whatever the theoretical merits or demerits of a liberal economy, its practical consequences included a ballooning of reckless speculation and shady business ventures as well as rents and bankruptcies that set the tone, in many respects, for urban life during the 1790s and beyond.

If, as Brown and some of his contemporaries feared, the integrity of the United States was being eroded by the money ethic, it had, of course, been compromised from the start by our enslavement of blacks and extermination of native Americans. Officially sanctioned slaveholding is perhaps the innermost of many concentric circles of paradox that justify Richard Chase's characterization of America as a "culture of contradictions."[19] By the time Brown began writing, this canker on the nation's conscience was already throbbing, as the congressional record indicates. Guilt and a growing fear of insurrection—heightened by Toussaint L'Ouverture's revolt that, between 1791 and 1803, claimed the lives of 46,000 whites[20]—led even southern states to discontinue or temporarily proscribe the importation of slaves throughout the 1790s. But the same fear, augmented by economic dependence, prevented America from abolishing slavery. Eli Whitney's invention of the cotton gin (1793), meanwhile, and the consequent burgeoning of the cotton industry, put a cap on prospects for manumission for half a century.

No less self-defining was the United States' conflict with the Indians. In retrospect, both the conflict and its outcome seem, as Alexis de Tocqueville ventured, inevitable.[21] The government's deracination and destruction of the Indians may not have been consciously planned. Hostilities were mutual; compromise solutions failed. Still, the effect of white incursions upon Indian lands squints toward genocide. The pre-Columbian population of what is now the United States has been estimated at one million. By 1800, 600,000 Indians remained; and by 1850, 250,000.[22] "Malnutrition and disease, with the former predisposing to the latter," accounted for much of the decline. Malnutrition resulted, however, from an eroded ecological basis of subsistence, as tribes and nations were driven from their homelands or persuaded to occupy distant, unfamiliar climes. Disease arose, in many cases, from contact with settlers. But massacres were also a factor in the Indians' demise.[23] Such massacres and relocations, generally thought of as nineteenth-century phenomena, were under way well before the turn of the nineteenth century. The forced removal of Indian tribes began in 1784; massacres accompanied the Revolutionary War effort.

During the 1790s, the weight of the newly formed government was thrown against the Indians, and their fate was, in effect, sealed. While

America under Washington pursued peace and neutrality toward Great Britain, France, and Spain, she pursued all-out war with the Indians on her western frontier. This war, which culminated in the Battle of Fallen Timbers in 1794 and the Treaty of Greenville in 1795, accounted for five-sixths of all federal expenses between the years 1790 and 1796 (about $5 million). The Treaty of Greenville gave the Indians $10,000 —and the United States title to the southeastern corner of the Northwest Territory and to the land that now comprises Detroit and Chicago, as well as de facto access to land as far west as the Mississippi River.

Domestic slavery and the Indian wars weren't the only foci of violence during the Federalist Era. Armed response to political frustration was still a tradition, especially (but not exclusively) in the West. Shays's Rebellion in 1786, an armed attack by the western Massachusetts populace on the lawmakers, wasn't the last revolutionary brushfire America was to experience. The year 1794 witnessed the Whiskey Rebellion, an armed insurrection in four counties of western Pennsylvania to protest the federal government's tax on whiskey, a staple of western economy. The rebellion had a broad enough base that when the insurgents threatened to attack Pittsburgh, the town decided to join them rather than fight. The federal government, in response, summoned an army larger than any George Washington had commanded during the Revolutionary War.[24] Likewise, the Virginia and Kentucky Resolutions of 1798, in which Jefferson and Madison articulated a states' rights response to the Adams administration's Alien and Sedition Acts, brought in their wake preparations for war, at least in Virginia. As John Randolph later admitted, Virginia planned to offer armed resistance to federal enforcement of the acts. Although no moment of reckoning arrived, the episode suggests the willingness of Virginia gentlemen as well as western rabble to resort to force as a political solution.[25]

But the chief index to the national temperament in the 1790s—and, arguably, to the American psyche in general—was the French Revolution. That America-inspired revolution, whose amalgam of ideals and atrocities put political choices, for better or worse, at the head of society's agenda, was a glass in which America read her own distorted likeness. The result was a crisis in national identity played out in bipartisan conflict.

John C. Miller summarizes the immediate significance of the French Revolution for America as follows: "The French Revolution became the paramount issue in American politics when, early in 1793, France proclaimed itself a republic, declared war upon Great Britain, and appointed citizen Edmond Genêt minister to the United States. By abolishing the monarchy, France joined the ideological camp of the United States; by going to war with Great Britain, it raised the question of American aid under the Treaty of Alliance of 1778; and by sending Genêt to the United States, it precipitated a crisis in Franco-American relations."[26] Genêt's tactless diplomacy—he presumed, on the strength of the popular response accorded him, to bypass diplomatic channels—so irritated· Americans that when Britain declared war on France, many applauded: "The English declaration of war upon France produced a crisis in America, and sharpened party cleavage. The Federalists went with Great Britain and turned fiercely upon the democratic movement, assailing it with increasing venom. The democrats, on the other hand, became French partisans, and denounced all aristocrats with true Republican fervor, becoming more radical as French Jacobinism developed."[27] Britain and France thus became poles in a debate whose subject, for all intents, was revolutionary democracy.

During the Reign of Terror and the years immediately following (1794–98), a factionalized America vacillated between these two poles. Democratic Societies grew up in response to Citizen Genêt's visit, then declined. Although the clubs were extinct by 1795, they numbered, at one point, about forty, and were perceived by some as a serious political threat. Federalists and old Tories likened them to the Committees of Correspondence that had engineered the Revolution a generation earlier. President Washington himself regarded them as "the most diabolical attempt to destroy the best fabric of human government and happiness that has ever been presented for the acceptance of mankind," and felt that, if not counteracted, they "would shake the government to its foundation."[28]

Meanwhile, a continuing succession of dramas involving Great Britain and France aggravated the country's schizophrenia. America's sympathy for France, which reversed itself following the atrocities of 1793–94, temporarily revived in 1795–96 as a result of British naval depredations and the Federalist administration's policy of concession to Britain: "The heated public discussions provoked by Madison's Commercial Resolutions, Clarke's Non-Intercourse Resolution, and the appointment of John Jay as Minister Extraordinary to Great Britain, set free such a torrent of anti-British feeling that the spirit of republicanism lifted its head with renewed vigor."[29] With America "on the verge of civil war,"[30] John

Jay negotiated a treaty to forestall war with Great Britain over the issue of impressment. Jay's Treaty (1795), however, by effectively renouncing freedom of the seas and allying the United States with England against France, provoked such rage at home that "the people all but rose *en masse*": "Marching mobs, mass meetings, . . . and burning effigies" of John Jay, says one historian, "give no conception of the popular ferment. Never had the people been more agitated or outraged."[31]

The Federalists responded to the resurgence of republicanism by enacting, during the summer of 1798, the Alien and Sedition Acts. These decrees against the importation and propagation of democratic ideas in general, and against the Jeffersonian Republicans in particular, allowed the president to deport aliens and prescribed heavy fines for "those judged guilty of writing, publishing, or speaking anything of 'a false, scandalous, and malicious' nature against the government or any officer of the government."[32] The Sedition Act was used as a political weapon against Republican newspaper editors. The Republicans countered by drafting the Virginia and Kentucky Resolutions, state laws declaring the federal decrees null and void.

Historians stress the "quantity of combustible material ready for the torch" in 1798: "Never before had political passion risen to such heights in America, not even during the early days of the American Revolution; and never before had political ideas taken such hold upon the common people."[33] "The whole people seemed ready to rise up in arms,"[34] notes John Bach McMaster, while Vernon Stauffer records in detail the "reign of terror" that prevailed: "Editors and pamphleteers, statesmen and demagogues, tore at each others' throats as they had never done before and have never done since. . . . Insults and violence were everywhere. Mobs tore down liberty-poles which Federalist hands had erected and put in their place other poles bearing symbols of defiance to 'British faction' and Federalist government; or the action was reversed, with Federalists tearing down the standards of the opposition."[35] Morton Borden sums up the spirit of the times: "One well-placed match might have ignited an insurrectionary blaze which would have gutted the central government."[36]

The final reversal in America's sympathy toward France came in 1798, when France, angered at the Jay Treaty and mistaking the American temper once again, embarked on a policy combining maritime and diplomatic coercion. With war looming, France added insult to injury by demanding money and apologies from the three American envoys sent to negotiate a settlement. This episode—the XYZ Affair—electrified the American public: "The feeling of revulsion in the United States was complete. All innocent delusions were shattered; all veils torn away. What the French government desired was not political sympathy, not commercial cooperation, not a fraternal alliance between two sister republics in order that the flame of liberty might not perish from the earth; what it desired was *money.*" [37]

The deadlocked election of 1800 reflected, I would suggest, a paralysis and indecision that had lain for a decade behind the lurching political pendulum. This paralysis stemmed, perhaps, not only from the high diplomatic stakes, but from the extent to which America's identity and heritage were implicitly on trial. On the one hand, Federalist overreaction prompted fear for basic liberties; on the other, the French Revolution taught America to fear her own heritage of revolutionary idealism. America stood threatened, as it were, by opposite aspects of her national self.

Under Jefferson, America would continue as a "culture of contradictions." Jeffersonian democracy was especially fertile in paradoxes. Jefferson, in purchasing Louisiana, championed a looser construction of the Constitution than any Federalist had dreamed of—and this for reasons of expediency, not principle. Moreover, Jefferson's administration strove with England over New England commercial shipping interests, reestablished the United States Bank, and enacted high protective tariffs—moves Alexander Hamilton would, no doubt, have been proud of.

The nation, in short, resembled an adolescent torn between alternatives, fondly recalling, yet rebuking, her past; discovering, yet denying, her dangerous propensities; looking hopefully but anxiously toward the future. Paradoxes, meanwhile, defined her present. The events that forced these paradoxes to the surface reached a climax of sorts in the years 1798–1800—the years during which Brown wrote the four romances that are the subject of this study.

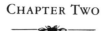

CHAPTER TWO

TOWARD

AN AMERICAN ROMANCE

Literature . . . has a relationship to social and intellectual
history, not as documentation, but as symbolic illumination.

ROBERT E. SPILLER, *The Cycle of American Literature*

Before we turn to the major romances, Brown's method and style call
for introduction. From the few remarks he made on the subject, Brown,
we know, sought to "enchain the attention and ravish the souls of those
who study and reflect." His projected reader was "the man of soaring
passions and intellectual energy."[1] The point, easily obscured by the
melodramatic verbs and participle, is that Brown sought to address not
only the heart but the mind. Emory Elliott enlarges on this ambition:
"In setting these goals Brown was following Beattie and the moral philosophers of the period who argued that the best fiction would affect . . .
the intelligent reader so deeply that he would feel compelled to review
the text carefully to seek answers to the moral issues raised."[2] Such
a theory of fiction counts on readers' actively engaging the text, not
merely basking in its sentimentalism or horror.

Brown also wished, we know, to write a national literature tracing
"the influence of public events on the character and happiness of individuals."[3] This suggests Brown perceived a close relationship between
history and art—an inference corroborated by various magazine pieces
and minor fictions he wrote. *Alcuin: A Dialogue,* Brown's first published book, begins in earnest with the question, "Pray, Madam, are you
a federalist?"[4] The conversation that ensues between the young male
protagonist and his hostess covers a range of social and political topics of importance to Federalist America, including women's rights and
the legitimacy of the exclusive office-holding and suffrage requirements
adopted by the new republic. Brown's two short stories "Thessalo-
nica" and "The Death of Cicero," moreover, fictionalize key moments
in classical history, and his sketches ("Sketches of the History of Carsol"

and "The History of the Carrils and Ormes") blend historical fact with fiction at great length. "National songs," Brown wrote in a letter to William Dunlap (November 28, 1794), "strains which have a particular relation to the political or religious transactions of the poet's country, seem to be the most precious morcels."[5] Brown's favorite poets and authors included Homer and Vergil, the continental satirists Scuderi and Marivaux, and the English "novelists of purpose"—Bage, Holcroft, Wollstonecraft, and Godwin: writers who mythologized history or made sociopolitical themes the subject of their fiction.

Brown himself attempted, in 1794, to write an epic poem on America (he had planned several). Epic ambitions may have colored his major fictions, all of which tend to feature a society under siege by an ineluctable evil. Distinguishing between his complementary literary interests, romance and history, Brown, in an essay published in his *Monthly Magazine and American Review,* remarked: "The observer or experimentalist . . . who carefully watches, and faithfully enumerates the appearances which occur, may claim the appellation of *historian.* He who adorns these appearances with cause and effect, and traces resemblances between the past, distant and future, with the present, performs a different part. He is a dealer, not in certainties, but in probabilities, and is therefore a *romancer.*" "The writer," he concludes, "who does not blend the two characters is essentially defective."[6] We might rightly expect, then, an interplay between "public events," historical themes, "political and religious transactions," and fictional concerns in Brown's romances. A look at two of his early efforts provides a glimpse into the ways in which fiction and history interact in his tales.

THE MAN AT HOME

In the months prior to writing *Wieland,* Brown completed two apprentice works intended to portray "American life and native scenes."[7] Publication of the first—the novel *Skywalk,* written during the last six months of 1797—was aborted following the publisher's death in the summer of 1798.[8] The second, entitled *The Man at Home,* appeared in installments in *The Weekly Magazine* during February, March, and April of 1798. Scarcely a novel itself,[9] the work nevertheless affords a bridge to Brown's major novels and a glimpse into his gestating technique.

Considering Brown's announced intent, this fiction seems, at first, surprisingly indifferent to the American scene. Except for its plague episodes, modeled on Philadelphia's yellow fever epidemic of 1793, the story could be set almost anywhere. *The Man at Home* is the disjointed narrative of a formerly well-to-do merchant who has gone into hiding because a friend whose debts he underwrote has defaulted. Variously characterized by critics as a tale of lofty crime set against the backdrop of a city in the grips of pestilence and a backhanded meditation on the wisdom of imprisoning debtors,[10] the narrative meanders far afield from any one concern, its negligible story line clouded by digressions on broomsticks, sailors' jargon, and the like. But at the edge of this rambling facade hovers the ghost of a theme.

To beguile his days, the narrator, Bedloe, in what is only the first of many echoes of Godwin's *Caleb Williams* in Brown's fictions, muses over the contents of a locked chest bolted to the floor of his chamber. Finally—and this is the climax of the piece, if it may be said to have one—curiosity prompts him to force the box open with an ax. The box looks empty, but further chopping discloses a false bottom. Concealed within is a manuscript that "unfolds the causes and exhibits the agents in a transaction of high importance in the American Revolution." [11]

"What event . . . so memorable," rhapsodizes the narrator, "as the disruption of Britain from the American colonies? How worthy and wise to investigate the causes that gave birth, and conducted to a prosperous issue, that revolution" (68). Revolution in general—and the American Revolution in particular—crops up throughout *The Man at Home,* the word itself ringing like a tripped siren.[12] The present owner of the narrator's cottage, we learn, came to America with a man whose son had fought and died in the American Revolution. De Moivre, a former tenant of the same cottage, had been an exiled French Revolutionary. He had lost an estate, moreover, in the St. Domingue insurrection. And when Miss De Moivre, on the narrator's advice, considers writing her memoirs and wonders what to record, the narrator urges her to "relate the dawning of the French alliance with the revolted colonies of England" (74), as if no better subject could be conceived.

Robert S. Levine, echoing Ronald Paulson, has ventured that revolutionary anxieties and impulses inform a number of late-eighteenth-century literary texts that don't, on the surface, seem to be about revolution. He notes, for instance, that *Caleb Williams* (1794)—the story of a young man who, after accidentally discovering his rich employer's murderous past, is persecuted ruthlessly, yet lives to turn the tables—"enacts some of the key truths and images of the French Revolution:

inversion, violence, unpredictability." [13] Likewise, *The Man at Home* may be said to sketch an implicitly revolutionary world in which abrupt change—economic as well as social—is liable to overturn a person's life at any time. (The commercial world of liens and debts and defaults by which Bedloe is undone *was*, of course, the product of a financial revolution in America.) The prospect of debtor's prison, moreover, testifies to the violence underpinning this treacherous world.

Various incidentals of Bedloe's narrative, however—particularly his allusion to the dawning of the alliance between the colonies and France—suggest an even more explicit concern on Brown's part with revolution, and prompt us to wonder whether *The Man at Home* might itself be a box with a false bottom, whose banal exterior camouflages an essentially American tale. Concerning the manuscript he discovers in the trunk's bottom, Bedloe says, "It has all the circumstantial and picturesque minuteness of a romance. . . . It is a sort of picture of the age at that period, and displays remarkable features in the condition of France, England and America" (69). Might the same be said of *The Man at Home?*

Consider as a historical fable this tale of one who contracts a debt whose implications he fails to discern. Had not America, in revolting against Great Britain, incurred such a debt to France—a debt that was to become, by the 1790s, an unexpected embarrassment, a commitment to be evaded? The Treaty of Alliance (1778) had constituted a formal agreement on our part to aid France in the future, in return for her immediate assistance—a commitment France had fulfilled. When France declared war on Britain in 1793 and called upon us to fulfill our pledge, however, we demurred in the face of the political dilemmas the summons entailed.

And of course America's debt to France, broadly considered, went far beyond the scope of the Treaty of Alliance. It included a philosophical heritage, a literature of Enlightenment, a vocabulary of natural rights and sovereignty—the makings, in short, of an ideology that, when joined with elements of our English heritage, had enabled us to undertake a revolution. No sooner had we set up our republic, however, than these revolutionary founding principles—indited, perhaps, without our fully appreciating their long-range implications—began, in turn, to cramp our conduct in the postrevolutionary era. In this respect, couldn't our plight be said to resemble that of Brown's Man at Home, whose task, in light of what he terms the "revolution" his fortunes have undergone, is to examine for the first time the wisdom of first principles and the meaning of an unforeseen confinement?

One further aspect of this work hints at a nationalist political focus. Keeping in mind that 1793 was the year during which the Reign of Terror in France drove America to the brink of faction, consider one Harrington's reaction to the narrator's bloody tale of faction in an "ancient republic" (81) and his blithe gratitude that "destiny had reserved us for a milder system of manners": " 'Not so fast,' said Harrington. 'You forget that the very city of which we are inhabitants [Philadelphia], no longer ago than 1793, suffered evils, considerably parallel to those that are here described. In some respects, the resemblance is manifest and exact' " (84). Harrington, we soon discover, is referring to Philadelphia's yellow fever epidemic, not to the factionalization that was rending its precincts. But his monologue, which ranges to "the evils which infest human society" (84), explicitly compares factional warfare to the plague. Brown, then, seems to suggest that faction is a "disease" endemic to republics. (No sooner, however, do we begin to conceive of the plague as a political metaphor than Brown introduces the character Wallace, who asserts that he is, of all things, "indebted to the yellow fever." It had, he remarks, forced him out of business; but in relocating, he had met the woman he has since married—"a young lady, who added three hundred pounds a year, to youth, beauty and virtue" [85].)

What, if anything, can we conclude from such a work? Perhaps only that Brown was ambivalent about the republic he inhabited and the revolutions that had shaped his world. Still, he seems to be groping, albeit haltingly, toward a fiction that would examine the "condition of our country"—from its naive generosity of spirit to its emerging ethics to its volatile economic system and political heritage to its apparent unconcern that any of these could confine as well as liberate. He seems, moreover, to see America's past as a "romance" that needed to be retrieved, reread, and reimagined if her present were to be fathomed. Given the diffuseness of *The Man at Home*, such inferences must remain conjectures. But in *Ormond* and *Arthur Mervyn*, Brown would indeed employ a yellow fever plague to suggest, among other things, political and social upheaval. Versions of the Man-at-Home parable recur, moreover, in *Wieland*, *Ormond*, *Arthur Mervyn*, and *Edgar Huntly*, all of which feature naive protagonists who undergo "revolutions" and confinements of one sort or another. In *Ormond* Brown scrutinizes an unexpected confinement brought about by an unexamined ethic. *Arthur Mervyn* examines whether self-concealment (in the broadest sense of the term: concealment of one's motives from others and even from oneself) offers a viable solution to postrevolutionary ethical enigmas. *Edgar Huntly* investigates the mythic and transforming consequences, social as well as psychological, of "opening the box." Even *Wieland,* despite its insular, familial locus, presents "a picture of the age at that period" and displays (I will suggest) "remarkable features in the condition of France, England and America" (69).

Brown's art, then—and perhaps this is one more lesson of *The Man at Home*—tends toward the symbolic. His fictions, as the recurring image of the locked trunk reiterates, are often boxes whose secret springs and false bottoms must be discerned; whose exteriors must be probed and reexamined in light of their guarded contents. These contents are not always social or political meditations; often, however, they are precisely that—America's "political systems . . . and social maxims" being Brown's self-declared subject. Proving symbolic associations is of course difficult. Robert E. Spiller has written, in words that apply especially to Brown's tales, "Literature . . . has a relationship to social and intellectual history, not as documentation, but as symbolic illumination." [14] To appreciate Brown's tales, we must engage correspondences, both historical and textual, the better to coax Brown's illuminations into view. That is, we must read his tales with imagination and enterprise—else they remain intriguing but empty (or merely cluttered) boxes.

I have introduced *The Man at Home* not only because its image of an apparently empty chest concealing an American romance seems to me to offer a clue to Brown's fictions, but also because I wish to suggest by the very tentative critique above some of the difficulties Brown's style and technique present. Brown is, for instance, an apostle of indirection. Understanding his work often involves scrutinizing circumstantial details and digressions (the story of "faction in an ancient republic," which in *The Man at Home* seems hopelessly peripheral to Bedloe's plight). Brown, I will suggest, employed digressions deliberately, if promiscuously; to do him justice, we must examine them. So too Brown's symbolic motifs—the locked box, the yellow fever plague—and his idiosyncratic rhetoric (the repeated use of the word "revolution" in *The Man at Home*). But at the same time that we attend to the minutiae of these tales, we must also be willing to consider them as fables, strip-

ping away circumstantial gratuities—and sometimes the author's or
narrator's purported intent—and retrieving their cultural contexts.

MEMOIRS OF CARWIN, THE BILOQUIST

One other minor fiction—*Memoirs of Carwin, the Biloquist*—warrants
mention before we turn to Brown's major romances. This fragment,
in which the character whose mischief catalyzes the chaos of *Wieland*
narrates his early history, was the last piece of fiction Brown published
(he used it as filler for *The Literary Review,* where it ran from November
1803 to May 1804, then in three further installments—July 1804 and
February and March 1805). Its first sequences, though, were completed
just before the publication of *Wieland,* according to Brown's letter to
William Dunlap, dated September 5, 1798. Fred Lewis Pattee reason-
ably suggests that Brown originally intended these sequences to form a
part of *Wieland*—Carwin's portion of the story—but that the narrative
ranged too far afield, and was therefore detached and developed sepa-
rately.[15] Its opening sequence, however, makes *Carwin* less remarkable
as a footnote to *Wieland* than as a prelude to Brown's oeuvre.

Memoirs of Carwin, the Biloquist recounts the narrator's childhood,
spent in the thrall of a cruel father; his discovery and mastery of the art
of ventriloquism ("biloquism"); his removal from his father's house to
an aunt's house in Philadelphia; his aunt's death; his ensuing friendship
with a rationalistic benefactor named Ludloe; his removal, as Ludloe's
guest, to Ireland; his subsequent journey to Spain; and the first phase
of his induction, under Ludloe's tutelage, into a secret European society
modeled on the Illuminati. In its relatively short compass, the narrative
raises several themes that recur in Brown's major works: the gradual
declension of venial habits (Carwin's imposture, for instance) into vices;
the dilemma of concealment vs. revelation (Carwin's quandary concerning whether or not to confess his biloquism)—a dilemma that will
acquire significance in *Arthur Mervyn* and *Edgar Huntly;* and the question, so pertinent to *Wieland,* of God's existence and agency in human
affairs.

The crux of *Carwin,* however—and, one suspects, Brown's main
reason for writing the piece—is the sequence culminating in Carwin's
abortive attempt, after developing biloquial abilities, to perpetrate a
hoax on his overbearing father. A parable of Enlightenment rebellion

masquerading as an adolescent prank, this episode serves as backdrop to a range of concerns Brown's other works will develop.

Carwin's father is a tyrant. Superstitious, anti-intellectual, Calvinistic (at least to the extent that he declaims his son's "incorrigible depravity" [276]), and cruel, he is everything the modern age defined itself against. He beats his book-loving son for reading and destroys his books. He enforces with "stripes" and "ignominious penances" a tedious regimen of farm duties. He considers all but the most basic education "useless or pernicious" (276). Carwin, by contrast, reveres knowledge and literature, detests the drudgery of farm life, and, by age fourteen, longs to be free of his churlish father. The perfect opportunity presents itself when his widowed aunt, who lives in the city, pleads to take him into her custody, offering to pay for his education and to bequeath him her slender patrimony. But Carwin's father, afraid his son will thereby inherit money he himself aspires to inherit, vetoes the proposal. So Carwin conceives a ruse. Knowing how superstitious his father is, he resolves to steal into his father's bedroom at night and, using biloquism, to feign the voice of his dead mother enjoining compliance with the aunt's request.

Given that Carwin chooses a violently stormy night as the most effective time to enact this plan, it's no wonder his enterprise takes on a Gothic air. Even granting the narrator's impressionability and theatrical flair, however, the portentous tone and language in which he casts the episode seem out of proportion with what he is ostensibly describing. The Gothic motifs combined with a rhetoric and imagery redolent of *Macbeth* suggest a truly sinister crime: "I could not divest myself of secret dread. My heart faultered with a consciousness of wrong. Heaven seemed to be present and to disapprove of my work; I listened to the thunder and the wind, as to the stern voice of this disapprobation. Big drops stood on my forehead, and my tremors almost incapacitated me from proceeding. . . . I crept up stairs, at midnight, and entered my father's chamber. The darkness was intense, and I sought with outstretched hands for his bed" (285). Carwin is presumably planning to hide at the foot of his father's bed (though why he must get so close is a mystery, considering that he has been honing his talent among the cliffs and canyons); but a flash of lightning shows he has become disoriented: "The brightness of the gleam was dazzling, yet it afforded me an exact knowledge of my situation. I had mistaken my way . . . my hands at the next step, would have touched my father's cheek" (285–86). David Lyttle has rightly identified the oedipal character of the episode.[16] We can't help suspecting that Carwin's subconscious intent, as he creeps up to his father's bed with outstretched hands, is to strangle the tyrant who has thwarted his hopes and made his life hellish.

But if the power of the scene stems largely from its Freudian overtones, surely its significance stems, at least in part, from its cultural context. Jay Fliegelman, in *Prodigals and Pilgrims: The American Revolution against Patriarchal Authority,* traces eighteenth-century America's repudiation of a range of established social forms. Religious awakenings, revised conceptions of God, economic liberalism, the War for Independence—all, says Fliegelman, resulted from and reflected a fundamental change of attitude toward authority: a change that emerged first in the household. As the doctrine of innate depravity waned and John Locke's environmental psychology gained currency, parents, Fliegelman suggests, came to view their children less as imps whose wills needed to be broken than as charges who matured in stages, whose characters were formed by their experiences, and who needed to be taught to think for themselves, to judge right from wrong. Affection and enlightened example therefore replaced blind authority and filial duty as child-rearing principles, and the son who, upon maturing, left the family hearth was no longer considered as "unnatural" as the father who sought to keep him back. This revised conception of authority called into question not only the traditional parent-child relationship, Fliegelman remarks, but also that of subjects to magistrates, of the American colonies to the parent-nation, and of man to God. Thus the colonies characterized their revolt against England as the just response of sons of liberty to an unnatural, tyrannical parent. Likewise, the "new light" preachers of the First Great Awakening, Fliegelman suggests, transformed the Old Testament Jehovah of their forebears into a less oppressive, more solicitous Father.[17] William G. McLoughlin, who traces the same phenomenon, enlarges on how pervasive the patriarchal mindset was in American life: "In New England the selectmen who ruled over the towns were called 'the town fathers'; the pastor was a father to his parish; the colonial magistrates were described as 'nursing fathers to the church' and fathers of the colony; the king was a 'father to his loyal subjects.' When dissenters in New England were brought to court for breaking the laws of the church or state, they were told they had dishonored the Fifth Commandment: 'Honor thy father and thy mother.' Lawgiving and law-enforcing officials were father surrogates and viceregents of God, who had 'ordained the powers that be.'"[18] This is the cultural-historical ground against which *Carwin* resonates.

The veiled drama of patricide in *Carwin* conjures this eighteenth-century context, and with it the constellation of repressive elements that made revolt against the patriarchal order inevitable: unreasonable and absolute exercise of authority; unwillingness, on the part of those in authority, to accept (let alone foster) maturity and independence among sons, subjects, parishioners; and a dim, demoralizing view of human worth. The young Carwin's determination, in the face of such a stifling universe, to think and, even more, to *speak* for himself—for his biloquism is at its simplest a finding of his voice[19]—makes him a subversive. But when that same youth approaches his father's bedside with hands outstretched, ready to play God and wrest control of his fate, he becomes something more: the prototypical American revolutionary. Brown's Gothic romances, on the whole, I shall argue, are *post*revolutionary fictions about the dangers of freedom, individualism, rationalism, and self-assertion. But *Carwin* evokes that prior trauma of rebellion toward which the other works cast, as it were, repeated backward glances.

And trauma it was. The bolt of lightning that apprises Carwin of his "situation" not only recalls him from his purpose, but sets the barn ablaze—suggesting to the young rebel that God still reigns (and, no doubt, that trifling with fathers amounts to playing with fire). Overwhelmed with guilt and awe, Carwin awakens his father to the imminent danger. No hand stays the bolt, however, that blasts the superstitious patriarch of *Wieland,* a book that, despite depicting a world in which rational, enlightened values have presumably triumphed, begins amid the same acrid whiff of smoke and ozone.

CHAPTER THREE

WIELAND:

DOMESTIC DEPRAVITY AND

THE EXTRAORDINARY SILENCE

In the murder of a brother . . . every
form of guilt is comprehended.

CICERO, *Pro Cluentio*

Wieland, or The Transformation: An American Tale traces the demoraliza-
tion and demise of an enlightened household in prerevolutionary Pennsylvania.[1] Based (Alexander Cowie suggests) on accounts of a religiously
inspired mass homicide that took place near Tomhanick, New York,
in 1781,[2] it raises into relief the alternate possibilities of divine intervention in human affairs and demonic perversion in the human heart.
The mystic Theodore Wieland, confounded by unexplained voices and
haunted by the memory of his devout father's mysterious death, possibly from spontaneous combustion, butchers his wife and children in
deference to what he believes is a divine command. He is apprehended,
tried, and imprisoned, but escapes, intent on completing the sacrifice he believes God has required him to perform by slaughtering his
sister, Clara.

The eighteen-year-old Clara, meanwhile, narrates this story in which
her own encounters with inscrutable voices have already involved her.
These voices—counterfeited, we later learn, by a ventriloquist named
Carwin—not only disrupt Clara's romance with Henry Pleyel, but
threaten her sanity. Clara is convinced Carwin is to blame for her
brother's atrocities. But Carwin, while confessing to having counterfeited voices on several other occasions, denies having prompted Wieland's savagery. When the crazed Wieland escapes a third time, accosts
Clara, and announces that she too must die by his hand, Carwin, by
counterfeiting a divine rebuke, saves Clara's life. Wieland commits suicide; Clara suffers a nervous breakdown. During her convalescence, she

is almost burned to death when her house catches fire, but an anonymous stranger—Carwin, quite possibly—rescues her. We learn from a postscript written three years later that Clara and Pleyel not only become reconciled, but marry and start life anew in Europe, each having fled America and the traumatic memories it holds.

As Larzer Ziff pointed out a generation ago, *Wieland* less expounds than queries the doctrines and philosophies of its time. Clearly religious revelation is suspect: Wieland's lunacy in murdering his family is self-evident. Lockean sensationalist psychology too comes under attack: Pleyel, despite an intimate knowledge of Clara's character, concludes from the evidence of his ears that she has deceived him; Clara is duped repeatedly by counterfeit voices. Rationalism itself is called into question: reason is shown to be insufficient in mediating sensory perception. Pleyel errs not only because his senses deceive him, but also because he draws certain eminently logical deductions that later prove false. But Ziff also noted a darker strain in *Wieland* than had previously been articulated—a strain that goes beyond philosophical skepticism: " 'Depraved' is the key word. . . . Besides the delusion of the senses . . . there is, ultimately, a depravity of the senses." What is the nature of this depravity? Ziff doesn't specify. He does intimate, however, that in *Wieland* "the virtue of maidenly reserve and the vice of masculine lasciviousness are child's play compared with the real horrors of life."[3]

Critics since Ziff have stressed Clara's importance and suggested, either implicitly or explicitly, that she too is transformed. But these discussions, however illuminating, haven't sufficiently described her transformation or traced its implications.[4] The discussion that follows builds on Larzer Ziff's intuition of inherent depravity by tracing Clara's transformation into a "creature of nameless and fearful attributes" (180). It further suggests that Clara's traumas and discoveries reflect the nation's; that *Wieland* is rooted in the combustible political and social atmosphere of the late 1790s. Finally it examines both the legacy of silence and "moral night" that succeeds Brown's revelation of universal depravity, and its corollary: the author's ambiguous role as creator and contriver, truth-teller and soothsayer in an ominously silent universe.

THE QUIET TRANSFORMATION

Wieland seems structured to culminate in Theodore Wieland's derangement. Yet even after delivering his lucid and detailed confession, Wie-

land remains inscrutable. His mystical mayhem dramatizes the dubiousness of subjective experience and even virtue—demonstrating, as it
were, that godliness can corrupt, and absolute godliness can corrupt
absolutely. But ultimately we see him from without; from afar. His
remoteness defies empathy.

Carwin, meanwhile, imported from Europe and dressed for a Satanic
role, proves something of a decoy. His "villainy" is more aptly described
as mischief. He is a seducer, a liar, an interloper—but not the paradigm of evil we have been led to expect; a character whose biggest sin,
perhaps, is a selfish curiosity indulged without regard to consequence.
Carwin, with his "mellifluent" voice, *is* important as an avatar of the
artist (about which more later). Moreover, as Edwin S. Fussell suggests,
his biloquism hints at a national transformation and suggests a larger
revolutionary/postrevolutionary tension in the book.[5] But Carwin is
essentially a function of plot, and remains on the periphery.

Our interest, then, devolves on Clara, and on her perception and
narration of the events she has experienced. Clara, in contrast to her
brother, is not easily swayed by superstition, nor is she given to brooding or solitary pursuits. On the contrary, she is sociable, strong-minded,
and sensible—well suited by her poise and presence of mind to be a
credible narrator of horrific events. She at first disbelieves the mysterious voice her brother claims to have heard. Hers is a rationalist credo:
"The will is the tool of the understanding, which must fashion its conclusions on the notices of sense" (35). Even as the tale progresses, Clara
maintains our respect by her resolution in the face of danger. Fearing
that an intruder lurks in her closet, she tries the door. Her very retell-
ing of so traumatic a story attests to her strength of purpose. At one
point she pauses, only to chide herself for cowardice, and proceeds: "I
mean not that dire remembrance shall subdue my courage or baffle my
design" (49).

The central transformation of the book is Clara's. It is rooted, in
part, in her maturation processes: arriving at womanhood, she is transformed. The darkness that obscures her outer world suggests the cor-
responding emotional confusion that envelopes her heart. Clara, for
instance, is both attracted to and repelled by Carwin, as is clear from
the extraordinary impression his voice makes upon her before she even
encounters him face to face. His appearance repulses, but his voice is a
"blend of force and sweetness" (52) that makes Clara weep. Despite the
abuse she piles upon him in the course of the tale, her initial fascination

is plain; Pleyel notices and remarks on it. Clara's feelings toward Pleyel too, though less ambivalent, are nonetheless confused. She goes to a play rehearsal planning to apprise him of her love, but returns home angered by his absence. One cannot help noticing, moreover, the way in which, time and again, Pleyel materializes in Carwin's wake, as if the two were alter egos: Clara, just after discovering Carwin in her closet, confuses the sound of their footsteps outside her door. Even more significant is Clara's ambivalence toward her brother. She both loves him and fears him sexually, as is suggested by the dream in which he tempts her into an abyss, and by the episode in which Clara becomes convinced he is hiding in her bedroom closet.

Clara, then, is ambivalent about all three men in her socially circumscribed world. During a sleepwalking episode, she dreams that her brother is beckoning to her from across a gulf, but awakens, instead, to the voice of Carwin crying, "Hold! Hold!" (62); Carwin no sooner disappears than Pleyel appears, calling to her "from the edge of the precipice" (64). Clara writes: "Thus was I distressed by opposite conjectures; thus was I tormented by phantoms of my own creation. It was not always thus. I can ascertain the date when my mind became the victim of this imbecility; perhaps it was coeval with the inroad of a fatal passion—a passion that will never rank me in the number of its eulogists" (83). This "fatal passion" invites conventional interpretation as love. It might be more appropriate, though, to identify it with the wider matrix of emotions attending sexual maturity in general. Clara's feelings for these various men include love, desire, fear, and animosity—though the last takes longer to become apparent. Deciding to grant Carwin a midnight interview, Clara resolves to bring along a knife, then reflects on the moral as well as physical danger she is courting: "Whoever has pointed steel is not without arms; yet what must have been the state of my mind when I could meditate, without shuddering, on the use of a murderous weapon, and believe myself secure merely because I was capable of being made so by the death of another!" (144).

These "opposite conjectures" that torment Clara threaten to banish not only her peace of mind but also her identity. "My mind seemed to be split into parts, and these parts to have entered into furious and implacable contention" (140), she reflects. Following Pleyel's tirade, she laments: "What an entire and mournful change has been effected in a few hours! . . . Yesterday and today, I am the same. . . . Yet in the apprehension of another . . . I had ceased to be the same. . . . I was

the colleague of a murderer, the paramour of a thief!" (113). Although
Clara has *done* nothing wrong, she is nevertheless assailed by incestuous
dreams, violent fantasies, and the imputations of a dear friend. "What
was it that swayed me?" (140), she wonders; "What purpose did I meditate?" (146). The worst conceivable, it would seem: figuratively, Clara
pursues her own brother; discovers murderers in her own closet.

The crux of Clara's transformation is her realization that she is no
longer mistress of the irrational feelings inside her. "Ideas exist in our
minds," she descries, "that can be accounted for by no established laws"
(87). That the mind is not merely the seat of reason is distressing; that
it can spawn unaccountable impulses is much more so. Still, as long
as we are not wholly at the mercy of such impulses, we need hardly
despair. . . . It is here that Brown's vision becomes truly dark.

Theodore Wieland is an introvert whose thoughts and heart remain
largely a mystery until his speech to the court. He is quiet, humor-
less, obsessive, and, like his father, given to religious meditation. His
atrocities, once revealed, awe us, but do not astonish us; we fancy we
recognize in his brooding personality the earmarks of the potential psychotic. It is rather Clara who elicits our concern throughout: we worry
about the effect the knowledge of her brother's agency in the slayings
will have upon her, because we identify wholeheartedly with her.

Clara bears up as well as can be expected following the murders.
Upon discovering her brother's role, however, she experiences "a new
dread . . . more insupportable than the anguish . . . lately endured"
(180). The source of this dread is crucial. Recalling the circumstances
that led her brother to his fatal act, Clara writes: "Had I not equal reason
to tremble? What was my security against influences equally terrific and
equally irresistible?" (179). Clara's horror stems not only from mortifi-
cation over her brother's complicity, but from the fear that she may find
herself summoned to commit a like crime: "I wondered at the change
which a moment had effected in my brother's condition. Now I was stu-
pefied with tenfold wonder in contemplating myself. Was I not likewise
transformed from rational and human into a creature of nameless and
fearful attributes? Was I not transported to the brink of the same abyss?
Ere a new day should come, my hands might be embrued in blood, and
my remaining life be consigned to a dungeon and chains" (179–80).

Empathy with her brother, combined with emotional distress, has
made Clara mistrust her ability to control her own actions. Yet all this

is not mere hysteria, for a disturbing propensity for violence *has* dawned on her. Its first fruits include a flirtation with suicide: "Death is a cure which nature or ourselves must administer. To this cure I now looked forward with gloomy satisfaction" (180). Clara recovers somewhat under her uncle's care. She cannot, however, dispel the suspicion that Carwin has somehow been responsible for her brother's conduct, and with an uncharacteristic vehemence remarks, "I thirsted for knowledge *and for vengeance*" (190, emphasis added).

Twice more Clara reiterates this sentiment: "The milkiness of my nature was curdled into hatred and rancour" (216), she says, and "my soul was bursting with detestation and revenge" (217). Nor does she stop here. Her craving for vengeance soon yields to blasphemy: "I invoked all-seeing heaven to drag to light and punish this betrayer, and accused its providence for having thus long delayed the retribution that was due to so enormous a guilt" (193). During a final visit to her old house, despair overtakes her, and she again premeditates, then resolves upon, suicide: "I knew how to find a way to the recesses of life. I could use a lancet with some skill, and could distinguish between vein and artery. By piercing deep into the latter, I should shun the evils which the future had in store for me, and take refuge from my woes in quiet death. I started on my feet, for my feebleness was gone, and hasted to the closet" (194). She is preparing to execute her design when Carwin appears. These mortal sins, however, are only the preliminaries. The final episode finds Clara confronted by her deranged brother come to murder her. "All that I have said [thus far] is preparatory to this scene" (221), she specifies, italicizing the significance of what is immediately to follow.

What follows is not only that Wieland's homicidal dementia is brought center stage, but that Clara finds herself ready to commit what is formalistically a comparable outrage: "Yes, I acknowledge that my guilt surpasses that of mankind. . . . What shall I say? I was menaced, as I thought, with death, and, to elude this evil, my hand was ready to inflict death upon the menacer. . . . O insupportable remembrance! hide thee from my view for a time; hide it from me that my heart was black enough to meditate the stabbing of a brother!" (223). "In the murder of a brother . . . every form of guilt is comprehended," Cicero had written in *Pro Cluentio,* a work Brown alludes to early in *Wieland.* Circumstantial justification notwithstanding, Clara's readiness to commit so mythic a crime suggests that there is nothing too heinous for the human breast to contemplate; that evil is no random lunacy, as Wieland's crimes, viewed superficially, might suggest, but rather an aptitude possessed by all, ever liable to surface. Brown spares Clara (and us) the final horror, arranging, as one critic notes, for her to drop the knife, and for Wieland to pick it up and kill himself.[6] But Clara, acutely aware of her own implication in this tragedy, underlines its wider significance: "My hands were sprinkled with his blood as he fell" (232).

The real evil in *Wieland,* then, lies not merely in the atrocities committed by the deranged brother, but in the frightful, if unrealized, impulses that surface in his sister—impulses whose source, apparently, is human nature, the familial bond, and innate psychosexual processes in which we all partake. This fundamental evil demands emphasis, for even as Carwin diverts our suspicion from Wieland, Wieland's own atrocities, on casual reading, obscure the even more disturbing transformation at work within Clara. By portraying her potential for evil, Brown delivers a more damning indictment than Matthew Lewis, Ann Radcliffe, or even William Godwin dreamed of. Whereas these Gothicists indicted individuals or social institutions, Brown indicts humankind. Whereas they accused the aggressor, Brown incriminates the victim. In the world of *Wieland,* "no human virtue is secure from degeneracy" (241).

Wieland, then, negates the optimistic philosophy and psychology of the Enlightenment, presenting man as naturally depraved, prey to evils beyond his control. *Wieland* first sets forth the "power of blackness" that Melville was to speak of half a century later, and which seems, in retrospect, to haunt American literature. The reader is left to resolve the balance between the book's dark insinuations and the patently contrived ending Brown bids for in the final pages—an ending that attempts, almost by brute force, to banish "moral night" and restore a rational and morally comprehensible universe. What is certain, however, is that by the end of the tale America has been abandoned. It is in Europe that Clara and Pleyel start life anew. What, if anything, does this emigration signify? Or, even more fundamentally: Why the book's subtitle, "An American Tale"?

PICKING UP THE KNIFE

Wieland is grounded in history from the start. Not only is it set on the eve of the American Revolution; its protagonist is also equipped with a family history that reads like America's. David Brion Davis, recalling the elder Wieland's life and death and the family circle that has succeeded him at Mettingen, notes:

> The story thus far is almost an allegory of American colonial history. It includes disrupting economic changes in Europe, religious fervor which was not unrelated to these changes, frequent references to predestination and to stern self-analysis, the vision and failure of spreading truth among the savages, unexpected economic success, and even the well-known figure of a temple (or city) on the hill. The parallel continues with the disorganization and self-consumption of the original religious fanaticism and with the appropriation of the temple by rationalistic descendants. Finally, the continental Enlightenment appears in the character of Henry Pleyel, "the champion of intellectual liberty . . . who rejected all guidance but that of his reason."

"Such a drama of historical allegory cannot be pushed too far," cautions Davis, "but it is important to note . . . that Brown was concerned with the problems of a society which imposed few limitations on self-expansion." [7]

Davis is wise, no doubt, to qualify his reading. Yet Brown, we have seen, was intrigued by a literature in which fiction and history intersect. And he was familiar with the strategy of allegorizing history. Jeremy Belknap, in *The Foresters* (1796), a book subtitled, like *Wieland,* "an American Tale" and reviewed by Brown in his *Monthly Magazine and American Review,* had allegorized the colonization, rebellion, and confederation of America. Brown, in praising Belknap, alludes to the "pleasing and popular form" of allegory, a form he elsewhere applauds as the "native region of the poet," whether employed in verse or prose. [8] *Wieland* itself features a debate between Wieland and Pleyel concerning the merits of Cicero's *Pro Cluentio,* a work in which the incests and familial murders committed by a powerful clan effectively allegorize the dissolution of the Roman republic. [9] Wieland and Pleyel explicitly debate the work's allegorical status, and the validity of making "the picture of a single family a model from which to sketch the condition of a nation" (30). The passage, which occurs early in *Wieland,* would seem to invite us to entertain the possibility that Brown's ensuing drama of familial atrocity may have wider implications.

This, however, is precisely where Davis's reading flags. Indeed, most critics who have considered *Wieland* in a historical light have failed to engage its central drama.[10] This is true even of Edwin S. Fussell's "*Wieland:* A Literary and Historical Reading," perhaps the most detailed analysis in this vein. Fussell's essay identifies the transformation of *patria* that Brown and his generation had experienced as the real antecedent of the novel's subtitle. Suggesting that, figuratively speaking, the newly nationalized writer of Brown's era was, like Carwin, a biloquist—a British "speaker" become American—and stressing the almost causal role writing had played in the American Revolution, Fussell sees this novel that pivots on biloquism and the writing act as embodying a revolutionary/postrevolutionary tension. With Clara Wieland as a "daughter of the American Revolution" in conflict with Carwin, an "American revolutionary and postrevolutionary writer," Carwin's destruction of the Wieland family becomes, Fussell suggests, an image of America's revolutionary devastation—even as Brown's "horror and contempt" for the author's powers becomes a "product of postrevolutionary backlash." Fussell concludes by noting a paradox: "Writing is both the cause and the effect of action: . . . the American Revolution . . . , at least partly caused by writers, . . . necessitates an American literature to justify it and to ensure its fruits to posterity." [11]

Fussell, in highlighting a historical context for Brown's plot, gives new dimension to Carwin and to several of the book's motifs—biloquism, in particular. His identification of various political tensions in *Wieland* is vital. But Fussell skirts the drama of Clara's transformation and confrontation with her lunatic brother, concentrating instead on a character who is, at last, more red herring than protagonist. Granted, the Carwin of *Memoirs of Carwin, the Biloquist* is the very prototype of a revolutionary. But *Memoirs of Carwin, the Biloquist* is a separate fiction altogether; the Carwin we encounter in *Wieland* is, despite iconoclastic traces and a romantic mien, no more a towering revolutionary than he is a towering villain. Rather it is Clara who most embodies the revolutionary/postrevolutionary tensions Fussell discerns.

In Brown's Gothic romances naive young protagonists often undergo transformations in which a dark side of their personalities comes to the fore. But the characters aren't initially aware they harbor the propensities that later engulf them: fundamentally, they don't know themselves. For Brown, I have suggested, a similar lack of awareness characterized America. That, at least, is the thrust of *An Address to the Government . . . ,* a work which, as we have seen, voices concern over the nation's soporific vulnerability. There can be little doubt that Brown's romances, published on the heels of the French Revolution, reflected anxiety over the atrocities that had resulted from that America-inspired upheaval. As Davis remarks, "The [French] Revolution showed what [Brown's own] earlier ideas *might* have brought about." [12] Yet Brown's America, her revolution accomplished and its gains institutionalized, had presumably escaped such a fate. Why, then, should Brown have been uneasy?

The Maxwell-Stuart-Conway subplot, in which Brown describes Maxwell's semisuccessful seduction of Mrs. Stuart and enunciates what the previous few hundred pages have dramatized—that "no human virtue is secure from degeneracy" (241)—provides a bridge, however unlikely, to the historicity of *Wieland*. Regarding Mrs. Stuart's transferal of affection, though not of favors, Brown writes: "This revolution in her sentiments was productive only of despair. Her rectitude of principle preserved her from actual guilt, but could not restore to her her ancient affection, or save her from being the prey of remorseful and impracticable wishes" (241). Mrs. Stuart "falls," in other words, even though she stops short of committing the deeds she thinks about. The same kind of guilt compromises Clara: though she does not actually wield the knife against her brother, the realization that she has been on the verge of doing so traumatizes her and constitutes a virtual "fall." A similar moral corruption, Edmund Burke ventured, tinges society at large any time immoderate religious or political goals are advanced: "The worst of these politics of revolution is this; they temper and harden the breast, in order to prepare it for the desperate strokes which are sometimes used in extreme occasions. But as these occasions may never arrive, the mind receives a gratuitous taint." [13] Burke's point, and the point of Brown's digression—that a "revolution in sentiments," even if it is not taken to the limit, carries irrevocable consequences—bears not only on Clara, but also on postrevolutionary America.

Colonial America, like Clara, had, in maturing, undergone a change; had found her new self alienated from, then threatened by, her former (British) self; had picked up the knife, as it were—albeit reluctantly and defensively—and squared off against her former self, that elder-kinsman-turned-antagonist, Great Britain. Fortunately, while our revolution triumphed (thanks to France), our republicanism (unlike France's) remained within bounds. *But,* Brown seems to warn his readers, even if we hadn't, like our ideological brother France, become a fanatical butcher (and this, I submit, is the second historical antecedent of Wieland's mania), we ought not be blind to the residual possibility, or to the violent transformation we *had* undergone. For, as Mrs. Stuart (who also stopped short of infamy) discovers, a "revolution in sentiments" *anticipates* the worst.

The violent transformation dramatized in Brown's climax, I am suggesting, echoes a complex national transformation. Wieland's threatening posture toward Clara simultaneously conjures two contrasting historical moments: first, the revolutionary era, during which America, like Clara, had been obliged to take up arms against her former protector and kinsman; and second, America's postrevolutionary, republican era, whose haunting specter was that of her zealot-"brother"-turned-indiscriminate-murderer, revolutionary France. Given that *Wieland* was written in the umbra and penumbra of these two revolutions, it isn't surprising that the political transformations they embodied should hover behind the tale's literal transformations. But more compelling reasons support such a reading.

America in the mid-1790s was, we know, factionalized almost to the point of civil war. Partisanship became especially intense during 1798, the year Brown was writing *Wieland*. During this time England and France, as noted earlier, were virtual poles in the American political psyche, the Federalist and Republican parties identifying themselves with Britain and France respectively. By evoking these polarities, Brown evokes the factionalized America of his own day. At bottom, the nation's division reflected a crisis that went beyond parties and politics: the Republic's need to come to terms with her revolutionary heritage. America scarcely a generation earlier had cultivated incendiary attitudes in response to a threat from without. By 1798, however, she was endangered perhaps as much by her own volatility as by any external threat. Historian John Patrick Diggins notes that "after the Revolution, the colonists, having resorted to power to overthrow whatever power did not come from themselves, had now to confront the problem of their own power, coming face to face with themselves and with the even more demanding problem of self-control." [14] Even as Clara is afraid of becoming as violent as her brother, America too was acutely afraid of being "transported to the brink of the same abyss" as her brother-republic France. Brown characterizes Wieland's lunacy with the politically loaded words "revolution," "overthrow," and "anarchy" (154, 162, 171). Clara's drama, then, suggests the larger drama of a republic in transition, beset by postrevo-

lutionary conflict and threatened by her own revolutionary heritage—
her older self, once removed: a self she must kill or perhaps be killed by.

The problem, of course, is that to "kill" one's violent self is to *become*
that self, to become a killer. Hence Clara's paralysis. Her knife-wielding
posture suggests both revolution *and* reaction. She has to choose between two extreme alternatives, two dangerous selves. "Murderers
lurked in my closet," says Clara midway through the tale. "One resolved
to shoot, and the other menaced suffocation" (58). Both politically
and psychologically, this icon of twofold danger mirrors the nation's
juncture. This was, after all, an era during which George Washington,
without a trace of irony, denounced western Pennsylvania tax rebels as
"armed banditti" and was, in turn, vilified by democratic opponents as
having been a "secret traitor" during the War for Independence; during
which John Adams was slandered as "the blasted tyrant of America"
and, in turn, approved of laws discriminating against refugees and
restricting freedom of speech.[15] To Washington, Adams, and their sup-
porters, America's republican self seemed to have lost its wits, and
needed (literally, the Alien and Sedition Acts suggest) to be sequestered;
to the Republicans, the Federalists constituted the deranged relative.

Brown's America was—to borrow an image from *Wieland*—a temple
on a cliff. Her primary challenge was to retain her balance: to avoid
being toppled by European wars or domestic crises. Hence George
Washington's admonition to shun faction at home and permanent alli-
ances abroad. But as crises erupted and faction increased, a studied
balancing act must have seemed more and more difficult, if not futile.
"My mind seemed to be split into separate parts," says Clara, "and these
parts to have entered into furious and implacable contention" (140).
Perhaps decisive action—a fratricide, if not a suicide, of sorts—*was* necessary. Brown does not answer this dilemma in *Wieland*—although, as
we shall see, he does in *Ormond. Wieland,* Brown's Scylla and Charybdis
myth for the young Republic, is primarily a plea that she wake up to the
danger on either hand. The conclusion repeats this motif: Clara, literally
asleep in her bed, barely escapes when her house catches fire. Simultaneously threatened by flames and by suffocating smoke, she is unable to
break the spell that stupefies her. And though Brown contrives a *deus ex
machina* to save her, her house burns to the ground.

This apocalypse and Clara's subsequent expatriation suggest grave
skepticism on Brown's part toward the American enterprise. Even

Clara's fairy tale preservation (carried through the flames to safety in the arms of a dark stranger, she is soon reunited and then eventually united with Pleyel) is rendered ironic by the change she undergoes. Once in Europe Clara adopts a moralistic, phony-sounding—Carl Nelson has said a "thrown"—voice,[16] and, with it, a habit of rationalizing irksome truths. Regarding the feelings she harbors for Pleyel even after he has married another, she says: "I continued to love him, but my passion was disguised to myself; I considered it merely as a more tender species of friendship, and cherished it without compunction" (238). Such explicit rationalizing forms an ironic coda to a tale that has hinged on the importance of discerning the truth behind appearances, of knowing oneself. Clara's figurative biloquism recalls the stance articulated earlier by her uncle, who advises Clara against disabusing her brother of the belief that God has prompted his deeds: that self-deception may be necessary for survival. It proves so, at least, for Wieland, whose delusion that his behavior was divinely prompted sustains him even as it subverts his mind. And America? Was America prepared to confront herself, or would she seek instead to transform unpalatable self-truths into the platitudes of history? Considered in light of the tale's conclusion, Edwin S. Fussell's previously cited paradox takes on an aura of necessity, the revolutionary writing act requiring, as it were, a postrevolutionary rewriting act, a sedative historiography.

Vying with this disheartening possibility is a still grimmer one: that the American experiment may simply be doomed beyond recall. Allusions to the crumbled glories of Rome, for instance—and particularly to Wieland's revered Cicero, whose death in an insurrection signified the triumph of anarchy and darkness—bode ill for the Wielands' neoclassical polity. Brown's occasional allusions to *Macbeth*,[17] moreover, melodramatic though they seem, remind the American reader that for centuries striking at a king meant nothing less than upending nature, and that hands thus bloodied defied cleansing. In addition, Brown's earlier intimations that fire signifies God's displeasure (consider the elder Wieland's death) makes the burning down of Clara's house smack of divine mandate rather than accidental mishap.

Brown's "American Tale," then, traces depravity not merely to an Old World villain (Carwin) or an overwrought zealot (Theodore Wieland), but to the normative, rational protagonist, Clara Wieland; it records her progress toward infamy culminating in an ironic confrontation with her brother/self that carries overtones of America's own ironic confrontation with her revolutionary self; it suggests that even a limited revolution contains the germ of future blight; and it hints that America may be doomed, even as Clara is doomed, twice-over: first, by a fatal ignorance of self, and second—ironically—by self-knowledge, once it has been afforded. By sending his surviving characters back to Europe, Brown as good as denies the possibility of rectifying the New World's "fall," of returning an adolescent America to a state of bliss. Even any *apparent* resumption of sanity, of balance, Brown seems to say, will come about through Old World artifice, not genuine convalescence. The only genuine hope *Wieland* extends is that Clara and America may, in time, learn, as Carwin perhaps learns by the tale's end, to use a revolutionary, transforming power with discretion.

Silence in the Temple

Separation of church and state notwithstanding, religion and politics have long overlapped in America. From the New England theocracy pursuing its errand in the wilderness to the War of Independence, which William G. McLoughlin has called "the secular fulfillment of the religious ideals of the First Great Awakening,"[18] to the quasi-religious sense of national mission that the Republic assumed in the nineteenth century, America has prided itself in being a "nation under God"—a "Christian Sparta,"[19] a New Canaan charged by "God's peculiar prerogative" with "the cause of all mankind."[20] In the 1790s, however, as Alan Heimert notes, "the religious and political concerns of Americans impinged on each other more directly, and also in many more subtle ways, than at nearly any other moment in our past."[21] Several historians have suggested, indeed, that the outbreak of evangelical revivalism known as the Great Revival, or Second Great Awakening, which began at about the time partisan discord crested (1797–1800) and continued through the Jacksonian era, derived largely from the decade's political anxieties.[22] Thus Samuel Keene, Jr., noted, upon returning to Kentucky in 1801 after several years' absence, that the people there had "substituted the Rage of Religion for the Rage of Politicks."[23] What is clear, at least, is that related cultural tensions churned both the secular and spiritual waters.

Anxiety over the future, says McLoughlin, lay at the heart of the Second Great Awakening. There was in the nation, he notes, deep-seated "disagreement about how to proceed, especially after George Washington passed away in 1799." Conspiracy fears (concerning Jacobins, Freemasons, deists, the Bavarian Illuminati) were rampant. Faction, sectional cleavages, and a "rising egalitarianism in sharp conflict with the old hierarchical structure of society" were straining the national fiber.[24] And underlying all, Donald Mathews has suggested, was a pervasive sense of frustration: "The Revolution had created great anticipation for the future; but the kind of future people wanted was not easily realized. The result was a vague uneasiness."[25]

Even the doctrinal divisions that fueled the Second Great Awakening reiterated broader tensions. "Most unsettling of all," writes McLoughlin, continuing his catalog of turn-of-the-century crises, "was the philosophical conflict between the world view of the Calvinists and the new Enlightenment rationalists." For the latter, America's history from the Revolution to the founding of the Republic had testified to the people's ability to determine their future by exercising their will, reason, and agency. But the former remained convinced that God alone orders events on earth; that man is corrupt, his understanding clouded and his will fettered; and that the rationalists, including Jefferson's Republicans, were the dupes of radicals.[26]

Rifts within Calvinism itself telescoped related social cleavages. Liberal "new lights," who held that God's will can be perceived through reason or an inner spirit, validated human spiritual potential; "old lights," skeptical of the mind as well as the heart, looked exclusively to the Scriptures and the church for guidance.[27] Like the Calvinist-rationalist split, this dispute, which had simmered for half a century, was bound up with the larger issue of individualism and the debate over human nature, and echoed the Revolutionary-era quarrel over natural vs. legal rights. And to the extent the Calvinist division focused on whether the average person was to play an active or passive role in the church, it mirrored the larger controversy over whether the common man was to play an active role in the polis, or ought to resign himself to taking cues from his betters (i.e., the [Federalist] political "elect").[28] Both outside and within the Calvinist churches, indeed, the Second Great Awakening expressed a yearning among the common people for admission into the ranks of the saved as well as a conviction that, as Russel B. Nye observes, "government and religion were both rooted in the individual"—attitudes that have been linked to Jeffersonianism and ultimately Jacksonianism.[29] Hence the message of revivalist firebrand Charles Grandison Finney that salvation was available to everyone who would reach out and seize it—a stance that only made explicit what was implicit in the sermons of Finney's more circumspect New England colleagues Nathaniel Taylor and Lyman Beecher.[30]

Small wonder, then, that *Wieland,* a romance fraught with post-revolutionary anxieties, should be preoccupied with religious themes as well. I don't mean to suggest that Brown was deliberately invoking the context of the Second Great Awakening—a phenomenon that, in 1798, was little more than a glimmer in the Reverend Timothy Dwight's eye. But as the product of a historical moment pregnant with revivalist sentiment, *Wieland,* I would argue, reflects many of the religious doubts and cultural tensions that were soon to coalesce in the Second Great Awakening. McLoughlin, citing Anthony F. C. Wallace, outlines the early symptoms of a great awakening:

> One by one, people lose their bearings, become psychically or physically ill, show what appear to be signs of neurosis, psychosis, or madness, and may either break out in acts of violence against family, friends, and authorities or become apathetic, catatonic, incapable of functioning. . . . Often [these] anomic individuals destroy themselves by drugs, alcohol, or suicide. By their friends, and by society in general, these early victims of social disjunction are seen as deviants. . . . But as the number of these individuals increases, the institutional bonds of society begin to snap. Families are the first to suffer.[31]

Madness, violence, suicide, deviance, family breakdown: the description is a virtual synopsis of *Wieland.*

Awakenings, McLoughlin adds, result not from external events like wars or depressions, but from "critical disjunctions in our self-understanding."[32] The dramatic core of *Wieland,* I have suggested, is Clara's—and America's—discovery of a deep self that defies Enlightenment assumptions; *Wieland,* in short, is a study in disjointed self-perception. During awakenings, McLoughlin continues, society's first response to the splits it is experiencing is to reassert the old-time religion, and to "find scapegoats in [its] midst (aliens, witches, conspirators, foreigners, traitors)."[33] This is precisely how Theodore and Clara respond to increasingly stressful circumstances. Theodore becomes obsessed with the God of his father, and Clara, in trying to account for the evils that have overwhelmed her, scapegoats Carwin—even as the Reverends Timothy Dwight and Jedidiah Morse, in 1798, were scapegoating the Illuminati (with whom Carwin, according to *Memoirs of Carwin, the Biloquist,* is associated).

Even more fundamentally, the questions *Wieland* poses reflect doubts of Awakening magnitude: Is God an interventionist or laissez-faire deity? Do we dare heed our intuitions—be they religious or revolutionary promptings, mandates to save or sacrifice souls? How do we know that what we take to be the voice of God (or nature) isn't merely our own voice, its perverse monotone disguised as an oracular stentorian? And what of the external voices that accost us—those of preacher or pamphleteer, church father or founding father, newspaper writer or novelist? How many of these are the voices of false prophets, demagogues, conspirators, "double-tongued deceivers" (244)?

Carwin, of course, embodies this last dilemma so pertinent to a republic, in which citizens, to play their role, are obliged to read, listen to, and assess a din of competing and often inscrutable voices. Edwin S. Fussell, as remarked earlier, has linked Carwin with the postrevolutionary writer.[34] And, indeed, Carwin's biloquist mischief suggests, as Jay Fliegelman has observed,[35] a mordant inversion on Brown's part of the revolutionary dictum *Vox populi, vox Dei* ("The voice of the people is the voice of God"). More intriguing, though, is the dilemma *Wieland* raises concerning the *internal* voices people hear. For in questioning the voices of reason and revelation, Brown brings a fundamental Revivalist tension to the fore.

Like Thomas Paine, who declared, "My own mind is my own church,"[36] the rationalistic Pleyel rejects "all guidance but that of his reason" (25). "I yielded not but to evidence" (135), he says to Clara, while wrongfully accusing her of pursuing an affair with Carwin—and the words, we can't help but feel, would make an apposite epitaph. Theodore Wieland, on the other hand, venerates "moral necessity and Calvinistic inspiration." This dichotomy isn't absolute. Intelligent and well read—a classicist, in fact, who delights especially in Cicero— yet, like his namesake, the German poet Christoph Martin Wieland,[37] "in some respects an enthusiast" (35), Theodore attempts, as Calvinism had attempted, to integrate reason and revelation. "But the Enlightenment's deification of reason," writes Russel B. Nye, "forced the Calvinist into a dilemma. What if reason denied . . . revelation?"[38] Wieland's solution, in fact, recapitulates that of Jonathan Edwards and others, who, as Nye remarks, "found beyond reason . . . a suprarational revelation in 'a Spiritual and Divine Light, immediately imparted to the soul by God.'"[39] Indeed, Wieland's complex spirituality, comprising what Norman S. Grabo has termed "'new-light' inspiration"[40] as well as devotion to an arbitrary and vengeful Jehovah, incorporates the new-light/old-light tensions at the heart of turn-of-the-century Calvinism—even as his dialogues with Pleyel evoke the Calvinist-rationalist axes of the Awakening.

Calvinist-rationalist tensions animate *Wieland* from the start, the elder Wieland's bizarre incineration bringing into focus the question of whether the world operates according to fixed laws instituted at the Creation, as the deists held, or according to an ever-present divine agency. Clara, trying to make sense of her father's death, muses: "Was this the penalty of disobedience? —this the stroke of a vindictive and invisible hand? Is it a fresh proof that the Divine Ruler interferes in human affairs, meditates an end, selects and commissions his agents, and enforces, by unequivocal sanctions, submission to his will? Or, was it merely the irregular expansion of the fluid that imparts warmth to our heart and our blood, caused by the fatigue of the preceding day, or flowing, by established laws, from the condition of his thoughts?" (19). Neither answer seems compelling.

As to the possibility that the elder Wieland's body has caught fire spontaneously according to "established laws," one detail jars: his arm has been smashed ("His right arm exhibited marks as of having been struck by some heavy body" [18]). Would Brown have us believe that is how spontaneous combustion works? Rather, his depiction conjures up the God of the prophet Jeremiah: "Is not my word like as a fire? saith the Lord; and like a hammer that breaketh the rock in pieces?" (Jer. 23: 29). (This yoked image signifying divine compulsion and power recurs in the literature of religious enthusiasts and reformers in America, from Quakers to revivalists to abolitionists.[41]) But the notion that an arbitrary Calvinist God has smitten a devout disciple is almost as difficult to credit as the idea that this same God has commanded Theodore Wieland to slaughter his family.

Clara's spiritual vacillation further dramatizes these Calvinist-rationalist tensions in which the novel is conceived, but which it seems unable to resolve. John G. Frank calls Clara a deist,[42] and that is probably as good a description as any for the unobsessive, rationalist faith in which she seems, at first, to rest—her doubts notwithstanding. But the memory of her father's death infects Clara's spirit, and the events that befall her erode her confidence in rational explanations. Conceiving first the belief that a good angel attends her, and later that an evil emissary assails her, she becomes, at last, almost as inclined as her brother to credit supernatural causes. Her spiritual transformation parallels her emotional transformation into a potential killer: she follows in her brother's footsteps in both respects.

But Clara's spiritual evolution doesn't end here. The Clara who narrates the book's tragic events is neither a blithe rationalist nor a believer in spirits. In fact her narrative begins in a vein of cynicism verging on tacit apostasy: "I address no supplication to the Deity," she says. "The power that governs the course of human affairs has chosen his path. The decree that ascertained the condition of my life admits no recall. No doubt it squares with the maxims of eternal equity" (5). No doubt it squares. Her tone, however, imports differently. Though she seems inclined to beg the question, Clara clearly wants nothing to do with this Deity: she declines, despite the ordeal ahead of her, to invoke His mercy, His sustenance, or even His name—"the Deity" being about as impersonal and abstract a form of address as one can employ. This attitude, which contrasts sharply with the pietism Clara takes refuge in at the close of the novel, makes us wonder about Brown's attitude toward his material. Had he, in writing *Wieland,* moved beyond the terms of the cultural debate he found himself articulating?

Wieland's denouement, which purports to explain the book's mysteries, fails altogether to resolve the debate between rationalism and Calvinism. Brown's attempt to restore the light of day with a rationalistic explanation for the strange voices—ventriloquism—rings false, as does the conventionally moralistic tone Clara adopts in the closing pages. Moreover, Brown's explanation raises as many questions as it answers, especially since it is disallowed at the crucial juncture: Brown leaves the fatal ninth voice—the command to kill that Wieland claims led him to slaughter his family—unaccounted for. Did Wieland imagine it? Did Carwin utter it and lie afterward?

A close look at *Wieland* suggests, I believe, that, the novel's proto-Revivalist context notwithstanding, neither the Calvinist nor the rationalist God is in His heaven; that the spiritual injunction "Seek, and ye shall find," so ironically impeached by the elder Wieland's death, is further undercut by the novel's conclusion; in short, that Brown has sketched a world in which humankind seems to have been left to its own devices.

John Calvin was haunted, as biographer William Bouwsma points out, by two images of angst that recur in his writings: the labyrinth and the abyss. The labyrinth, Bouwsma says, imaged the papal church, whose constricting theological assumptions Calvin sought to leave behind. The abyss, on the other hand, was "a symbol of Calvin's horror of the unlimited. It suggested the absence of boundaries and the unintelligibility of things," and represented the anarchic potential of the faith he was pioneering, "the direction in which he was advancing and therefore that unknown future whose indeterminate horrors usually seem more frightening than the remembered and finite troubles of the past."[43] Because related tensions (past vs. future, institutions vs. individuals, constraint vs. freedom) define the Gothic novel, it is perhaps not surprising that both images turn up in Brown's romances. The abyss, however, assumes special symbolic status, both in *Wieland* and *Edgar Huntly.* Because Calvinism and American society as a whole had, by the time Brown was writing, removed itself far from traditional theological moorings, one can't help wondering if the abyss that beckons to Clara Wieland didn't evoke for Brown some of the same horror that Calvin's abyss epitomized.

For if the young Republic prided itself on the liberties it had secured, it also feared the liberties it had taken—religious as well as political. The Revolution, as noted, had been anticipated by the First Great Awakening, a radical restructuring of America's churches in the course of which, McLoughlin has said, "the individual became his own church."[44] But by the 1790s the consequent loosening of the community's spiritual bonds seems to have reached a point where many Christians perceived a crisis. The Presbyterian Assembly of 1798, for instance, noted "with pain and fearful apprehension a general dereliction of religious principles and practice among our citizens, a visible and prevailing impiety and contempt for the laws and institutions of religion"[45]—a theme that, as Russel B. Nye points out, thundered from hundreds of pulpits.[46] "Even more alarming," says Winthrop S. Hudson, "was the aggressive Deism of Thomas Paine, Ethan Allen and Elihu Palmer," who had "launched a frontal attack upon the whole concept of revealed religion."[47] Nor, apparently, was this picture of religious laxity and rebellion merely a figment of overwrought clerics' imaginations. A visitor to Princeton in 1799 found "only a few undergraduates" who made any pretense to piety, and Timothy Dwight, then president of Yale, felt obliged to debate publicly the truth of the Bible with skeptical students and to devote a series of two hundred sermons to the subject of "infidelity."[48] Richard Hofstadter notes that "the American colonies at the end of the eighteenth century were perhaps the most unchurched regions in all Christendom."[49]

What was Brown's attitude toward God and religion during this era of apostasy and awakening? We know that he was raised a Quaker and that, during the early and middle 1790s, he was influenced by radical doctrines—those of, among others, his mentor and best friend Elihu Hubbard Smith, a deist. Brown's close friend and biographer William Dunlap testifies, on the other hand, that many of the "plunging tenets and dangerous doctrines" Brown entertained during these years gave way, later on, to more conformist and conservative views.[50] Bernard Rosenthal, however, citing a letter dated October 24, 1795, from Brown to another close friend, Joseph Bringhurst, notes that while Brown probably died a Christian, his early radicalism "was more pronounced than is usually indicated."[51] In the letter, Brown suggests to Bringhurst that "the belief in the divinity of Christ and future retribution" has been pernicious to mankind.[52] David Lee Clark adds to this picture of the young writer as a skeptic: "Like Voltaire, . . . [Brown] was mortified that the apparently intelligent accepted the view that the Lisbon earthquake was the expression of the wrath of a benevolent God because the city contained a few wicked people. The religion which called for the adoration of such a God was in Brown's mind a dangerous religion." We know, furthermore, that Brown succumbed to despair and an even greater skepticism following the yellow fever epidemic of September 1798. This epidemic ravaged New York, where Brown was staying, killing Elihu Hubbard Smith. Brown himself was stricken, but recovered. Clark writes: "[Brown] came to question the goodness and power of God, and to look upon man as insignificant in the scheme of the universe."[53]

Brown's subsequent fiction registers some of this skepticism. In *Ormond* and *Arthur Mervyn,* the image of a plague-ridden Philadelphia becomes a virtual correlative for a morally infected and hapless cosmos. *Edgar Huntly,* moreover, explicitly incorporates the issue of religious skepticism. The protagonist, we learn, has saved a number of letters from his deceased friend Waldegrave expounding skeptical doctrines that the latter eventually abjured—letters Waldegrave has asked Edgar to destroy, but which Edgar, who has adopted some of the doctrines, is loath to part with. Kenneth Bernard has suggested that this episode may play a more important part in the unfolding drama than most critics have allowed.[54] The novel also offers what could almost be considered a veiled parable of resentment against God. Edgar, prior to the ordeal recounted in the second half of the book, has undergone shock and disappointment. Not only has his brother-in-law-to-be been brutally murdered, but the money Edgar and his fiancée have been relying on for their marriage—money left unassigned by Waldegrave's will—has suddenly been reclaimed by its apparent owner, so that Edgar is forced to call off the wedding indefinitely. Thus distressed, Edgar sleepwalks, falls into a pit, and, upon awakening, complains: "Methought I was the victim of some tyrant who had thrust me into the dungeon of his fortress, and left me no power to determine whether he intended I should perish with famine, or linger out a long life in hopeless imprisonment."[55] Brown, then, it seems safe to conclude, was alternately quarreling with and doubting the God of his fathers and the Deity of his fellows during the middle and late 1790s.

Wieland, of course, unlike Brown's other romances, was completed prior to the demoralizing plague of September 1798. Yet, as Clark reminds us, Brown had witnessed two earlier incursions of yellow fever in Philadelphia—one in 1793, the other in 1797. It seems reasonable to assume, as Clark does, that these scenes of horror had already tainted Brown's outlook by the time he began *Wieland*.[56] *Wieland*, quite clearly, is preoccupied with the problem of evil—its sources, rampancy, and spiritual implications. The novel generates an undertow of skepticism, moreover, that flows not only from its intimations of innate depravity, but from its imagery and plot.

Brown's use of light and darkness, for instance, reiterates the dilemma of whether or not God interferes in human affairs. Throughout *Wieland* Brown associates light with God. The elder Wieland's strange death is accompanied by gleams, rays, and "blazing light" from a fire that, like the fire in the bush from which Jehovah spoke to Moses, burns but does not consume ("No part of the building was on fire" [17]). His identification, moreover, with the mysticism of the Camisards and Albigenses—French sects that, like Brown's own Quakers, revered light as the symbol if not the literal manifestation of divine goodness—accentuates Brown's association of light and God. Clara further underlines it. Addressing her brother in the temple one night shortly after he first hears the seemingly supernatural voice, she remarks, "How almost palpable is this dark! yet a ray from above would dispel it." Theodore's response makes plain, on the other hand, the significance of darkness: "Ay," he says, "not only the physical, but moral night would be dispelled" (36).

Rays, gleams, glimmerings, lusters, and effulgences abound in *Wieland*. But they expire with maddening regularity, the recurring motif of a flickering light followed by darkness reinforcing an aura of skepticism. When Clara awakens from her sleep near the summerhouse, she hears a voice, then sees a gleam that flickers and dies. Returning home to keep an interview with Carwin, she sees in her window a light, shortly extinguished. Brown first employs the motif in relating the elder Wieland's death. Clara's uncle, responding to an explosive noise, runs to the temple. "Within the columns he beheld . . . a cloud impregnated with light. . . . He approached the temple. As he went forward, the light retired, and, when he put his feet within the apartment, utterly vanished. The suddenness of this transition increased the darkness that succeeded in a ten-fold degree" (17). It is this succeeding darkness, its intensity multiplied by the disappearing light, that is symbolically suggestive: such is the loneliness that ensues if the God of Abraham and Isaac proves to be a fiction.

Silence as well as darkness pervades *Wieland:* an "anxious silence" (45) that grows despite Carwin's biloquist pranks—and is, in fact, thrown into relief by them, much as the darkness is increased by the expiring gleams. Pleyel remarks the "extraordinary silence" of his European fiancée, until assured by an unidentified voice in the night that "her silence is the silence of the tomb" (44). Wieland recounts how, after he was addressed by a voice resembling his wife's, "the deepest silence ensued" (33). Catherine demands the meaning of Pleyel and Wieland's "silence" and wild gazing, not knowing that what was apparently her own voice has just been the medium of tragic news. Clara notes, prior to her final confrontation with Wieland, that "silence reigned through my habitation" (193).

Like the darkness that signifies "moral night" (36), the silence of *Wieland* conveys a spiritual desolation best captured in the image of Pleyel questioning the mysterious voice to no avail: "the deepest silence was all the return made to my subsequent interrogatories" (45). Little more than an atmospheric embellishment in most Gothic novels, the motif of silence, like that of darkness, evokes in *Wieland* the specter of a world without God. As Clara says of her imagined guardian angel, "Who could say whether his silence were ascribable to the absence of danger, or to his own absence?" (147). An irony of plot intensifies this "extraordinary silence" further.

From the outset, *Wieland* has taken shape against an implicitly Old Testament backdrop. The setting is Edenic; the characters include a devilish conniver with a beguiling voice and subtle mind, and an Abraham-like devotee who believes God has required him to prove his

faith by sacrificing his family. The book's skeptical undertones notwithstanding, this backdrop persists, nourishing faint expectations. Indeed,
as the Lockean rationalist view held by Clara and Pleyel is progressively
discredited, the outside possibility that an inscrutable Jehovah might
actually be manipulating events grows, however imperceptibly, by de-
fault. For Brown's readers, surely, that possibility must have seemed
less remote than for us, in that they were closer in time and spirit to a
culture that perceived itself in typological terms.

New England's Puritan settlers, that is to say, had envisioned themselves (as Sacvan Bercovitch and others have shown) as latter-day Israel-
ites, God's chosen people charged with building the New Jerusalem—a
conceit their ministers elaborated in countless sermons that drew parallels between New England's unfolding history and that of the Old Testament Jews. These parallels, and the rhetorical framework of which they
became the foci, served to define and consecrate the Puritan enterprise
in America—an enterprise that, Bercovitch has shown, was transmit-
ted in only somewhat secularized form to the young Republic.[57] (The
Second Great Awakening, indeed, would be the transmitter.) *Wieland's*
biblical overtones, in short, would likely have struck familiar mythical,
if not theological, chords, even among non-Calvinist readers.

As we approach the denouement of *Wieland,* then, three, not two,
possible explanations for Theodore's atrocities present themselves: he
has succumbed to insanity; Carwin, in some unknown way and for
equally unknown ends, has preyed upon and manipulated him; or God
has indeed required a sacrifice of him, as Wieland claims in a remarkably
lucid confession that is the more compelling because he has nothing to
gain by lying. As the ending unfolds, the question of who is ultimately
responsible for Wieland's deed—and particularly the remote possibility
that God has orchestrated it—absorbs us.

What Carwin's confession makes plain is that, in at least eight cases
out of nine, the voice purported to be God's has been a counterfeit,
an illusion worked up by a busybody. God has not been speaking to
Wieland, and almost certainly did not order him to massacre his family
(Brown stops short of precluding the possibility altogether). Our first
reaction is one of relief: God is not a bloodthirsty giaour; he does not
require us to prove our faith by sacrificing children and loved ones.
But behind this relief comes the realization—obscured, admittedly, by
the sensationalism and suspense of the episode—that, if God has not
prompted Wieland's crimes, neither has He prevented them: rather,
a slaughter of innocents has taken place unhindered in God's name.

Wieland's denouement, which parodies the Abraham-Isaac story and shatters the fragile expectations set up by the novel's Old Testament subtext, constitutes a reverse epiphany, a conspicuous failure of the Deity, whose agency has been in question since the opening pages, to manifest Himself.

This failure, even more than any subtheme or network of imagery, causes the skepticism that haunts *Wieland* to metastasize. Could a merciful God, Brown seems to ask, remain aloof to infanticide? And, conversely, given the horror of Wieland's infanticide, can one still posit a merciful God? Or has the last lamp lit against moral night in this unrelentingly nocturnal work been extinguished?

To be sure, Clara's miraculous, last-minute rescue from her deranged brother seems, on the contrary, to testify to a watchful and merciful God who hears His children's prayers and responds. Recalling her confrontation with Wieland, Clara writes: "I spoke, but my words were half formed:—'Spare me, my brother! Look down, righteous Judge! snatch me from this fate! take away this fury from him, or turn it elsewhere.' . . . Supplicating eyes were cast upward; but when my prayer was breathed I once more wildly gazed at the door. A form met my sight; I shuddered as if the God whom I invoked were present. It was Carwin that again intruded" (226). Clara's prayer, of course, *is* answered: she is spared, and Wieland's fury is directed elsewhere—against himself. However, the fact that Clara's plea to God conjures up only the all-too-human Carwin seems rather an ironic indictment of the God who has absented His aid for so long. In both the literal and practical sense, it is Carwin, not God, who answers Clara's prayer—and who continues to stand in for an otherwise deaf and dumb Deity.

The shadow of a death-of-God theme is visible even in the deep structure of this novel that so repeatedly records the demise of fathers. Witness not only the elder Wieland's spontaneous combustion and Wieland's own suicide, but also Clara's grandfather's suicide (we are told he threw himself from a cliff) and Maxwell's assassination of Stuart (Louisa Conway's father). Set against and penned in an atmosphere of historical patricide, *Wieland* is not only punctuated throughout by the untimely deaths of various fathers, but imprinted with the suggestion that, in dying, these characters do but follow their Heavenly Father into oblivion.

The Second Great Awakening was to renew and consolidate America's sense of national purpose by inaugurating a civil religion based on a democratized Christian God and founded on the belief "that Americans are a peculiar race, chosen by God to perfect the world."[58] This religious nationalism, whose roots, as noted, lay deep in colonial Calvinism, would underwrite the political doctrine of Manifest Destiny, the economic goals of industrial capitalism, and the social tendency toward "romantic perfectionism" that has so colored the Republic's history. *Wieland,* however, poses a contrary, highly skeptical vision of God and the American experience—one that stresses the abyss on whose verge the nation's temple has been erected.

THE "AUTHOR OF THIS . . . DEVASTATION"

Considering the ominous tenor of his first major novel, one wonders, finally, in what light Brown must have viewed the medium that had given form to, if not elicited, such dire intimations. If, as *Wieland* dramatized, acts of good intent could have evil consequences, what of the morally equivocal venture of romance writing?

Brown, like many other fiction writers of his time, insisted that his writing had a moral purpose: "In my literary moods," he remarked, "I am aiming at making the world something better than I find it."[59] His prefaces routinely purport to uplift the reader, teach discipline, and expose ethical pitfalls. Given that in the 1790s the reading and writing of fiction was still frowned upon as licentious,[60] this manifest moralizing is, perhaps, only to be expected. Nevertheless, such prefaces may also have betrayed anxieties about the moral dilemmas fiction writing posed— anxieties Brown's fictional preoccupations could only have multiplied.

If his romances are any indication, Brown was almost certainly dubious about his medium and role. Consider his frequent characterization of the reader as voyeur. In *Edgar Huntly* Edgar, after entering Clithero's chamber, prying into his trunk and digging up his strongbox, peruses Clithero's memoirs. In *Wieland* Carwin not only reads Pleyel's personal correspondence but steals into Clara's room to read her books and personal jottings. Pleyel, meanwhile, spies over Clara's shoulder as she writes in her journal. The act of reading is repeatedly conveyed as something shameful, necessitating secrecy, while writing is portrayed—at least in this last instance—as an almost provocative posture.

Or consider Brown's use of the penknife as a prop in *Wieland* and *Ormond.* Seized as a weapon of defense by both Clara Wieland and Constantia Dudley, the penknife is an icon of ambiguous purpose, and hints at a lethalness in the writing act—as if the pen Brown wields is somehow akin to the penknife Clara wields. Consider, too, the frequency with which Brown uses the term "author" to mean originator—almost invariably, the originator of evil. Carwin, for instance, is referred to repeatedly as the "author of evils" (50, 94, 244). *Wieland* refers, in addition, to "the author of this unheard-of devastation" (160), "the author of all this misery" (161), the "author of this destruction" (159), "the author [of suffering]" (190), "the author of my peril" (189–90), "the author of this black conspiracy" (190), and "the author of this treason" (143). It is difficult not to sense artistic self-contempt in such persistently negative contextualizations.

Brown, then, it would seem, was generally anxious about his enterprise. And the Gothic themes that obsessed him no doubt intensified his anxieties. But their most implacable source may well have been a dilemma concerning artistic responsibility that Carwin helps bring into focus. Carwin is, as suggested earlier, an avatar of the artist. His "magical and thrilling" voice (68–69) and protean nature—he transforms himself from an "Englishman by birth" (69) into a Spaniard, and finally into an American rustic—identify him as an actor. His most frequent biloquial utterance—"Hold, hold!"—mimics Shakespeare's *Macbeth,* and he is, as often as not, the antecedent of the pejorative "author" phrases cataloged above. Carwin's biloquism, however, reflects the artist's/author's enterprise still more fundamentally. Both biloquist and artist project illusions, "transformations" that masquerade as realities. And in so doing they incur responsibilities. If the biloquist is irresponsible—or the artist merely mistaken—much mischief can result.

One of Carwin's crimes, certainly, is a blasphemous presumption: he counterfeits the voice of God. (Since, according to Judeo-Christian tradition, God is the Creator, the Author of our being, the Voice that created the world, there is a sense in which every artist and author flirts with presumption by inventing and projecting imaginary worlds and characters.) But because the divine presence Carwin counterfeits is ironically impeached, his crime goes beyond presumption to false prophesying, counterfeiting the voice of a God who may not exist: "I had filled your mind," he tells Clara, "with faith in shadows and confidence in dreams" (211). Every Gothic novelist, one might of course argue, does likewise, implicitly reifying the existence of God if only by invoking His opposite. The Gothic novelist, even more than other fiction writers, depends on a kind of biloquial ability to project a supernatural presence into every nocturnal landscape and winding staircase, to throw the whisper, if not the voice, of spirits at strategic moments. Not even Mrs. Radcliffe's rationalistic endings can undermine the supernaturalist myths by which the genre is defined.

But when Brown, controverting the expectations of the genre far more than Radcliffe did, depicts a world in which God is either dead or doting, he risks an artistic guilt commensurate with Carwin's audacity. For in telling what he presumes is the truth, he risks doing to the reader what Clara's uncle cautions her against doing to Wieland: disabusing him of an illusion that may be essential to his existence. Clara's uncle puts the matter bluntly: "What is it that enables him to bear the remembrance [of his deeds] but the belief that he acted as duty enjoined. Would you rashly bereave him of this belief?" (186) Later on, Clara, mourning her dead brother, explicitly regrets this aspect of his fate: "Oh that thy phrenzy had never been cured! that thy madness, with its blissful visions, would return" (213). Clara, indeed, as we have noted, survives her own ordeal by learning to counterfeit "blissful visions," to transform truths. Her final moralizing, with its implicit denial of every ambiguity raised earlier, seems to illustrate her transformation into one whose need to justify herself dictates feigning a new voice. Her lines are those of someone who has labored for sanity's sake to accept an illusion:

> It will not escape your notice, that the evils of which Carwin and Maxwell were the authors, owed their existence to the errors of the sufferers. All efforts would have been ineffectual to subvert the happiness or shorten the existence of the Stuarts, if their own frailty had not seconded these efforts. If the lady had crushed her disastrous passion in the bud, and driven the seducer from her presence, when the tendency of his artifices was seen; if Stuart had not admitted the spirit of absurd revenge, we should not have had to deplore this catastrophe. If Wieland had framed juster notions of moral duty, and of the divine attributes; or if I had been gifted with ordinary equanimity or foresight, the double-tongued deceiver would have been baffled and repelled. (244)

Clara's succumbing to self-deceit, however, suggests that the need to create protective fictions may be universal.

Brown, then, at least implicitly doubts whether humankind, however deceived (or self-deceived), ought to be undeceived—even of a belief in shadows; whether the counterfeiting of illusions isn't crucial to survival. "An illusion which makes me happy is worth a verity which drags me to the ground," wrote Christoph Martin Wieland in *Idris and Zenide* (canto 3). To say so, though, is to spurn the notion of art as truth-telling, and to redefine it either as therapy or a form of propaganda, an instrument whose role is to perpetuate mass illusions for utilitarian reasons. Brown tables this last prospect in *Wieland*—a novel whose virtue is to dramatize dilemmas, not to propose answers. (He will return to it in *Edgar Huntly*.) Clearly, however, to ratify self-deceit and artifice as a *modus operandi* is to risk re-entering the cycle of Wieland's madness. *Arthur Mervyn*, we shall see, investigates an ethic of strategic transformation and self-deceit. So ambiguous, though, is the happy ending Arthur seems to achieve that it suggests the insolubility of the dilemmas involved.

In *Ormond,* the next book we will consider, Brown conceives an experiment to test the prescriptions Clara voices at the close of *Wieland*. Brown postulates a heroine capable of repelling seducers, spurning vengefulness, and holding fast to the principles of virtue. (Constantia Dudley does all this and more.) This tack both succeeds and fails; but the experiment reveals much about the nature of virtue and the difficulty of charting a moral course.

CHAPTER FOUR

ORMOND:

FEVER IN THE LAND

What Brown's fictions convey is an ambiguous warning to
Americans, and by implication, to all men, that the course of
action for a nation or an individual must be based on a balanced
wisdom which is aware of its own dark potentialities.

ARTHUR G. KIMBALL,
Rational Fictions:
A Study of Charles Brockden Brown

In *Ormond; or The Secret Witness* the young Constantia Dudley, paradigm
of virtue and common sense, confronts two consecutive dangers, the
first a yellow fever epidemic that ravages Philadelphia, and the second a
scheming seducer—the titular Ormond. Ormond, after courting Constantia with limited success and murdering her father to enhance his
own influence, decides, in the face of further frustration occasioned by
the interloping narrator, Sophia Westwyn, to rape Constantia. Trapping
her alone in an empty house, Ormond makes plain his intention, despite her threat to commit suicide rather than submit to dishonor. But
the curtain, which closes as Ormond vows, "Living or dead, the prize
that I have in view shall be mine," reopens over his prostrate form—
Constantia having forgone suicide to plunge a penknife into his chest.[1]

From the first, *Ormond* has been a Rorschach blot for critics. Its structure and characterization have been alternately lauded and damned.[2] Its
literary mode has yet to be agreed upon.[3] Its theme has long been moot.[4]
As of 1974, the novel's protagonist was still in question.[5] Critics have
tended to view *Ormond* simplistically as a tale of virtue tried and triumphant or to address the book obliquely, concentrating on such peripheral
concerns as feminine pedagogy and Godwinian philosophy.[6] More recent
critics—in the absence, perhaps, of a clearer critical framework—have
summoned increasingly eccentric interpretations or dismissed the book
out of hand as an incompetently crafted mélange of abortive themes,
confused archetypes, and hasty improvisations.[7] Close studies of the

book's structure and imagery, however, as Paul Witherington points out, have been lacking.[8]

Warner B. Berthoff's 1954 dissertation on Brown is an exception to this bleak picture. Berthoff sees the novel as a venture in symbolism: "[Brown's] symbols for society, from which the manners and the motives of Constantia and Ormond take color, are worked out in the two major events recorded in the first section: the defrauding by Thomas Craig of Constantia's father, which sinks the Dudley family into desperate poverty, and the epidemic which infests the whole city and exposes Constantia to the perverse fulfillment of death." He considers the yellow fever plague "a medium of trial and revelation, in which whatever is latent—the weakness of an individual constitution, the secret truth about society—is shocked into the open." *Ormond*, he contends, depicts "a struggle for power by the good and evil alike"—a struggle carried out within a society whose poisoned moral atmosphere requires "an ethic of individual integrity and self-development," but whose hostility "drives those who seek to live by this ethic to choose between a self-inclosed sterility and an unnatural violence."[9] In addition to recognizing the book's symbolist core, Berthoff suggests that *Ormond* doesn't so much dramatize an ethic—Constantia's virtue—as present "a fable about the ethical life."[10] He locates Constantia, moreover, at the center of this fable, where she belongs, rather than casting her in a supporting role to the charismatic Ormond. Finally, he acknowledges an ambiguous tenor to the ending, Constantia's preservation notwithstanding.

Ormond is indeed a symbolist work, perhaps the first in American fiction. It represents a thematic extension of discoveries set forth in *Wieland* concerning the depravity latent in everyone and operative in all realms of experience—personal, domestic, and political. If *Wieland* culminates in a vision fraught with skepticism and shocked self-recognition, *Ormond* seeks both to embody this vision in symbolic terms and to scrutinize it further: to see if, as it were, there hasn't been some mistake. In *Ormond* Brown probes whether a determined pursuit of virtue and reason isn't at least theoretically possible; whether the dilemmas dramatized in *Wieland* are as irreconcilable as they appear. Both in its form and content, then, *Ormond* is an experimental novel.

This chapter will investigate the experimental techniques Brown employs in *Ormond*—particularly the device of the yellow fever plague. It will also explore the discoveries Brown makes concerning the viability of virtue and reason as absolutes in human conduct. And it will try to synthesize the domestic and political implications of a tale whose human drama is but one step removed from various social, political, and historical dramas in which turn-of-the-century America was involved.

"EVIL, POLITICAL AND PHYSICAL"

Brown's outline of *Wieland* suggests that at the start he had no clear conception of the vision he was to arrive at by the novel's end. From all indications, the book was begun with the conventional sentimental-Gothic model in mind: Carwin was to play the traditional villain; the Wielands were to be his victims—Clara ("Caroline," originally) playing a decidedly minor role.[11] As the romance evolved, however, the depravity that Carwin seemed to embody came to defy localization, migrating first to Wieland, then finally to Clara. This evolution of focus is reflected in Carwin's waning significance as the tale progresses, and amounts, one suspects, to a discovery on Brown's part of the full implications of his vision.

At the outset of *Ormond,* however, Brown had already articulated a vision of evil, of humanity, of America. Many of the problems of this second major work, I would suggest, stem from an attempt to give appropriate form to this vision. The yellow fever motif is Brown's attempt to express a comprehensive vision of evil in a single symbol. Perhaps the conscious nature of his enterprise is what thwarts him, for in knowing what he wants, Brown tends to demand too much, to insist that his symbol function simultaneously on several highly specific planes of reference. Brown is so specific about these planes that the symbol verges, at times, on multiple allegory. The experiment, however, not only provides an index to Brown's literary development but adumbrates the course of nineteenth-century American fiction as well.[12]

Brown introduces the yellow fever motif early in the text. It is intertwined, though, with a related motif that demands independent scrutiny—a motif that, although overshadowed by the yellow fever symbol, functions in its own right before and after the plague episode. Beneath the surface of *Ormond* is a fable of incest so deviously broached that one is scarcely inclined to credit it at all. This incest motif is first enunciated when Stephen Dudley, his fortune plundered by the duplicitous Thomas Craig, succumbs to a species of depravity whose exact nature Brown delays specifying.

Mr. Dudley's character disintegrates, we are told, because of his misfortunes. But it is the death of his wife, following upon financial upset, that shatters his equilibrium. No sooner does Mrs. Dudley die than Constantia is beset by "evils . . . to which it is likely she would have yielded, had not their approach been intercepted by an evil of a different kind." The intercepting evil proves to be Dudley's blindness. Our immediate concern, though, is the initial evil associated with Dudley's character transformation (26).

Brown piques us with ambiguous rhetoric for several pages before ascribing Dudley's dissolution to demon drink. A closer look at Brown's diction, however, discredits this explanation. Brown describes Dudley's desolate state of mind as follows: "The pressure of grief is sometimes such as to prompt us to seek a refuge in voluntary death. We must lay aside the burthen which we cannot sustain. If thought degenerate into a vehicle of pain, what remains but to destroy that vehicle? For this end death is the obvious, but not the only, or, morally speaking, the worst means. *There is one method of obtaining the bliss of forgetfulness, in comparison with which suicide is innocent*" (26, emphasis added). Can Brown really be suggesting that drunkenness is more reprehensible than suicide? Vague innuendoes follow: "The strongest mind is swayed by circumstance. . . . There is no firmness of integrity, perhaps, able to repel every species of temptation. . . . Yet temptation is successful chiefly by virtue of its gradual and invisible approaches. We rush into danger, because we are not aware of its existence. . . . Our opposition grows fainter . . . and the man becomes enslaved by the most sordid vices . . . who would have been imagined liable to any species of depravity, more than to this" (26–27). Again, the characterization of Dudley's "depravity" belies the explanation: Is it likely an aging man would be ignorant of the consequences of drink—would "rush into danger" unaware? Why, moreover, would this temptation be characterized by "gradual and invisible approaches"? Was someone unobtrusively stocking Dudley's brandy cellar one bottle at a time? This incongruity between the crime and its characterization becomes complete when the narrator concludes that "in the many-colored scenes of human life, none surpasses [this picture of Dudley's lapse into drink] in disastrousness and horror" (27). Such apparent overstatement can only be reconciled by looking beyond Brown's explanation to one that lies between the lines.

When the indictment of drunkenness is finally lodged, it is embedded in a series of vague, sensationalized, and ambiguous phrases:

Mr. Dudley's education had entailed upon him many errors; yet who would have supposed it possible for him to be enslaved by a depraved appetite, to be enamored of low debauchery, and to grasp at the happiness that intoxication had to bestow? This was a mournful period in Constantia's history. . . . I cannot describe the manner in which she was affected by the first symptoms of this depravity, the struggle which she made to counteract this dreadful infatuation, and the grief which she experienced from the repeated miscarriage of her efforts. I will not detail her various expedients for this end, the appeals which she made to his understanding, to his sense of honor and dread of infamy, to the gratitude to which she was entitled, and to the injunctions of parental duty. I will not detail his fits of remorse, his fruitless penitence and continual relapses, nor depict the heartbreaking scenes of uproar and violence, and foul disgrace that accompanied his paroxysms of drunkenness. (27)

Brown's melodramatic rhetoric camouflages a lexis of prurience. Phrases like "a depraved appetite," "enamoured of low debauchery," and "dreadful infatuation," though perhaps figuratively suggesting drunkenness, also reverberate with sexual overtones. And the word "miscarriage" raises questions. Given the context of the story (a father bereaved of a wife and confronted with a maturing sixteen-year-old daughter), another possibility—incest—suggests itself.

Especially when Dudley's blindness is introduced as, of all things, "a fortunate event," on the grounds that "it dissolved the spell, by which he was bound, and which, it is probable, would never have been otherwise broken" (27–28). Why, one wonders, should blindness break the spell of liquor? On the other hand, in the absence of visual stimuli an incestuous attraction might understandably give way to more appropriate emotions. Brown remarks on the new filial relationship: "The genius and eloquence of [Constantia's] father, nourished by perpetual exercise, and *undiverted from its purpose by visible objects,* frequently afforded her a delight in comparison with which all other pleasures were mean" (29, emphasis added). In the course of the tale Brown's insinuations about the nature of Stephen Dudley's affection for Constantia become more pronounced. We learn that Dudley "never reflected on his relationship to her without rapture" (174) and that "the emotions which [Constantia's image] excited sprung but in part from the relationship of father" (181–82). Brown later adds: "The filial passion is perhaps instinctive to man; but its energy is modified by various circumstances. Every event in the life of Constantia contributed to heighten this passion beyond customary bounds" (215). After her father's murder, Constantia consoles herself with the dubious solace that "her father had only exchanged one form of being for another: That he still lived . . . to enter the recesses of her thought" (216)—a fancy which, late in the tale, the narrator makes more explicit while recalling her earlier despair at ever finding Constantia alive: "From [the Dudley's] house I wandered to the field where the dead had been promiscuously . . . interred. . . . The father and child had been placed in the same cart and thrown into the same hole" (249). This vision of father and daughter "promiscuously . . . interred" completes one phase of a motif which, in various guises, haunts *Ormond.*

Incest motifs were not unusual in fictions of the early Republic. Anne Dalke, citing eight early-American novels (Brown's not among them), has theorized that depictions of incest projected "political anxiety" over the erosion of a well-defined social system.[13] And indeed, more than any other of Brown's fictions except *Arthur Mervyn* (in which an incest motif recurs), *Ormond* presents a social landscape in which individuals and families carom from one socioeconomic plane to another. (Witness how the Dudleys and Thomas Craig, whom Dudley employs and is robbed by, trade places.) The political connotations of incest will be explored at greater length below. At present I wish only to gesture in their direction as a prelude to observing that, by functioning as an archetype of "evil, political and physical" (35), the incest motif both parallels and reinforces *Ormond*'s major motif—the yellow fever plague.

This veiled drama of incest, meanwhile, displays two of Brown's characteristic prose strategies—an orientation toward symbolism and an ambitious use of diction to complement, if not to achieve, a symbolic dimension. Brown's diction lends itself, as often as not, to parody and criticism; yet there are passages in which his melodramatic rhetoric camouflages allusions—hence the baroque renderings. ("Amorous contagion," for instance, may be a laughable rendition of "love," but its metaphoric significance would be lost if the conventional substitute were employed.) One marvels, for instance, at how, in the passage quoted above, Brown uses the vocabulary of sickness—e.g., such terms as "symptoms of . . . depravity," "fits of remorse," "continual relapses," and "paroxysms of drunkenness"—to describe Dudley's dissoluteness, all but anticipating the yellow fever symbol shortly to be introduced. At such times Brown's diction seems to strain toward symbolic levels by itself, unassisted by dramatic elements.

Ormond opens, then, with the suggestion that evil, alive in society at large, is dormant in even the virtuous breast. The incursion of yellow fever into such a world seems almost poetically justified.

Brown introduces the yellow fever motif as a symbol from the outset. Constantia first encounters the plague as a literal fact—yellow fever having caused the death of a bookseller acquaintance, Mr. Watson. The abstract nouns Brown uses to refer to the plague, however ("the evil," "the malady" [34]), suggest a wider intent. Constantia's dawning recognition of this epidemic, meanwhile, parallels her dawning recognition of evil in the world at large—evil with which she has had little prior experience: "She lived at no great distance from the seat of the malady, but her neighbourhood had been hitherto exempt" (34). The yellow fever plague, then, is both a real pestilence that kills people and a correlative for a generalized evil.

Brown specifies the scope of his symbol in the following paragraph: "Contagious diseases, [Constantia] well knew, periodically visited and laid waste the Greek and Egyptian cities. It constituted no small part of that mass of evil, political and physical, by which that portion of the world has been so long afflicted. That a pest equally malignant had assailed the metropolis of her own country—a town famous for the salubrity of its airs and the perfection of its police—had something in it so wild and uncouth, that she could not reconcile herself to the possibility of such an event" (35). Thus phrased, the "event" extends beyond the pale of a disease epidemic: Brown associates it with that "mass of evil, political and physical" that has always haunted the world. Its potential victim is both the individual—Constantia—and America, a nation "famous for the salubrity of its airs and the perfection of its police."

Brown develops his symbol well enough at first, establishing the plague as a historical fact, then raising it to the status of a timeless, generative evil, the cause of poverty, famine, economic paralysis, and fear— for these are the scourges it wreaks on Philadelphia and has wreaked, Brown would have us know, on other cities through the ages. This abstract meaning persists even after the plague sequence, when we find Ormond using the language of sickness to characterize human society in general: "A mortal poison pervaded the whole system, by means of which every thing received was converted into bane and purulence" (112). Brown's goal, however, is finally more narrow and ambitious: to symbolize "evil, political *and* physical."

He begins by linking the two parameters through the improbable, but surprisingly convenient, common denominator of geography.[14] France and Italy, the two countries that, as Stephen Dudley notes, yellow fever epidemics have ravaged with particular ferocity, are also, as it happens, notorious settings of political upheavals. Dudley discourses on "the revolutions of Italy" (28), as the character Martinette de Beauvais does later on the French Revolution. So when Dudley, fearing the incursion of the plague in his own country, bemoans "a truth too plain to be disguised"—namely, that "the tragedies of Marseilles and Messina will be reacted on this stage" (36)—a political meaning, the threat of revolution, throbs behind the literal one. (History, ironically, elaborates the figure even better than Brown is able to: the plague that struck Philadelphia in 1793 may well have been introduced by French refugees fleeing Cap Francais and the St. Domingue revolution in progress there during July 1793.[15]) This association between political and physical subversion is reinforced by such lexical gambits as "the reigning disease" (44, 61, 70) and "strength of constitution" (71)—phrases that link the body and body politic.

The identification of fever with political upheaval, meanwhile, was one Brown's contemporary readers would likely have understood, for the image of disease as a figure for revolutionary populism was a staple of late-eighteenth-century political rhetoric. During the Revolutionary War, for instance, Thomas Hutchinson, the last governor of Massachusetts colony, referred in a letter to the democratic spirit that was afoot in the town meetings as an "infection."[16] Benjamin Rush, in "The Influence of the American Revolution" (1789), spoke likewise of "the contagion of rebellion,"[17] as Edmund Burke did of the "distemper" of revolution;[18] and William Ellery Channing noted, upon arriving at Harvard, that "the French Revolution had diseased the imagination . . . of men everywhere."[19] *The Federalist Papers,* indeed, are rife with references to the "ill-humors" of democracy, "the pestilential influence of party animosities," and the "disease" or "malady" of faction that tends to "infect" the "body politic."[20] Literally speaking, then, Constantia's health is in danger; figuratively, however, her moral well-being and America's political well-being are at risk.

Brown seems also to bid for the sexual connotation of the word *physi-*

cal as part of the matrix of meaning surrounding the fever. (He had done so once before, in the short story "Jessica.") At first we only infer the association because the sentimental-Gothic plot, which juxtaposes alternating threats to Constantia's health and virtue, activates it. Before long, however, Brown makes the link implicit, comparing the virtually romantic sentiment Constantia displays for Sophia to a "febrile affection" and characterizing marriage as a "remedy" and "cure" for physical passion (104). Finally the identification becomes explicit: "Sexual sensations," Brown writes, "associating themselves, in a certain way, with our ideas, beget a disease which . . . is a case of more entire subversion of the mind than any other" (160). The last phrase, of course, suggests the common denominator between these realms of meaning: much as sexual passion can overwhelm individual self-discipline and reason, political passion can overwhelm and undo a political system. Federalist rhetoricians, indeed, routinely conflated political and moral subversion, both of which threats they traced to France, the era's paradigmatic hotbed of rakes and rebels. Thus the Reverend Timothy Dwight's July 4, 1798, jeremiad alleging a French "contagion" abroad in America asked, "Shall our sons become the disciples of Voltaire, and the dragoons of Marat; or our daughters the concubines of the Illuminati?" [21]

Brown, it seems clear, is depicting a society in which traditional institutions (church, state, class) and attitudes (the "deference to paternal authority" [5] that defined Stephen Dudley's world) have given way to new and untested freedoms, both individual and political—freedoms that define the world of Constantia. But who knew where these freedoms would end? Perhaps in a society of godless seducers and schemers like Ormond; perhaps in a nation of con men like Thomas Craig, ruthless ideologues like Martinette de Beauvais, or disposable victims like Ormond's suicidal mistress, Helena Cleves. Brown's yellow fever motif aspires to correlate this range of related anxieties, domestic as well as political, that stemmed from what Federalist America perceived as the deliberate subversion of cherished forms and values. What the yellow fever motif resolves into instead, however, is a kind of several-tiered allegory—physiological fact plus "physical" (i.e., sexual) trope plus political metaphor.

So ambitious a device seems doomed from the start. What plot can sustain such elaborately envisioned and intertwined correspondences? Perhaps it is frustration with the difficult task he has set himself that leads Brown to embark on two digressions, the first concerning the

Whiston family and the second, the Baxter and Monrose families. These digressions, troublesome to generations of readers, in which Brown arrogates freedom from plot at the expense of plot, make little sense except as attempts on Brown's part to shore up a flagging symbol.

The first of these digressions concerns the Dudleys' neighbor, Whiston, "a young man . . . who divided his gains with an only sister who lived with him, and who performed every household office" (44). When Whiston, having earlier displayed symptoms of the plague, fails to pay his customary visit to the Dudley household, Constantia, fearing the worst, calls at his house. She finds his sister Mary alone on her deathbed, deserted by her brother: "It appeared that Whiston had allowed his terrors to overpower his sense of what was due to his sister and to humanity," observes the narrator (48). Whiston's cowardice costs him dearly, for he too is infected, and dies horribly: "Whiston, deserted by every human creature, burning with fever, tormented into madness by thirst, spent three miserable days in agony. When dead, no one would cover his body with earth, but he was suffered to decay by piecemeal" (48).

More conspicuous still is the Baxter-Monrose digression. This narrative four times removed is told by Constantia's friend, former employee, and neighbor Sarah Baxter, who loses a husband and her two eldest daughters to yellow fever. Constantia discovers her distress, aids her, and is, in turn, assisted by Sarah in her own time of illness. The friendship that ensues leads Sarah to relate the unusual circumstances under which her husband fell ill. Sarah's story concerns the Baxters' neighbors, a Frenchman named Monrose and his "daughter" (actually, foster child) Mlle Monrose. Baxter wakes one night to a strange glow emanating from Monrose's house, and goes to investigate. Perching on the fence that divides their properties, Baxter watches, transfixed, as a thoroughly composed Mlle Monrose appears, framed in candlelight, hauling what appears to be a dead body from the house to a newly dug grave. Baxter's horror is complete when the veil slips from the corpse's face, revealing Monrose himself. At this sight Baxter panics, scrambles from the fence, and returns home, only to display immediate symptoms of the yellow fever that claims his life some eleven days later. Brown quotes his fate as "an example of the force of imagination" bringing to fruition "seeds . . . [that otherwise] might perhaps have lain dormant" (71).

Would that we could read both episodes simply as illustrations of the plague's horrors. (They are, of course.) But as Brown presents them, they affect us less as documentary sketches than as moot morality plays,

Gothic dream sequences in which no one speaks, in which cause and effect can scarcely be discerned or trusted. Their obscurity, the many questions they give rise to, and their narrative remoteness make us wonder whether we have even been told all the facts. The Baxter-Monrose subplot in particular seems, like the portrait on which Constantia later muses, rife with a "species of mute expression" (77).

Their inscrutability notwithstanding, both episodes expand the yellow fever symbol by linking the disease with the breakdown of morals and social forms. Whiston abandons his sister; Baxter, for reasons never made clear, resembles a would-be criminal (or, at the very least, a peeping-tom): "A man, perched on a fence, at midnight, mute and motionless, and gazing at a dark and dreary dwelling, was an object calculated to rouse curiosity. . . . An observer would be apt to admit fearful conjectures" (68). For both Whiston and Baxter, then, the yellow fever they contract seems a consequence of, if not a correlative for, their dubious conduct.

Both digressions also underscore the "force of imagination." The seeds of evil, Brown implies, lie dormant in many people but don't necessarily flower. An overindulged imagination, however, can activate their growth. Here Brown implicitly links his symbol of evil to the process of artistic creation—to his own morbidly imaginative enterprise of "bookmaking." (The yellow fever sequence begins, we recall, with the death of Mr. Watson, a bookseller.) This self-censuring reflexiveness is seen in a more complex light elsewhere in *Ormond* in the implied characterization of the artist as "secret witness." Brown may even have sought to animate these digressions with "political" and "physical" significance—though here we tread, admittedly, on the thin ice of inference. The Whiston episode, for instance, in which a brother deserts his sister in her hour of need, enjoys just enough of a parallel in history to suggest a guilty cultural nightmare on America's part for what many believed was our betrayal of a legal and ethical commitment to aid our sibling republic France when the Revolution came under attack. An even more tailored political correlative hovers about the Baxter-Monrose subplot, in which Baxter plays the quintessential postrevolutionary American role of the paralyzed fence-sitter who watches, fascinated yet horrified, while a symbolic drama of regicide transpires in a neighbor's yard. Mlle Monrose, that is to say, who is later revealed to be the French revolutionary Martinette de Beauvais, coolly buries the corpse of her French "father," that "venerable figure . . . of tarnished splendour" (63).

Nor, perhaps, can we avoid wondering about the familial politics of these episodes. In a romance that opens with a drama of veiled incest and ends (I shall argue) with the specter of symbolic incest, what are we to make of a tale about an isolated brother and sister that ends in the sister's bedridden exigence and the brother's figurative ostracism and literal abomination? What are we to make of the Monrose-Mlle Monrose relationship, and of the "fever" that Baxter—himself the father of "two daughters, nearly grown to womanhood" (61), both of whom succumb at about the same time he does—contracts by spying on the Monroses' house at midnight? Is the relationship between the foster daughter, Mlle Monrose, and the "father" with whom she lives mute and ambiguous enough, perhaps, to provide a frame for, if not to trigger, Baxter's darkest fantasies? Does the image of an apparently ungrieving daughter summarily disposing of a dead father take on for Baxter the aspect of a paralyzing reproach for his own forbidden fantasies?

Whatever Brown's intent in these episodes, his plot and purpose fail in the interim. In the first place, the Baxter-Monrose subplot strains our credulity: we scarcely believe Baxter's strange surveillance, his inexplicable panic, or the improbable way in which he contracts the plague. The sequence seems artificial; its symbolism, stilted. Even more importantly, Brown's focus lapses. Sandwiched between these two potent digressions, the episode that ought to command attention—Constantia's own bout with the plague—goes almost unnoticed. Constantia, we are told, gets sick and recovers, but whatever dramatic or symbolic significance this event might have had for the tale isn't realized. Brown overloads his subplots, but slurs his climax, and this, more than his use of digressions per se, is the real measure of his failure in the first half of *Ormond*.

VIRTUE DECONSTRUCTED

The yellow fever, then, an abstract symbol of "evil, political and physical," as well as a literal motif, signifies various spheres of action or emotion—sexual, political, and perhaps even aesthetic (the "force of imagination")—that, when indulged beyond ordinary bounds, pose a threat to the health of the individual and society. The incest motif that precedes the fever symbol, moreover, performs a like role. Not only does it embody "physical" evil; as suggested earlier, it too constitutes a political metaphor. America's successive abuses at the hands of late-eighteenth-century Britain and France might be figuratively characterized as "violations." Britain's taxation policies—and, even more, the high-handed paternalism those policies spoke for—"violated" the daughter colony. Later, having successfully rebuked the king's intentions and established herself as an independent nation (with the help of her political sister France), America found herself threatened anew—this time by the fraternal nexus she had recently cherished. These violations, or prospective violations, in which America played an ambiguous and adolescent role herself (America's flirtation, as it were, with France both before and during the 1790s is a matter of record), are echoed structurally in the presumptions made on Constantia, first by her father, and later by the Frenchman Ormond. Together they represent antipodal dangers between which America had to steer her course.

The Baxter-Monrose subplot, meanwhile, marks the culmination of the symbolist treatment that defines the first half of *Ormond.* The yellow fever's significance becomes further clarified as the tale progresses, but no new associations are appended. Brown keeps the symbol alive through diction and imagery: the "symptoms" of love (161), love as an "incurable infirmity" (162), love as a "source of . . . maladies" (160), and so forth. Stretched to its limit, however, this predominantly symbolist approach shades off into other modes of development.

Remarkable though it is, Brown's symbolist experiment fails to the extent it ossifies into an unwieldy allegory. Later novelists such as Hawthorne and Melville would likewise explore the limits of allegory (Hawthorne in, for instance, "The Minister's Black Veil," Melville in *Mardi*) and the possibilities of symbolism (*The Scarlet Letter, Moby-Dick*), and would discover that the latter allowed the writer to juggle abstract ideas and spheres of allusion without becoming mired in fast correspondences. Whereas allegory harked back to an older world of fixed values and beliefs, the symbolism of a work like *The Scarlet Letter,* by recognizing competing moral assumptions, acknowledging uncertainty, and offering multiple interpretations of events, better reflected modern experience. *Ormond* anticipates this symbolist tack in American fiction.

The yellow fever symbol, meanwhile, is not the novel's only structural device. Brown's symbolist exposition yields to a closely related dramatic exposition featuring Ormond the seducer. A series of formal correspondences and dramatic ironies, moreover, links Constantia to Ormond and to the evil he embodies, preparing the way for her to succumb to his advances, discovering her own capacity for evil in the course of her seduction. Brown, however, resists the temptation to replay the

drama of Clara Wieland's gradual transformation. Postulating an inviolate heroine, he instead conducts an appellate hearing on the question of
universal depravity, reexamining reason and virtue—absolutes already
impeached in *Wieland*—to see if there isn't at least the possibility of
living a "healthy" life despite the plague. This hypothetical question
is also an anxious meditation on the American enterprise—for Constantia's history, like Clara's, recalls key national dilemmas. The book's
overall structure, then, echoes the "political" and "physical" concerns of
its chief symbol.

Brown's investigation leads to a surprising assessment of the paradoxes surrounding virtue as well as passion. He gropes, ultimately,
toward a compromise ethic resembling the "virtuous expediency" espoused by Plinlimmon in Melville's *Pierre, or The Ambiguities.* Thus
Ormond evolves not only beyond the terms of *Wieland,* but beyond its
own initial premises. Its ending, however, accentuates the ironies that
flank this stance even as it confirms the need to act in spite of them.

Many critics have denied any relationship between the seduction and
plague sequences in *Ormond,* and have faulted Brown on this account.[22]
The evidence, however—here as in *Edgar Huntly,* a romance that has
drawn similar fire for its disjointedness—is on Brown's side.

Ormond personifies the plague. Even as the fever represented "evil,
political and physical," Ormond is a seducer and a revolutionary, one
who entertains "unauthorized conceptions of matrimonial and political
equality" (140). Ormond's vaunted disregard for distinctions of class recalls the arbitrary progress of the epidemic and the "terror with which
all ranks appeared to have been seized" (35). His foreign extraction and
philosophical outlook—based on the axiom that a contagious corruption taints society—further the analogy. Ormond is, like the fever, a
prototype of evil: insidious, virtually invisible (consider his penchant
for disguise and surveillance), seemingly omnipresent, he penetrates
people's thoughts the way the fever penetrates their bodily defenses.
The plague incarnate, Ormond is an indiscriminate killer.

Constantia's progressive infatuation with Ormond soon becomes as
evident as was her prior compulsion to court the plague.[23] Even before her first audience with Ormond on behalf of his mistress, Helena,
Constantia shows herself predisposed in his favor, his profligacy notwithstanding: "The treatment which Helena had received from him,
exclusive of his fundamental error, betokened a mind to which she did

not disdain to be allied. In spite of his defects, she saw that their elements were more congenial, and the points of contact between this person and herself more numerous than between her and Helena" (146). It isn't long before we learn that "the image of Ormond occupied the chief place in her fancy, and was endowed with attractive and venerable qualities" (157).

Constantia's affinity for Ormond is, however, but the reflection of a deeper relationship signaled by a network of formal correspondences that joins the two: for, apparent contrasts notwithstanding, Constantia and Ormond have much in common. Both, for instance, rid themselves of intellectually inferior admirers (Balfour and Helena). Neither shows much patience with formalities. Both visit each other under assumed purposes (Ormond visits the Dudley household disguised as a chimney sweep; Constantia visits Ormond pretending concern over Craig's whereabouts). Each seeks to dissuade the other from continuing an ill-advised intrigue (Constantia knows Ormond is keeping Helena as a mistress; Ormond thinks Constantia is Thomas Craig's brother's jilted mistress). Ormond is characterized as an actor; theater imagery informs Constantia's speech. When, following Helena's suicide, Constantia inherits Ormond's estate, it's as if the virtual kinship between them is at last objectified.

Such extensive structural parallels imply, of course, that Constantia may share other, more distressing similarities to Ormond. Nor is Brown coy about revealing this implication: in a key exchange between the two, Ormond asks Constantia, "Is there no part of me in which you discover your own likeness?" (167). Such a question seems to adumbrate Constantia's surrender to Ormond's wiles. Brown, however, resists this obvious denouement, subliming Constantia's virtue the better to scrutinize it.

Constantia is no typical sentimental heroine. As her name suggests, her virtue remains adamant. She does not "fall." But her reaction to Ormond's incisive question betrays a mind-set that raises grave questions about her moral posture. Constantia, that is, refuses to acknowledge *any* similarity between herself and Ormond. And Brown, by qualifying the extent of her self-awareness, makes us wonder about the nature of her virtue.

The extent of Constantia's self-awareness sets *Ormond* apart from *Wieland,* whose drama consists largely of its heroine's growing awareness of her own potential for depravity—an awareness that, for Clara, develops for some time before culminating at the moment when she stands, penknife in hand, ready to dispatch her brother. In *Ormond,* however, the heroine is characterized instead by her knack for submerging self-recognition. Constantia's willful self-blindness juxtaposed with Ormond's generally unblinking perception both of others and of himself generates an instructive irony. Constantia's penchant for suppressing disturbing self-truths is dramatized in the scene following Ormond's abandonment of Helena Cleves, and Helena's subsequent suicide. For Ormond, Helena's suicide operates like a prism, diffusing his thoughts and feelings; for Constantia, on the contrary, it obscures self-awareness.

Even before that crucial episode, Constantia's encounters with Ormond, it becomes plain, have subtly altered her thinking. At one point, for example, she entertains doubts about the necessity of marriage that, prior to her acquaintance with Ormond, would have been uncharacteristic: "In her present reflections, . . . the eligibility of marriage seemed not so incontestable as before. . . . At present, there is a choice of evils, and that may now be desirable which at a former period, and in different circumstances, would have been clearly otherwise" (156–57). The narrator enlightens us further concerning this change in Constantia:

> In no case, perhaps, is the decision of a human being impartial, or totally uninfluenced by sinister or selfish motives. If Constantia surpassed others, it was not because her motives were pure, but because they possessed more of purity than others. Sinister considerations flow in upon us through imperceptible channels, and modify our thoughts in numberless ways, without our being truly conscious of their presence. . . . The image of Ormond occupied the chief place in [Constantia's] fancy. . . . A bias was hence created that swayed her thoughts, though she knew not that they were swayed. To this might justly be imputed some of the reluctance which she now felt to give Ormond to Helena. (157)

Constantia's growing passion for Ormond, then, quietly undermines her allegiance to virtue; she remains, however, "free from the consciousness of any secret bias" (167)—unaware, that is, of her shifting thoughts.

When Helena Cleves, following Ormond's brusque repulse, commits suicide, she enacts what can only be a mutual fantasy on the part of both Ormond and Constantia. How they confront this fact is significant. Immediately after he spurns Helena, Ormond goes to Constantia and confesses his passion for her, to which she responds with "excitements of grief" (167). Upon discovering Helena's suicide, Ormond reacts with characteristically brutal honesty: "Thou hast done my work for me. . . . I am satisfied" (171). Constantia, meanwhile, thanks to Helena's generosity, inherits Ormond's estate (which he had deeded to her, and she, to Constantia). Constantia thereby falls heir, quite literally, to Ormond's favors and to the fruits of what she herself has termed a murder on Ormond's part. (On learning of Ormond's abrupt disavowal of Helena, Constantia had accused him of planting "a dagger in her heart" [168].) And what is Constantia's reaction to this ironic turn of events? "She justly regarded the leisure and independence thus conferred upon her as inestimable benefits. It was a source of unbounded satisfaction on her father's account" (174). Whereas Ormond acknowledges his role and motivations, Constantia rationalizes her role as surviving usurper.

Constantia's blindness to her own motives and mental processes becomes increasingly evident as the tale progresses. Of her acceptance of the benefits conferred on her by Ormond after Helena's death the narrator says: "It created no bias on her judgment, or, at least, *none of which she was sensible*" (176, emphasis added). Constantia, moreover, after first embracing a perceived likeness to Ormond's sister, the revolutionary Martinette de Beauvais, denies all likeness after Martinette's recital of blood-letting ventures she has engaged in threatens to taint Constantia by association: "Constantia shuddered and drew back, to contemplate more deliberately the features of her guest. Hitherto she had read in them nothing that bespoke the desperate courage of a martyr, and the deep designing of an assassin. The image which her mind had reflected, from the deportment of this woman changed. The likeness which she had feigned to herself, was no longer seen" (207). Ormond, at last, in his penultimate interview with Constantia, unmasks her willful blindness: "Just now, I pitied thee for want of eyes: 'Twas a foolish compassion. Thou art happy, because thou seest not an inch before thee or behind" (255). It is the narrator, Sophia Westwyn, however, who passes judgment: "Rightly to estimate . . . danger and encounter it with firmness are worthy of a rational being; *but to place our security in thoughtlessness and blindness is only less ignoble than cowardice*" (263, emphasis added).

That Ormond should serve as an oracle of accusation in this matter is ironic, of course, for even he exhibits a species of self-blindness. Ormond is blind to his own susceptibility to passion—and therefore to the true mainsprings of his reasoning. (Shortly after introducing Ormond, Brown writes: "His conclusions . . . were not uninfluenced by

improper byasses; but of this he himself was scarcely conscious" [123].)
In fact, instances of self-blindness pervade the novel. Martinette proves
blind to the fact that her revolutionary ideals have dehumanized her.
Dudley's blindness is, of course, a literal fact as well as a metaphor for
his inability to spot Craig's duplicity.

Brown, in universalizing a figurative blindness, all but negates the
possibility of a disinterested virtue. For if virtue and rational idealism
derive from an unwillingness or inability to look at the true nature of
events or motives, then they are false and potentially fatal facades. Even
a virtue such as Constantia's begins to appear off-white, perhaps even
to mask hidden intents (the conceit is Brown's: Sophia's mother, we are
told, delighted to assume "the mask of virtue" [226]). At the moment
of her father's murder, Constantia is complacently relishing acquiescing
to her father's proposal of a trip to Europe. This filial acquiescence, however, is also a decision to travel figuratively in the continental footsteps of
Ormond and Martinette, Constantia's conscious motives notwithstanding. Brown underlines this irony with a lexical ploy reinvoking those
evils "political and physical" that Constantia is presumably eschewing
by obeying her father's will: "No change in [Constantia's] external situation had been wrought, and yet her mind had undergone the most signal
revolution. The novelty as well as the greatness of the prospect kept her
in a state of elevation and awe, more *ravishing* than any she had ever
experienced" (212, emphasis added).

In questioning the possibility of virtue, Brown undertakes roughly the
same task Hawthorne was to undertake in *The Blithedale Romance*. In that
novel Hawthorne, placing his characters in a utopian community apart
from the corruptions of society, asks whether humankind is capable of
living an ideal life, given the proper milieu and the will to do so. Brown,
however, appends an even more audacious question: If such a life *were*
possible, would it be worth living? In fact, he places Constantia's commitment to virtue in such a paradoxical light that we are forced to doubt
its advisability altogether.

The yellow fever symbol, I have suggested, signifies the danger of un-
regulated passion, both private and public. A virtuous constraint, then,
would seem to be the antidote. That, after all, was the prescription of
clerical and Federalist leaders as well as republican philosophers, who
postulated that a republic depended on its citizens' virtue in lieu of a
tyrant's arm. However, a vigorous self-constraint, Brown implies, can

have its own liabilities, precisely because of the internal walls it requires. This dilemma is best approached in context, though, for *Ormond* sets forth a range of behavioral paradoxes whose net effect is to suggest the danger of all extremes—and the relativity of ethical absolutes.

Consider Sophia's remark, late in the tale, that a lack of religious training may be to blame for Constantia's naiveté toward Ormond. Smacking of triteness and contrivance, this sudden observation has puzzled and frustrated critics. Some have seized desperately upon it as the novel's elusive theme.[24] Others have chalked it up to careless craftsmanship on Brown's part.[25] Neither explanation suffices. The opposite theme—religious fanaticism—is implicated, to be sure, as a dangerous form of passion in *Ormond* (not to mention *Wieland*). Quakerism, for instance, is indirectly implicated in the Baxter-Monrose subplot: Monrose's house, Brown tells us, once belonged to William Penn, whom he refers to elsewhere as that "incorrigible enthusiast."[26] Brown further impugns religion in several minor character portraits: the lecherous Father Bartoli; the protean devotee Madame de Leyva; her hypocrite husband M. de Leyva (having learned that his wife had run off with a Protestant, "De Leyva . . . , who was sincere in his religion as well as his love, was hasty to avenge this injury" [203]). But, given this broad suggestion that religiosity tends to mask, if not inflame, passion rather than to control it, Brown's apparent broaching of the need for religion bewilders. Religion, Brown would seem to suggest, is both a transparent corruption *and* a necessary corrective.

Taken as a deliberate paradox, however, this contradiction assumes its proper place within a larger scheme. For Brown, in the course of *Ormond,* renders paradoxical every aspect of the fever symbol. For example, imagination, though portrayed as an agent in the spread of the plague (the "force of imagination"), is also the means by which Constantia circumvents the plague: Brown highlights her ingenuity in procuring a cheap, plentiful food source without which she and her father would have starved. Moreover, imagination saves Constantia during her final encounter with Ormond, when she uses a penknife to dispatch her assailant.

Physical passion exhibits a similar paradox. The threat of incest hinted at earlier in the novel becomes inverted in the relationship of Sophia Westwyn and her loveless mother, lack of parental love proving almost as damaging as its overindulgence. So, too, love in general: plainly it can constitute a dangerous passion, as shown by Ormond's homicides and Helena's suicide. Yet the absence of love—sterility and isolation—poses a grim alternative. Even friendship partakes of this paradox. Sophia's obsessive friendship for Constantia represents a dangerous extreme, a "febrile affection" (187); yet friendship is elsewhere shown to be essential for human survival—in time of epidemic, for instance. This spirit of paradox besets political enterprise as well. Martinette, for example, kills remorselessly in the name of humanity and liberty. Or consider the French Revolution, with its excesses and devastation, juxtaposed (at least implicitly) against the less rapacious and presumably justified American Revolution. Martinette has in fact fought in both.

These dramatic paradoxes are summarized in the paradoxical aspect of the plague itself—a bane whose presence (in a dynamic we've seen before in *The Man at Home*) actually benefits Constantia, though it bereaves and destroys thousands:

> Such is the motley and ambiguous condition of human society, such is the complexity of all effects, from what cause soever they spring, that none can tell whether this destructive pestilence was, on the whole, productive of most pain or most pleasure. Those who had been sick and had recovered found, in this circumstance, a source of exultation. Others made haste, by new marriage, to supply the place of wives, husbands and children whom the scarcely-extinguished pestilence had swept away.
>
> Constance, however, was permitted to take no share in the general festivity. Such was the color of her fate, that the yellow fever, by affording her a respite from toil, supplying leisure for the acquisition of a useful branch of knowledge, and leading her to the discovery of a cheaper, more simple, and more wholesome method of subsistence, had been friendly, instead of adverse, to her happiness. Its disappearance, instead of relieving her from suffering, was the signal for the approach of new cares. (73)

These several paradoxes culminate in the paradox of virtue: for, if the fever cannot be altogether condemned, neither can the febrifuge be completely condoned.

The climax of *Ormond* dramatizes the triumph of virtue over vice. Constantia, menaced by Ormond, who has announced his intention of raping her, is forced either to yield her virtue or to kill herself or her attacker. She kills Ormond and remains inviolate, an apparently resplendent example of virtue triumphant. Brown undermines the victory, however, by deemphasizing Ormond's death and lingering, instead, on Constantia's subsequent entrapment in the house she grew up in. Peering through the keyhole in the aftermath of the assault, Constantia's friend and would-be rescuer, Sophia Westwyn, narrates:

> Presently I heard a voice within exclaim, in accents of mingled terror and grief, "Oh, what will become of me? *Shall I never be released from this detested prison?*"
> The voice was that of Constantia.
> . . . My sensations scarcely permitted me to call, "Constantia! For Heaven's sake what has happened to you? Open the door, I beseech you!"
> "What voice is that? Sophia Courtland! Oh my friend! *I am imprisoned! Some daemon has barred the door, beyond my power to unfasten.*"
> (289, my italics)

Having murdered the man whom, she confesses, she might have loved under the proper circumstances, Constantia awakens to discover her house a prison. Her imprisonment within her own walls suggests her emotional bondage to a stifling ethos. Constantia's virtue is her prison—a prison to which some "daemon" (not *demon: daemon,* on the contrary, means a "guardian spirit") has confined her.[27]

Constantia's survival takes on greater irony in light of the connotations imprisonment has acquired in the story. During the height of the plague she had feared her father might be imprisoned by their landlord, McCrea, for failing to pay the rent. Sophia describes Constantia's fears as follows: "The horrors of a prison had not hitherto been experienced or anticipated. The worst evil that [Constantia] had imagined was inexpressibly inferior to this. . . . It was better to die than to go to prison" (103). Constantia, in other words, has figuratively secured for herself a fate worse than death, her triumph over Ormond notwithstanding. Brown anticipates the theme of emotional imprisonment, meanwhile, by weaving a network of "fetter" imagery into his tale. When Constantia reproaches Ormond for his refusal to marry Helena, he pleads a contrary emotional attachment with the words, "See you not that I am fettered?" (165). Loath, moreover, "to put fetters on [his] usefulness" (166), Ormond seeks to avoid "wedlock" (179) altogether. This fetter motif is linked particularly to Constantia's mental and emotional well-being. Stephen Dudley refrains from rearing Constantia to a particular religious faith in order that she might develop "a mature and unfettered understanding" (180). Ormond, however, in his penultimate interview with Constantia, suggests that quite the reverse has occurred: "Heaven grant . . . thy disenthrallment from error, and the perpetuation of thy happiness" (259). Prior to assaulting Constantia, he reiterates the image: "Poor Constantia, . . . the toils that beset thee are inextricable" (275).

Virtue, then, is not merely a form of blindness; when carried to an extreme, it can be a form of self-imprisonment. Our initial relief for Constantia's safety yields, on second glance, to concern over the dubiousness of her self-deliverance. If it is her fortune to remain inviolate, it is also her fate. Her virtue is a two-way fortress. In sidestepping rape, Constantia stumbles, as Warner Berthoff suggests and as Brown's imagery implies,[28] toward sterility and isolation. Hence, the "incurable malignity in her fate" (264).

FRENCHMAN'S GAMBIT

If a self-denying virtue poses dilemmas in the personal sphere, it does no less in the political sphere. Constantia's confrontation with Ormond, at least, suggests as much.

That confrontation is adumbrated by the Baxter-Monrose subplot. A repetition of motifs (the glimmering light, the corpse, the male interloper, the ritual of "unveiling," the protagonist's ultimate entrapment within his or her own walls) is only part of a similarity that extends to the symbolic level. In the climax as well as in the Baxter-Monrose episode the suggestion of incest hovers over the encounter. Brown elsewhere emphasizes the extensive similarities between Constantia and Martinette. Besides "similitude in age and sex" [186], Constantia and Martinette share similar educations—including instruction in the sciences—and similar histories. Both have been, while adolescents, the objects of an incestuous (or quasi-incestuous) passion: Constantia, as suggested earlier, of her father's, and Martinette, of her spiritual guardian, Father Bartoli's. Both are, at various times, improbably and miraculously reunited with the foremost objects of their affections: Constantia with Sophia, and Martinette with Wentworth. Lastly, and perhaps most significantly, both are associated with France and Italy (Constantia has been schooled in French and Italian; Martinette has spent time in both countries). This association links Constantia and Martinette not only to each other, but also to the fever motif (as noted earlier, Brown specifies that previous outbreaks of the plague have ravaged Marseilles and Messina). Again, such correspondences imply other less flattering and superficial similarities between the virgin and the revolutionary. The revelation, therefore, that Martinette is actually Ormond's sister activates a hint of incest that is, if anything, more explicit here than it was in *Wieland* (in which the brother-sister relationship was patent, but the sexual nature of the confrontation only implicit). A corollary is the almost fratricidal nature of Constantia's self-defensive murder.

Like the Baxter-Monrose subplot, moreover, the climax of *Ormond* invites political reading—though here we must backtrack briefly to retrieve the thread of Brown's political theme. Brown, as suggested earlier, attempts a dual allegory of "physical" and "political" dimensions. So, as the fever motif wanes, Ormond emerges as the fever incarnate. Seducer and revolutionary, he embodies both a sexual and political threat. Owing to the centrality of the seduction motif, however, the political side of Ormond's identity becomes increasingly nominal. To be sure, Brown's sporadic references to Ormond's membership in a secret society patterned on the Illuminati shadow forth Ormond's identity as a revolutionary. And the popular mythology concerning the Illuminati was certainly fertile enough, in 1799, for Brown to have counted on his readers' making that inference.

The Order of the Illuminati, a fraternal society touting rationalist ideals, had been founded in 1776 by Adam Weishaupt, a law professor at the University of Ingolstadt. Its purpose was to combat the stifling power of the Bavarian Jesuits. Although it boasted three hundred members at one point, the organization was crushed in 1786 by the Bavarian government.[29] Its ghost, however, lived on. During the 1790s the defunct society became the whipping boy of reactionaries the world over. Paul C. Rodgers, Jr., observes: "Nourished by the very absence of solid confirmatory evidence, the shadowy spectre of Illuminism became a scapegoat for all manner of tumultuous change. . . . Political commentators credited it with fomenting Jacobinism and the enormities of the French Revolution."[30] John Robison, in a book published by Brown's New York publisher, George Forman, some six months prior to *Ormond,* set forth alleged proofs of the society's existence, of its responsibility for engineering the French Revolution, and—even more significant—of its presence in America.[31] Robison's allegations gained general credence in America when two prominent clergymen, Jedidiah Morse and Timothy

Dwight, enlarged upon them from the pulpit. Dwight's sermon "The Duty of Americans at the Current Crisis" characterized Illuminism as a "contagion," a system "dedicated to the overthrow of religion, government and human society, civil and domestic," and charged that "there are even in this state, persons, who are opposed to the government."[32] Dwight's brother Theodore even went so far as to publicly link the Illuminati to "Thomas Jefferson, Albert Gallatin, and their associates."[33] That Brown was aware of this developing mythology cannot be doubted: both Dwight and Morse were fellow guests at the Friendly Club.[34]

The problem with Brown's Illuminati motif is that he only alleges, never manages to dramatize, Ormond's secret-society connections. Ormond may be involved in subversive projects that are likely (Brown tells us) to influence the future of the Western world, but Brown *shows* us nothing of them. Ormond's political identity lapses, the Illuminati motif notwithstanding. Formalistically, Brown solves this problem by creating a character to play the role of Ormond's revolutionary counterpart: Ormond's sister, Martinette. Through Martinette, Brown is able not only to develop the political aspect of his theme but to link these political overtones to the American experience, for Martinette, we are told, has fought in the American Revolution. Through her Brown also adumbrates the implicitly American dilemma Constantia will face in the climax: a dilemma involving the actualization of ideals through violence and the paradoxes of liberty that result.

Constantia's personal history, meanwhile—and, hence, the book's overall structure—virtually allegorizes the political history of late-eighteenth-century America. Her youth is marked by a crisis involving filial violation and culminates in a crisis involving violation by the Frenchman Ormond. Throughout the trials that intervene, Constantia tries—as did America—to steer a middle course, to preserve both her independence and her principles. In so doing, however, she remains blind to the violent potential latent in the liberal spirit she alternately flirts and identifies with, and to which she feels beholden—a liberal spirit embodied, for Constantia, in Ormond, and, for America, in France. This political allegory is corroborated by the theme of maintaining independence that is developed sporadically throughout the novel. Early in the tale Constantia becomes preoccupied with "maintaining her independence inviolate" (88). Rejecting marriage, at one point, because it would impede her from administering her property (America's own impetus for self-determination is ironically recalled),

Constantia rationalizes her decision: "Homely liberty was better than splendid servitude" (85). The climax of *Ormond* completes both the political allegory suggested above and the theme of maintaining an inviolate independence.

Ormond, by dropping all pretense of high-minded intent and beneficence and attempting to force Constantia's compliance to his wishes, recalls France's coerciveness toward America in 1797–98—even as Constantia's response reflects the nation's. Having taken umbrage at the Jay Treaty, which America signed with Great Britain and ratified in 1796, France, as Vernon Stauffer notes, adopted toward the United States "a policy of coercion, of which two chief instruments were the destruction of American commerce upon the high seas and the overbearing and insolent conduct of diplomatic negotiations." This policy of coercion—and particularly the diplomatic outrage of the XYZ Affair—when laid before the American public (in April 1798) caused an unprecedented outcry:

> The result was, to the discomfiture and disgrace of the Democrats in particular and to the alarm of the country in general, that the United States was made aware of the fact that its government was being driven into a corner from which, as far as a human mind could foresee, the only avenue of honorable escape would be recourse to arms. . . .
>
> To the sense of injustice was added the burden of fear. The idea began to take possession of the minds of leaders of thought in America that France had darker and more terrible purposes in her councils than the blighting of American commerce in retaliation for the treaty-alliance which had recently been concluded with Great Britain; she sought . . . to visit upon this nation . . . overwhelming disasters. . . . [France's] ravenous appetite could not be satisfied.

Once the full extent of France's intentions became apparent, America's revulsion, Stauffer continues, was complete: "All innocent delusions were shattered; all veils torn away." Consequently, "The passion for war with France became the one passion of the hour" [35]—one that eventuated, in fact, in an undeclared war.

With this political scenario in mind as well as the fact that Brown wrote *Ormond* only months after the XYZ Affair, consider Constantia's crisis. Upon Ormond's arrival at her house, Constantia rebukes him on the grounds that "your recent deportment but ill accords with your professions of sincerity" (275). But she soon notes a fundamental change in his attitude as well as his behavior: "There was something in the looks and accents of Ormond, different from former appearances. Tokens of an hidden purpose and a smothered meaning, were perceptible" (277). Her apprehension becomes fear when she finds herself menaced with threats, backed, indeed, into a corner: "Now did she perceive herself sinking in the toils of some lurking enemy" (277). That enemy—the Frenchman Ormond—proceeds to claim from Constantia credit and more for having dispatched her parent: "For killing him," says Ormond, "I may claim your gratitude. His death was a due and disinterested offering on the altar of your felicity and mine" (281). This tack failing to persuade her, Ormond proceeds in a more ominous vein: "What thou refusedst to bestow it is in my power to extort" (282). Constantia, realizing that "stratagem or force was all that remained, to elude or disarm her adversary" (282), resorts to the knife. In murdering Ormond, Constantia metaphorically enacts the sentiment of an American public outraged at France's presumption and willing at last to do whatever was necessary to sever an increasingly painful tie.

Historians have noted a permanent change in the tenor of American politics toward the turn of the century. This change, Vernon Parrington observes, involved a trend toward pragmatism: "The doctrine of the ethical absolute . . . quietly yielded to the more practical conception of expediency." [36] This trend is identified, ironically, not with the "realistic" Federalists, but with Jefferson's Republicans. Historians Charles and Mary Beard find pragmatism and compromise to be the characteristic feature of Jefferson's presidency, highlighting Jefferson's own remark, "What is practicable must often control what is pure theory," and summarizing his administration thus: "Jefferson, a practical man as well as a theorist, steered the ship of state by the headlands, not by distant and fixed stars." [37] America, during these difficult years, rejected her revolutionary heritage, the alliance with France that was its vestige, and the idealism both bespoke, and turned to a more practical ethic, a politics of survival. *Ormond* allegorizes this tack in the nation's course.

Given the trials to which extremist values (an adamant virtue, revolutionary idealism) seem prone, the tempering of absolute ethics with expedience would seem to offer the obvious alternative—and maybe even the only possible solution to the dilemmas *Ormond* investigates.

Ormond's query to Constantia, "Yet why should you not shun either extreme?" (167), suggests this course, and the introduction of Sophia Westwyn, the narrator, seems to second it. Mature and circumspect, Sophia is a virtual paradigm of the golden mean. Her experience of the world lets her perceive Ormond's character at a glance, yet has neither blunted her conscience nor made her cynical. She affirms the need for religion as a "security" and "bulwark," yet her friendship for Constantia testifies to her capacity for passionate response as well as considered restraint. Moreover, the fact that she is married suggests she has achieved that satisfactory resolution of opposing drives that seems denied to others in the novel. Here, Brown seems to suggest, is a balanced, healthy personality, a character well equipped to guide both reader and protagonist through the moral dilemmas the novel so insistently poses.

No such luck. This paradigm Sophia, we soon learn, is herself prey to a "master passion"—her love for Constantia. "I have indeed much to learn," she admits. "Sophia Courtland has never been wise. Her affections disdain the cold dictates of discretion, and spurn at every limit, that contending duties and mixed obligations prescribe" (250). Sophia, in fact, whose name signifies "wisdom," disclaims wisdom and confesses an ultimate allegiance, not to restraint and "the cold dictates of discretion," but to passion: "And yet, O! precious inebriation of the heart! O! preeminent love! what pleasure of reason or of sense can stand in competition with those, attendant upon thee? . . . surely thy sanction is divine; thy boon is happiness!" (250).[38] Sophia's romantic paean to that "precious inebriation of the heart" is potentially the most radical moment in the book, given the symbolic and philosophical context that precedes it. Far from repudiating the fever or merely flirting with the pestilence, Sophia apparently elects sickness over wellness. However, it is the very "sickness" of the attitude that undermines its validity, for, as several critics have observed, Sophia's friendship for Constantia verges on obsession: "I could not bear to withdraw my eyes from her countenance. If they wandered for a moment, I fell into doubt and perplexity. . . . The ordinary functions of nature were disturbed. The appetite for sleep and for food were confounded and lost amid the impetuosities of a master passion. . . . I would not part from her side, but eat [*sic*] and slept, walked and mused and read, with my arm locked in hers, and with her breath fanning my cheek" (250). Sophia's "master passion" not only recapitulates the thesis that passion, when indulged, tends to proceed beyond acceptable limits and to necessitate the very constraints it eschews; it also confirms the inexorability of the plague and forces us, furthermore, to review Sophia's narrative in light of her all-consuming love for Constantia.

Nevertheless, the possibility of a Sophia-like character free of such a flaw seems to interest Brown, judging from the next fiction he immersed himself in—*Arthur Mervyn*. Arthur, as we will see, begins as a naif-cum-bluenose, but experiments with the possibility of a tempered idealism that Sophia seems to suggest. *Ormond*, however, although backhandedly suggesting the Melvillean alternative of a "virtuous expediency," declines to affirm even this possible solution. There is as much pathos in this work, with its scrupulous search for a way out of the virulent darkness, as there is terror in the blackness that emanates from *Wieland*.

EPILOGUE: THE SECRET WITNESS

The significance of the subtitle of *Ormond*—"The Secret Witness"— is clarified during the climax when Ormond confesses to having spied upon private interviews involving Constantia and others. This device of Ormond's secret spying is central both to the plot and to the rational explanation of events.

Ormond's witnessing is not unique, however. In point of fact, there are several secret witnesses in *Ormond*. Stephen Dudley, standing unseen behind a door, witnesses Thomas Craig pick up a letter and curse its broken seal—an action which, in light of his later conduct, identifies Craig as a fraud. Baxter secretly watches from his perch on the fence as Mlle Monrose buries M. Monrose's corpse in the dead of night. Shortly after Constantia's ordeal with Ormond, Sophia Westwyn, peeking through a keyhole, views Constantia, her hair disheveled and clothes awry, looking as though she has just been ravished. Even Constantia is, at one point, invited by Ormond to "be a looker-on" (151)—as if to suggest her inclusion within the ranks of secret witnesses. And behind these overt instances lurks the specter of the Illuminati, who purportedly elevated spying to the status of philosophical rubric and *modus operandi*. [39]

One wonders, therefore, whether the obvious identification of Ormond as *the* secret witness isn't too delimiting; whether the significance of the subtitle doesn't lie in the larger pattern of secret witnessing suggested by these several instances. Their common denominator seems to be the epiphany of evil they record: an epiphany that, while primarily

a shock of recognition, is also, perhaps, a shock of self-recognition—
since a "secret" witness is one who both becomes privy to hidden truth
and himself has something to hide. These epiphanies are usually initia-
tory, the evil proving so contagious that to look upon it is, in effect,
to be stricken by it. Dudley's depravity, for instance, manifests itself
shortly after his discovery of Craig's duplicity, and Baxter no sooner
witnesses the effects of the plague on the Monroses than he contracts it.
All Brown's romances, in fact, meditate the consequences of consciously
recognizing evil. There is a fatalistic consistency to the way his seekers
are corrupted and consumed by the issue of their quest.[40]

In light of these considerations, an otherwise incidental and isolated
titular motif becomes significant. Besides presenting an ironic metaphor
of initiation, the secret-witness motif also poses theological doubts and
questions the role of both the artist and his audience. Brown's secret-
witness motif, for instance, impeaches the Deity. No sooner does Brown
identify the seemingly omniscient Ormond as the secret witness (260)
than the narrator refers, in passing, to the Deity as "that divine and
omniscient Observer" (262). Irony accrues from the association of God's
all-perceiving watchfulness with Ormond's sinister surveillance.

Brown's irony cuts deeper. As with the revelation in *Wieland* that
God did not utter the mysterious commands and that His voice was
absent during the horrors that transpired, the secret-witness motif in
Ormond implicitly faults a God who merely observes in *secret*—that is to
say, in silence[41]—the evil at large, without interfering to rectify it. In
this light, Sophia's assertion that "the study of concealment is, in all
cases, fruitless or hurtful" (262) becomes a more-than-perfunctory criticism, condemning even divine reservation. As in *Wieland*, this whisper
of apostasy is reinforced by a motif of dead, dying, or absent fathers.[42]

It is reinforced too when Sophia, in the course of her meditations,
proceeds from Constantia's victimization at the hands of Ormond, to
Constantia's victimization at the hands of Providence, to mankind's
victimization at the hands of Providence:

> I did not labour to vanquish the security of my friend [Constan-
> tia]. As to precautions, they were useless. There was no fortress,
> guarded by barriers of stone and iron and watched by centinels
> that never slept, to which she might retire from [Ormond's] strata-
> gems. If there were such a retreat, it would scarcely avail her
> against a foe, circumspect and subtle as Ormond.

I pondered on the condition of my friend. I reviewed the incidents of her life. I compared her lot with that of others. I could
not but discover a sort of incurable malignity in her fate. I felt as if
it were denied to her to enjoy a long life or permanent tranquillity.
I asked myself what she had done, entitling her to this incessant
persecution. Impatience and murmuring took the place of sorrow
and fear in my heart. When I reflected that all human agency was
merely subservient to a divine purpose, I fell into fits of accusation
and impiety. (264)

Sophia recants in the paragraph that follows; still, her lapse suggests the
scope of Brown's conceit. In *Ormond* as in *Wieland,* human device sup-
plants a secretive Deity, leaving the protagonist in a quandary of doubt
and fear. This deposing of the Deity is one of the direst transformations
in Brown's fictions.

The secret-witness motif also implicates the author, since fiction writing involves private scrutiny of character and situation. This is especially
true in *Ormond,* for the book specifically scrutinizes the mental processes
at work behind various masks, such as Constantia's virtue and Martinette's idealism. Here the author is not just an inadvertent observer,
but a highly self-conscious voyeur, hiding behind the narrator's skirts,
insinuating dark motives. As such, he is all the more rueful an heir to
discoveries made in his capacity as secret witness—discoveries that, as
they concern his creations, concern him.

The self-reflexiveness of the secret-witness motif is dramatized by the
fact that the various secret witnesses cited earlier are all types of the
artist. Not only is the theatrical and poetic Ormond a prototype of
the artist: Dudley is a painter; Sophia is the narrator and ostensible
writer of *Ormond;* Baxter is a victim of "the force of imagination." Meanwhile, the persistently negative contexts in which the term "author"
appears in *Ormond* reiterate Brown's morbid perception of the artist's
identity and enterprise. Phrases like "the authour of injury" (91), "dis-
tresses of which he was the authour" (92), "the authour of this new evil"
(217), "the authour of his fate" (278), and "the authour of this new impediment" (278) suggest an awe of the power of the pen and a nagging
fear that by depicting evil the author unleashes it.

The Protestant milieu in which Brown wrote clarifies Brown's awe of
the writer's wizardry. The poet's role had always been sacred: by naming, the poet conferred existence. Judeo-Christian tradition mytholo-

gized the poet's role, picturing the Creation as an act of divine poesis. This traditionally sacred aspect of the word was felt by eighteenth-century Americans to such an extent that the writer of fiction was condemned not only for trading in lies, but for arrogating divine privilege, for tampering with the divine order.[43] Brown, a child of the Enlightenment, was perhaps willing enough to ignore public rebuke, superstitious or otherwise. He could not, however, ignore his own dark findings; nor, it would seem, could he reconcile his role as the "authour of . . . new evil," the namer and, therefore, creator of depravities. Perhaps the self-doubts Brown's secret-witness figure exemplifies stem from the irony with which the discoveries he was making as a writer conformed to and confirmed the cultural bogey.

Brown clearly felt, along with many contemporary critics of fiction, that duplicity inheres in the author's task, since art often involves conscious posturing, deliberate assumption of identities. Michael Davitt Bell has commented at length on the extent to which Brown's romances hinge on a tension between sincerity and duplicity, with such villains as Carwin and Ormond emerging as "figure[s] of the artist as master of duplicity."[44] The written artifact especially can lie, as Thomas Craig's successive forgeries demonstrate. But it is not, finally, the conscious forgeries of Craig or even the duplicities of Ormond that disturb as much as the unconscious duplicities of Constantia—and, possibly, Sophia as well. Because she is the narrator, Sophia's motives compel consideration. To what extent is her love for Constantia a cataract on her—and, consequently, our—vision of Ormond? of Constantia? The inevitable corollary to this question, as Brown himself seems to have been well aware, is: To what extent do the author's secret motives and unconscious needs constitute a similar cataract on his and our vision? Such unwitting duplicity is captured in the figure of the artist as *secret* witness.

Constantia's knack for rationalizing problematic truths suggests that unconscious duplicity is universal. I ventured earlier that Brown's blindness motif, most troublingly exemplified in Constantia, implicates everyone for their unwillingness to look upon motives and desires. The secret witness is but the mirror image of the motif; an inversion, yes, but also a version. For a "secret witness" is one who sees, but pretends not to; who "witnesses"—that is, observes—but refuses to "witness"— to publicly acknowledge. (Both motifs are united in Stephen Dudley, who sees but blinks at the first signs of Craig's deception and goes blind shortly thereafter.) We are all, Brown implies, secret witnesses of our impulsive selves, watching fascinated, then pretending to have seen nothing.

As readers we stand in double jeopardy. The final irony of Brown's secret-witness motif is that it incriminates the reader for eavesdropping on dark scenes and dusky revelations. As was true in *Wieland,* the act of reading, like the act of writing, imbibes an aura of guilt; becomes a shared, conspiratorial venture. Consider Dudley's reading of the letter addressed to Craig—a piece of prying that, although justified, seems to precipitate not only Dudley's economic ruin but also the moral depravity that is its indirect consequence. We, too, in reading *Ormond,* peruse what is, formally speaking, a letter addressed to a private individual—one I. E. Rosenberg.[45] Does a similar moral taint accrue to us as a result of our viewing familiarly the skeletons in another's closet? Do we not as readers witness the uncovering of truths that implicate us? Sophia's last words constitute, in effect, a personal address to the reader: "Of Constantia's personal deportment and domestic habits *you have been a witness.* . . . It is sufficient to have related . . . to you the knowledge *which you have so anxiously sought*" (293–94, my italics). Brown denies the reader the prerogative of casual involvement, insisting instead, as some of America's most sophisticated authors would, on universalizing the artist's trauma.

CHAPTER FIVE

———·✹·———

ARTHUR MERVYN:

SICKNESS, SUCCESS, AND

THE RECOMPENSE OF VIRTUE

When I perceive the least inclination to deceive,
I suspect a growing depravity of soul that will one day
be productive of the most dangerous consequences.

CHARLES BROCKDEN BROWN, *The Rhapsodist*

One of the ironies of *Ormond* is the extent to which it remains within the framework of the sentimental-domestic novel of analysis, paying homage to its archetypes and assumptions even as it deposes and inverts them. For instance, the novel retains the motif of seduction, but with a reversal: the victim kills her seducer. In similar fashion Ormond's obsession for Constantia ironically validates the cult of sentiment, though Ormond otherwise mocks sentiment. Helena Cleves seems a romantic simpleton alongside the strong-willed Constantia and Ormond, both of whom explicitly deny the power of love. That power, however, drives their behaviors as much as it drives Helena's.

But the thematic centerpiece of the sentimental-domestic novel is marriage, and marriage, in *Ormond,* is conspicuously absent. It figures as a theme, to be sure, in a more abstract sense, for the book is very much about the need to achieve a resolution of opposites, a compromise between extremes such as passion and restraint, revolution and reaction, idealism and expediency. The absence of marriage in *Ormond* suggests Constantia's failure to satisfactorily resolve such tensions.

In *Arthur Mervyn* there is marriage. Arthur is one of the few characters in Brown's fiction to wed (though the book concludes just before the marriage occurs). More importantly, Arthur seems to achieve the figurative marriage that eludes others, to satisfactorily combine self-interest and ethics, innocence and experience, constraint and desire. The ambiguousness of this "marriage," in fact, is the central riddle of *Arthur Mervyn*.

In *Arthur Mervyn; or Memoirs of the Year 1793* an eighteen-year-old rustic piqued by an awkward domestic situation leaves home to find his fortune in Philadelphia. The youth, Arthur, finds his fortune, all right, but not without undergoing a half-dozen nearly fatal escapades, including a bout with yellow fever, a head wound that almost results in his being buried alive, a prolonged association with a multiple felon named Thomas Welbeck, a midnight plunge in the Delaware River, and a point-blank pistol assault by a crazed madam. Such a tissue of improbabilities—narrated, moreover, by a half-dozen separate speakers, several of whom tell stories within others' stories (at one point the reader is at four removes from the principal speaker)—threatens to become a tale told by several idiots, signifying nothing. But Arthur's singular presence and the moralizing tone he brings to the novel unifies it, while the melodrama of his career propels the reader through its narrative and episodic matrices.

It is the ambiguity of Arthur's career, though, that fascinates and puzzles. Arthur is a moral enigma. The original "fool of virtue," he is a prig with an uncanny knack for being found on the wrong side of town. What pilgrim ever seemed so intent on walking the straight and narrow path, yet dallied in so many compromising culs-de-sac? (At one point he stands covered with blood, secretly disposing of a corpse; at another, he sits on the bed of a presumed prostitute, holding her hand; yet in every case his motives are "unquestionably pure"—as he is quick to point out.) Or, if you will, what fortune-seeker ever kept up so sanctimonious a patter?[1] Here is Arthur, prostrated by yellow fever and threatened with death by the murderer Welbeck unless he give up certain found money: "Mr. Welbeck, said I, my regard to your safety compels me to wish that this interview should terminate. At a different time, I should not be unwilling to discuss the matter. Now it will be fruitless. My conscience points out to me too clearly the path I should pursue for me to mistake it. As long as I have power over this money I shall keep it for the use of the unfortunate lady, whom I have seen in this house. I shall exert myself to find her, but if that be impossible, I shall appropriate it in a way, in which you shall have no participation."[2] Is Arthur selfish or selfless to a fault?

The more Arthur is compromised by appearances, the more we wonder about his actual motives. The same Arthur who voluntarily risks his life entering a plague-ridden city to locate and assist a virtual stranger, the friend of a friend, also consorts with and abets a self-confessed killer, even helping him flee the scene of the killing. The same Arthur who, immobilized with fever, anguishes over his tormentor's spiritual welfare later spurns the love of the sweet Eliza Hadwin to marry a wealthy "night-hag" (his best friend's characterization [2:432]), the former proprietress of a brothel. Such ambiguities crop up like weeds around the sunflower of Arthur's virtue.

By the end of this two-part novel, Arthur has not only weathered the plague and the corruption of the city, but has come out on top, with money, a wife, prospects, and a clean conscience into the bargain. This last is no surprise: Arthur wouldn't have it any other way. On the other hand, as recent critics have noted, Arthur's final happiness is, at best, questionable: plagued by sleepwalking and nightmares, he seems troubled at heart as he prepares to wed the maternal widow, Achsa Fielding.

Whereas criticism of Brown's other novels has alternately lurched and foundered, criticism of *Arthur Mervyn* has progressed almost dialectically over several decades. R. W. B. Lewis posed the thesis. Mervyn, he said, is an American prototype—a "foolish, young innocent: the first of our Adams."[3] Lewis's Arthur Mervyn, though, is a pre-lapsarian Adam, a good boy who learns about evil without ever stumbling. Warner Berthoff countered that Mervyn is no naive innocent, but a "chameleon of convenient virtue," an ironic hero who, for all his scruples, gets on quite well in the morally poisonous atmosphere of the city. Berthoff finds Arthur "a moral sharper of the most invincible sort"—and all the more American for it.[4]

Critics of the 1960s and 1970s synthesized these viewpoints, finding Mervyn either self-deluded or morally schizophrenic—both an innocent *and* a con man[5]—and locating his Americanness in the paradox: "The contradictions of America *are* this virtual orphan."[6] Critics during the last decade also reassessed the structure of *Arthur Mervyn*. Instead of apologizing for Brown's technical shortcomings, they scrutinized his narrative technique and the social context in which he was writing, defended his eclectic mode, and cataloged his image patterns—veil imagery, candle imagery, wound and pen motifs.[7] Modern criticism has so upgraded both the content and form of *Arthur Mervyn* that it now vies with *Wieland* as Brown's most highly praised novel.

Nor should such a revaluation surprise. *Arthur Mervyn* is, in a sense, the most modern of Brown's fables, not only because of its narrative technique but because it so candidly and implicitly acknowledges the

deceptiveness of appearances, the indeterminacy of truth, and the un-
reliability of fiction as a truth-telling instrument. If one were to look
for likenesses, André Gide's works (*Lafcadio's Adventures*, or *The Counter-
feiters*, which develops, coincidentally, the same motif of forgery that
Brown uses in *Arthur Mervyn*) would come to mind sooner than those of
most nineteenth-century writers. Melville's duplicitous and successful
Confidence Man, to be sure, could be nephew to Arthur Mervyn. But
The Confidence Man is itself an exception in nineteenth-century American
literature, and seems, like *Arthur Mervyn*, more aptly grouped with such
modern novels as Thomas Pynchon's *The Crying of Lot 49* and Ralph
Ellison's *Invisible Man*.

Arthur Mervyn, like Ellison's Invisible Man, evolves a "blues ethic,"
an improvisational approach to moral situations that helps him survive
and succeed. Like *Invisible Man*, *Arthur Mervyn* is best understood as a
series of parables tracing the development of a prototypical American
identity. And like Pynchon's *The Crying of Lot 49*, *Arthur Mervyn* leaves
the reader with the sense that the conspiracy of appearances is at last
impenetrable; that the culture is simply awash in paradoxes.

In this chapter I will trace the evolution of Arthur's iridescent character as revealed in the sequence of parables that is his career. I will
also try to show that Arthur's Americanness, while comprising those
general features of the national character pointed to by Hedges, Justus,
Bell, et al., can be more specifically located in the social, economic, and
philosophical climate of turn-of-the-century America.

LEARNING TO PLAY THE PIANOFORTE

The ending of *Ormond* dramatized the liabilities of a blind commitment
to virtue and suggested the practical necessity of leavening virtue with
expedience in the interest of survival. The nature of this compromise is
the subject of *Arthur Mervyn*, a tale that traces the adventures of a youth
who, as critics suggest, is an embodiment of America, and who, like
America, manages, to all appearances, the seemingly impossible task of
being good and making good. Arthur's material success never dents his
sanctimonious facade, despite the many dramatic ironies that corrode
its edges.

But already the word "facade" falsifies a complex issue, for Arthur is
not merely a "moral sharper," a "chameleon of convenient virtue,"[8] any
more than he is merely a naïf. Arthur fascinates because he is both pro-

vincial messiah *and* con man: one who genuinely and disinterestedly tries to do what is right, often at great risk and sacrifice, *and* one who gets ahead, however improbably, and "lands on his feet"[9] time and again, with prospects in hand and money in his pockets. Hayseed and hustler, novice and master of the pen, voyeur and accomplice, child and adult— Arthur Mervyn is a fictional palindrome, an enigma who reads true from opposite vantage points simultaneously.

Brown in his preface to *Arthur Mervyn* says the book "confers on virtue the notoriety and homage that are due it." The remark is a gem of ambiguity, "notoriety" connoting infamy as well as fame, "homage" suggesting not only respect but monetary tribute, and the final clause acting as qualifier as well as conventional close. Brown's prefatory remark indicates the dual mask that virtue will wear throughout the novel.[10] The evolution, though, of this viable and adaptive virtue capable of incorporating money and morality, ethics and expediency, is gradual and complex. Arthur is not born with such extraordinary ethical coordination; he acquires it. Some critics have denied that Arthur develops in the course of the novel,[11] but a close reading shows Arthur is educated and altered by discoveries he makes concerning various ethical options— and particularly by the discovery that virtue not only can but must be alloyed with material considerations. Arthur's bout with fever is the symbolic watershed: he survives the plague, and his prospects improve. Not that Arthur does not remain, to outward appearances, the same naïf with a knack for landing on his feet in spite of himself; but he comes out ahead more consistently in part 2, where his transformation from sanctimonious adolescent to well-heeled saint[12] takes on a seamless quality.

Arthur's career begins with his leaving home and journeying to Philadelphia. En route he is forced to buy unwholesome food at unfair prices, so that he is broke before reaching the city. Once in the city, he loses his belongings, then is duped by a presumed friend to the extent that his life and reputation are jeopardized. These preliminary adventures dramatize Arthur's naiveté and ignorance. They are also, however, rife with subtexts. Arriving in the city at night, Arthur fancies himself in Milton's hell: "I, for a moment, conceived myself transported to the hall 'pendent with many a row of starry lamps and blazing crescents fed by napthe and asphaltos.'" He adds, moreover, that the change in surroundings he has experienced since leaving home "wore the aspect of miracle" (1:28). The following morning Arthur, having lost not only his belongings but his shoes as well, his symbolic nakedness recalling the shamed and fallen Adam ("It was Sunday, and I was desirous of eluding observation" [1:46]), jokes ruefully about the "barefoot pilgrimage" necessity has forced him to undertake (1:46).

Arthur is indeed a pilgrim—and his history an ironic *Pilgrim's Progress* in which didactic parables contrast with their opposite numbers, self-serving narratives. In the first of these parables Arthur, gulled by the nonchalant jokester Wallace, is locked in the merchant Thetford's bedroom. At a loss to explain his presence, Arthur hides in the closet when the room's occupants—a newly married couple—enter. From his hiding place, Arthur first hears the grieving bride tricked into adopting her husband's unacknowledged baby by another woman, then overhears a conversation concerning a plot to jilt a shyster called "the Nabob" out of $30,000. After the couple falls asleep, Arthur escapes undetected.

In this episode Arthur is initiated into a world where financial scheming is a way of life and duplicity taints the most intimate relationships. Irony accrues later when Arthur, in Welbeck's employ, realizes his master is the mark Thetford plans to defraud. This is not the half of Brown's irony, though: for Arthur's career not only places him in the midst of the frauds and deceptions he has overheard, it also casts him in the role of perpetrator. Arthur, that is to say, soon finds himself engaged in "jilting the Nabob." After Welbeck's presumed suicide, Arthur possesses himself of a book belonging to Welbeck, in which he discovers not $30,000, but $20,000. When Welbeck returns, ill but alive, to demand the money, Arthur refuses to return it. His reasons notwithstanding, Arthur's conduct links him formalistically to the criminals he has eavesdropped on earlier. The irony of this link is enhanced when we recall how Arthur, while hidden in Thetford's closet, had reflected: "By means as inscrutable as those that led me hither, I may hereafter be enabled to profit by this detection of a plot" (1:41).

Nor is this the only way in which Arthur becomes, in the course of the book, an ironic actor in the melodrama he overhears in Thetford's bedroom. Thetford, single and with a baby to care for, has contrived to find a woman to play the dual role of wife and mother. Arthur, in the final pages of the novel, manages a similar feat in marrying Achsa Fielding ("Was she not," he says, "the substitute of my lost mamma?" [2:429]). Of course the similarity is circumstantial—that is the nature of all truth in *Arthur Mervyn*—but its irony is no less powerful for that.

Especially significant is the glimpse this parallel affords into Arthur's paradoxical character: for if his own role is prefigured by the conniving Thetford, it is equally prefigured by the motherless infant— Arthur being both man-about-town and babe-in-the-woods simultaneously. The melodrama Arthur witnesses, then, from his womb-like closet, is symbolically his own. The evils he discovers he will soon be embroiled in.

Arthur Mervyn's initial transformation—for he undergoes several—begins shortly after his escape from Thetford's house, when, broke and shoeless, he peers through a knothole at the Welbeck mansion. Envy overcomes him. He confesses: "I had been entirely unaccustomed to this strain of reflection. My books had taught me the dignity and safety of the middle path, and my darling writer abounded with encomiums on rural life. At a distance from luxury and pomp, I viewed them, perhaps, in a just light. A nearer scrutiny confirmed my early prepossessions, but at the distance at which I now stood, the lofty edifices, the splendid furniture, and the copious accommodations of the rich, excited my admiration and envy" (1:47). In coveting Welbeck's house, Arthur, in effect, sloughs his country self.

The actual molting takes place the following day. Hired by Welbeck, he enters the fantasy mansion and, on Welbeck's suggestion, exchanges his fustian coat and check trousers for a white silk waistcoat, casimer pantaloons, and silk stockings. Says Arthur, "You may imagine, if you can, the sensations which this instantaneous transformation produced" (1:51). The change, though, is superficial—a prelude to more significant transformations. For if Arthur's worldly ambitions have surfaced, his conscience has scarcely acknowledged, let alone accommodated, these ambitions. Arthur may have shucked his country clothes effortlessly enough, but what of his country sensibilities? Clearly such a reshuffling of priorities demands more than a new waistcoat; it demands an ethical re-outfitting—something Arthur seems unlikely to survive.

Arthur, of course, not only survives, but thrives on the necessary transformation, the end-product of which is a special brand of moral ambidexterity whose genesis can be traced in Arthur's history. The metaphor, in fact, is Brown's: ambidexterity is a minor motif in *Arthur Mervyn*. Beholding Welbeck's "daughter" (mistress), Clemenza Lodi, at the pianoforte, Arthur records his fascination with her playing: "She played without a book, and though her base [*sic*] might be preconcerted, it was plain that her right-hand notes were momentary and spontaneous inspirations" (1:53). Upon hearing her, Arthur is not only transported; he is (once again) transformed:

> I am certain that no transition was ever conceived more marvel-
> lous and more beyond the reach of foresight than that which I
> had just experienced. Heaths vexed by a midnight storm may be
> changed into an hall of choral nymphs and regal banqueting; for-
> est glades may give sudden place to colonnades and carnivals, but
> he whose senses are deluded finds himself still on his natal earth.
> These miracles are contemptible when compared with that which
> placed me under this roof and gave me to partake this audience.
> I know that my emotions are in danger of being regarded as ludi-
> crous by those who cannot figure to themselves the consequences
> of a limited and rustic education. (1:53–54)

Arthur's obvious infatuation with Clemenza aside, his emotions do seem ludicrous—or at least hyperbolic—unless understood in light of his recent "transformation" and the inadequacy of his rustic morality (his "limited and rustic education") to accommodate new ambitions. His country conscience is a high hurdle in the path of success; but Cle-menza's piano playing affords him a glimpse of how to modify it. Her dexterity offers a clue to a new ethic, less constrained and more supple than absolute precept, and more viable than romantic illusionism:[13] an ethic geared to city life and modern survival.

Not for nothing was the pianoforte replacing the harpsichord toward the close of the eighteenth century. Unlike its predecessor, the piano-forte offered dynamic range. Brown, indeed, refers appreciatively, in *Alcuin: A Dialogue,* to the instrument's capacity "for conjuring up the 'piano' to melt, and the 'forte' to astound."[14] Its range makes it a con-venient, if unlikely, correlative for the ethical versatility Arthur will develop. It is Clemenza's playing, however, that demonstrates just how versatile the instrument can be. Her playing suggests, in short, that a performer's hands can function independently, yet harmoniously. For Arthur, the epiphany is ethical as well as musical. He senses that one can learn, as it were, to count coins with the left hand while blessing bread with the right. And if the right hand does not know, at any given moment, what the left is doing, so much the better.

Arthur does not master this lesson at once. In fact, even toward the end of the tale his technique lapses. Having returned $40,000 in missing money to its rightful owners, he discovers that a $1,000 reward had been posted for its return. The beneficiary of the $40,000, however, proves stingy, and refuses to pay Arthur the reward. Her husband's executor, Hemmings, muses: "Mrs. Maurice, to be sure, will never pay but on compulsion. Mervyn should have known his own interest better. While his left hand was stretched forth to give, his right hand should have been held forth to receive" (2:388). By the time he receives this refresher course, however, Arthur has long since acquired the necessary ambidexterity, honed his harmonic skills, and learned to simultaneously "melt" and "astound" the most astute auditor.

How is the new ethic to work? Improvisationally, rather than by preconcerted dictum. In a world in which "revolutions" of all kinds are the order of the day, the enterprising individual wants the liberty to exercise a creative discretion—to play each situation by ear. Beyond that ground rule, Arthur's description of Clemenza's recitation provides one further clue: "I found," says Arthur, "that after some time, the *lawless* jarrings of the keys were *chastened* by her own, more liquid notes" (1:53, my italics). This ability to "chasten lawless jarrings," to harmonize moral dissonance, will henceforth become Arthur's forte.

Brown develops a virtual iconography of the hand in the following chapter. Arthur relates how Welbeck introduced him to his task: "My maimed hand, so saying he showed me his right hand, the forefinger of which was wanting, will not allow me to write accurately or copiously. For this reason I have required your aid, in a work of some moment" (1:55). Arthur's "job" is a placebo. Welbeck's villainous character, though, justifies the melodramatic touch of a missing finger by rendering his crippled right hand a symbol of his deformed moral sense.

The moral ambidexterity Arthur eventually acquires is better appreciated in relation to Welbeck's deficient moral sense. A seducer-forger-fraud-murderer, Welbeck has prospered outwardly; his villainies have netted him money, luxury, and renown. But they have also destroyed his self-esteem and peace of mind:

I can talk and feel as virtue and justice prescribe; yet the tenor of my actions has been uniform. One tissue of iniquity and folly has been my life; while my thoughts have been familiar with enlightened and disinterested principles. . . . Ease and the respect attendant upon opulence I was willing to purchase at the price of ever-wakeful suspicion and eternal remorse; but, even at this

price, the purchase was impossible. . . . Anguish and infamy appeared to be the inseparable conditions of my existence. There was
one mode of evading the evils that impended. To free myself from
self-upbraiding and to shun the persecutions of my fortune was
possible only by shaking off life itself. (1:85, 90)

Welbeck, in other words, suffers not only from a missing forefinger but
from a partially amputated conscience. This partial amputation allows
him to get ahead, but also cripples him: Welbeck is assailed periodically
by a guilt that, in combination with lapses of luck, drives him to the
verge of suicide. Though he would make the devil's bargain—would
sacrifice his right hand, as it were, to his left—what remains of his
conscience throbs painfully. Figuratively as well as literally, Welbeck's
crippled right hand foils him.

Arthur, on the other hand, never knowingly transgresses against
conscience: "My peace of mind depended on the favourable verdict
which conscience should pass on my proceedings. I saw the emptiness
of fame and fortune when put in the balance against the recompense
of virtue" (1:71). The irony of the last sentence is priceless. Arthur's
need to reconcile moral virginity and material voracity—his sense that
"the recompense of virtue" is preferable to either "recompense" or
"virtue" alone—sets him above his tutor Welbeck, makes him a stream-
lined, nineteenth-century American avatar, rather than a handicapped,
eighteenth-century villain; a lawyer, rather than an outlaw.[15]

Figuratively speaking, then, the ethic Arthur glimpses requires two
good hands—one to wash the other. Arthur tries out the technique
directly. Charged by Welbeck to deliver a letter and return promptly,
the ever curious Arthur contrives, despite his instructions, to see the
inside of the house he is sent to. He satisfies his curiosity, yet refrains
from breaking his trust with Welbeck by this elaborate rationalization:
"[Welbeck] had charged me to leave the billet with the servant who
happened to answer my summons; but had he not said that the message
was important, insomuch that it could not be intrusted to common
hands? He had permitted, rather than enjoined, me to dispense with
seeing the lady, and this permission I conceived to be dictated merely by
regard to my convenience. It was incumbent on me, therefore, to take
some pains to deliver the script into her own hands" (1:63–64). In the
next paragraph, however, Arthur admits an ulterior motive: "I ought
to mention that my departure from the directions which I had received

was, in some degree, owing to an inquisitive temper: I was eager after knowledge, and was disposed to profit by every opportunity to survey the interior of dwellings and converse with their inhabitants" (1:64). Trivial though it is, this incident illustrates the dynamics of Arthur's ethics—a rationalizing right hand washing, as it were, a self-gratifying left. One senses the confession itself is part of the self-exculpation.

Arthur's moral imagination is tried in earnest when Welbeck kills Amos Watson and requires Arthur's help to bury the body, then escape. Such circumstances defy precept, and Arthur is at first uncertain how to act: "I was driven by a sort of mechanical impulse, in his footsteps. I followed him because it was agreeable to him and because I knew not whither else to direct my steps" (1:113). Welbeck plans to escape across the river to New Jersey, but is stymied when he discovers the only boat available has but one oar. Arthur, however, is not stymied: "This impediment was by no means insuperable. I had sinewy arms and knew well how to use an oar for the double purpose of oar and rudder. I took my station at the stern, and quickly extricated the boat from its neighbours and from the wharves" (1:114).

Arthur's timely intervention is a particularly ironic illustration of his flare for rationalizing. Arthur has just resolved to cast aside passive obedience and take charge of his options ("I had acted long enough a servile and mechanical part; and been guided by blind and foreign impulses. It was time to lay aside my fetters, and demand to know whither the path tended in which I was importuned to walk" [1:114]). The course Arthur chooses, though, is not conscientious objection but active complicity. Unlike that other captain Welbeck has so recently faced (Amos Watson), Arthur merely stammers a few timid questions, then voluntarily assumes the helm on Welbeck's behalf, his rationale bolstered by chivalrous sentiment: "To desert this man, in a time of so much need, appeared a thankless and dastardly deportment" (1:108).

Rationalization aside, the episode showcases Arthur's willingness and ability to improvise in morally confusing situations. The missing oar—analogous to Welbeck's missing finger—stymies Welbeck's present course as the moral handicap of a guilty despair has repeatedly hamstrung his career. (Moments later this despair leads him to attempt to drown himself.) Arthur, however, circumvents this handicap. By using one oar for a "double purpose," Arthur demonstrates the symbolic equivalent of his capacity to use virtue for a dual end: namely, as a guide, or rudder, but also as an oar, a means of getting ahead.

This guileless ability to coordinate crossed purposes simultaneously and improvisationally is the crux of Arthur's evolving ethos.

This ethos has its liabilities, though. When Welbeck leaps overboard, Arthur, startled, drops the oar. Left to the mercy of the current, "wholly unacquainted with the river" (1:115), Arthur drifts blindly: "How to help myself, how to impede my course, or to regain either shore, since I had lost the oar, I was unable to tell. I was no less at a loss to conjecture whither the current, if suffered to control my vehicle, would finally transport me" (1:116). Having forgone conventional moral moorings, Arthur learns the terror of being adrift at night out of sight of a shore.

Perhaps Arthur's retreat to the country and his subsequent bout of obsessive virtue is a reaction to this unsettling flirtation with situational morality. Or perhaps his plague-courting course stems, as Carl Nelson suggests, from an inordinate and recurring fascination with death.[16] In any case, although Arthur temporarily turns his back on the city ethic, he returns to savor the city's horror.

Arthur's mercy errand to plague-ridden Philadelphia, both laudable and foolhardy, is ultimately instructive. His confrontation with Welbeck—the culmination of the plague sequence and climax of part 1—constitutes a final lesson in ethics. For Arthur, though glimpsing the possibilities of a new ethic, has yet to see the need to jettison the old; has yet to learn Constantia Dudley's lesson: that an untempered virtue can be claustrophobically confining.

This final lesson occurs when, at the height of his contracted sickness, Arthur is accosted by Welbeck, who demands from him the money Arthur confesses to having taken from Welbeck's shelf. The episode—one of the most comical in all of Brown's writing—reduces to the absurd the melodrama of Arthur's dedication to virtue. Arthur, powerless and bedridden, courts murder by scrupulously volunteering to Welbeck the information that he has expropriated funds from Welbeck and will not give them back. Arthur then stokes the fire with a sermon on ethics and duty. When Welbeck, in a last effort to dupe Arthur into giving back the money, claims the bills are forged, Arthur completes his sanctimonious charade by torching the $20,000.

The questionability of Arthur's own title to the money aside, his conduct is not only unrealistic but suicidal. His rigid adherence to principle blinds him to all else, preventing him both from discerning

Welbeck's predictable sham concerning the "forged" bills and from seeing the obvious expedience of keeping quiet in the first place. His virtue
becomes a prison, a perverse confinement to which he has committed
himself, and which threatens his life. Arthur's obtuse righteousness is
pointedly answered by Welbeck: "Maniac! Miscreant! . . . Execrable
and perverse idiot! Your deed has sealed my perdition. *It has sealed your
own*" (1:210–11, my italics). At this moment the scene is interrupted
by several knocks at the door. Welbeck forgoes killing Arthur in order
to escape, convinced the hospital attendants and hearse porters will finish the job for him. Arthur outwits them—but almost kills himself in
the process. The scene in which this drama transpires neatly objectifies
Arthur's perverse sanctimony.

Feeble but determined, Arthur eludes the corpse collectors by hiding
in the attic. This convenient crawl-space, entered by a trapdoor and
retractable ladder, seems ideal, but for one drawback. Arthur narrates:
"I gained the uppermost room, and mounting the ladder, found myself
at a sufficient distance from suspicion. The stair was hastily drawn up
and the door closed. In a few minutes, however, my new retreat proved
worse than any for which it was possible to change it. The air was musty,
stagnant, and scorchingly hot. My breathing became difficult, and I saw
that to remain here ten minutes, would unavoidably produce suffocation" (1:211–12). Arthur tries the trapdoor, but to no avail. What he
thought to be a refuge is instead a trap. This episode, following on the
heels of Arthur's dangerously virtuous flirtation with Welbeck's rage,
suggests a parable of suicidal self-confinement and awakening. Even as
he has elected the confines of a rigid virtue, Arthur literally confines
himself in an untenable space—then awakens to his mistake.

Realizing terror had "rendered me blind to the consequences of im-
muring myself in this cheerless recess" (1:212), Arthur tries desperately
to open the door, but fails. Finally, lighting on a nail "imperfectly driven
into the wood" (1:212), he manages to raise the trapdoor enough to
ventilate the attic. This affords him both breath and vision, and, judging himself safe, he prepares to descend. Before descending, though, he
pauses to examine his hideaway and reflect on its possibilities: "It was
large enough to accommodate an human being. . . . Though narrow
and low, it was long, and, were it possible to contrive some inlet for
the air, one studious of concealment, might rely on its protection with
boundless confidence" (1:212). The trap, then, need not be a trap; it can
be a valuable place of concealment, if modified slightly. So, too, virtue.

A little tolerated "imperfection," Brown seems to suggest, can make the difference between a stifling ethic and a sterling expedient.

By now it seems clear that the source of Arthur's "fever" is the moral dilemma he has been wrestling. Life with Welbeck has been a series of temptations: wealth, luxury, sex—all have piqued Arthur's ambition and assaulted his virtue to an extent he, perhaps, would deny. The result has been moral paralysis and vacillation. Arthur has glimpsed and toyed with a new ethic, then retreated compulsively to the old—only to discover one more dangerous than the next. Arthur's bout with the fever suggests, on the one hand, a general moral malaise in Arthur as well as the populace at large; but it also suggests to Arthur the opposite: the "sickness" of a perverse dedication to an idealized virtue. Compare Arthur's account of his attitude toward his illness at the time of his illness with his later, terse assessment of that attitude:

> The foresight of my destiny was steadfast and clear. To linger for days in this comfortless solitude, to ask in vain not for powerful restoratives or alleviating cordials, but for water to moisten my burning lips and abate the torments of thirst; ultimately to expire in torpor or phrenzy, was the fate to which I looked forward, yet I was not terrified. . . . I felt as if the opportunity of combating such evils was an enviable privilege, and though none would witness my victorious magnanimity, yet to be conscious that praise was my due, was all that my ambition required.
>
> These sentiments were doubtless tokens of delirium. (1:213)

RECUPERATING AND RECOUPING

Arthur's desolate state, when Dr. Stevens finds him, is comparable to Constantia's, when Sophia glimpses her disheveled form through the keyhole. Both Constantia and Arthur must suddenly face the self-defeating element in their idealism and glory in their infirmity because they have lost or forfeited all else. However, Brown gives Arthur a second chance. Part 2 finds the nimble protagonist on his feet, making the most of his reprieve.

The recuperated Arthur, whether consciously or unconsciously, internalizes the lessons of part 1. He becomes a success, disencumbering himself of Eliza Hadwin, his country girlfriend, and engaging instead to marry the wealthy Achsa Fielding. Throughout these and other adventures, Arthur continues to assert his virtue, brushing away circumstantial ironies and adverse characterizations like so many gnats. Not only does he convert virtue from a trap into a refuge; he transforms what has been primarily a defensive ethic into an offensive tactic. In part 2, Arthur deploys his virtue like a martial art, confounding his adversaries with an aggressive passivity. The results of this moral and psychological jujitsu, as Warner Berthoff has observed,[17] lend a comic tone to part 2. Beneath the comedy, though, Arthur's invincibility continues to amaze.

Arthur visits Eliza's kinsman, the burly Philip Hadwin, and coolly informs him that his niece has burned the will naming Philip executor of his brother's estate and Eliza's guardian. Hadwin, a brawler whose anger has been primed by nasty reports of Arthur's character and intentions, vows to beat Arthur bloody. Arthur, however, by affecting a fearless and straightforward mien, manipulates Hadwin's anger to such an extent that he not only eludes a beating, but wangles a dinner into the bargain. One wonders at the fluency of Arthur's act, though—and at his motives for the visit. Perhaps significantly, while there he unearths the information that Eliza's estate is mortgaged.

A short while later, Arthur prowls a bordello in search of Clemenza Lodi. Roaming unannounced from room to room, his "virtuous intent" a battering-ram or doctor's note excusing the most eccentric behavior, Arthur gads about surprising negligently dressed women until he is shot by the madam. Again, one wonders what he is doing there. By his own admission, there is nothing he can do for Clemenza. Not one to miss an opportunity, though, he comes away carrying the calling card of his bride-to-be.

The self-justifying, self-aggrandizing nature of Arthur's virtue becomes, at last, impossible to ignore: his stated intent is compromised too consistently by circumstance to be taken for granted. When Arthur discovers his father has died, he at first grieves. Eventually, though, he realigns his views: "It was some time before my reason came to my aid, and shewed me that this was an event, on the whole, and on a disinterested and dispassionate view, not unfortunate. . . . He was now beyond the reach of my charity or pity; and since reflection could answer no beneficial end to him, it was my duty to divert my thoughts into different channels, and live henceforth for my own happiness and that of those who were within the sphere of my influence" (2:393–94). Reasonable enough. Yet it is also true that moral duty and reason, by reconstructing Arthur's apprehension of the event, accommodate his thinking to his interests. This, ultimately, is the goal of virtue in *Arthur Mervyn*.

Arthur Mervyn illustrates the evolution of a well-oiled rationalizing mechanism as the key to success and survival. Arthur succeeds because he becomes adept at disguising his true motives not only from others but from himself. Hence, unlike Welbeck, he avoids a gnawing guilt. Brown links the writing process to this rationalizing mechanism: "The pen is a pacifyer. It checks the mind's career; it circumscribes her wanderings. It traces out, and compels us to adhere to one path. It ever was my friend. Often it has blunted my vexations; hushed my stormy passions; turned my peevishness to soothing; my fierce revenge to heart-dissolving pity. . . . I must continue at the pen, or shall immediately relapse" (2:414). Other versions of the writing process presented in *Arthur Mervyn* include the minor motifs of forgery and translation, both of which highlight the penman's power to imperceptibly recast or paraphrase truth. Arthur, especially in this sense, is a "master of the pen"—and perhaps the ultimate forger. The formal device of Arthur's memoirs becomes especially suspect in this connection. To what extent are those patently self-justifying memoirs elaborate forgeries? The fact that Arthur usurps the narrative task at precisely the moment when Dr. Stevens's suspicions, only barely assuaged, show signs of recurring [18] throws further doubt on the nature and purpose of Arthur's narrative.

To write, then, is to rationalize. Arthur must "continue at the pen, or . . . relapse" because only the transforming, rationalizing mechanism embodied in the writing act stands between Arthur and his "illness": depraved passion, on the one hand, and a hysterical conscience on the other. Arthur's moral sense mediates as his pen "pacifies," checking the "mind's career" while hushing "stormy passion." (Welbeck's inability to write because of his missing finger assumes further significance in this regard.) The novel's swarming ironies dramatize the self-deceit at the core of such rationalizing. But it is a useful self-deceit, an adaptive blindness [19] ("I have *labored* to fatigue myself," says Arthur, "to deceive me into a few *tolerable* moments of forgetfulness" [2:413]). *Arthur Mervyn* is, in this respect, a comic version of *Ormond*, Arthur's self-blindness serving as a skeleton key to success whereas Constantia's was her prison.

Skeleton key, indeed. As several critics have noted, Arthur's final "ecstasy" is undercut by a morbid anxiety. On the eve of his marriage to Achsa, Arthur is plagued by nightmares and sleepwalking. Though he denies relevance to these dreams of oedipal vengeance, one cannot help but wonder how long he can successfully ignore his dubious acts and deepest desires. Is there a point at which the rationalizing mechanism, its premises of right and reason too severely compromised, breaks down? a point at which a hideous figure leaps from the mirror? Does Arthur's relinquishing the pen at last signify (as he himself has suggested) inevitable relapse?

Arthur's pilgrimage, then, is an ironic one. His spiritual journey leads away from absolute virtue toward a pliant, urban ethic of accommodation and self-justification. Virtue becomes, for Arthur, a technique to be explored and mastered, an instrument of unsuspected potential and, at last, a weapon capable of disarming adversaries and justifying any course. Given Arthur's earlier statement—"My peace of mind depended on the favourable verdict which conscience should pass on my proceedings" ($1:71$)—it is probably inevitable that conscience should assume a pacifying rather than clarifying role. Inevitable, but no less disturbing for that.

To the extent *Arthur Mervyn* portrays depravity less as a diabolical bent than as a propensity for rationalizing actions and remaining blind to one's motives, it refines the doctrine of innate depravity suggested in *Wieland.* However, the novel seems more intent on characterizing mundane depravity than on dramatizing its more freakish manifestations. *Arthur Mervyn* presents everyday moralizing in its most ironic light.

A NATIVE APPARITION

Arthur Mervyn, though less concerned than *Ormond* or *Wieland* with establishing political-historical allegories, not only reflects the time and place in which it is set, but also suggests an attempt on Brown's part to characterize a changing America in the person of his protagonist. The fleeting similarity between Arthur's name and age—he is eighteen at the time of the tale (1793)—and America's may well be coincidental. His personal history, however, beginning with his altercation with his father and including his leaving his father's house, seeking independence and soliciting the help and friendship of the French-speaking, French-dressing Welbeck, recapitulates America's national history much as the history of the Wieland family recapitulated America's colonial history.

Moreover, by highlighting in his subtitle ("Memoirs of the Year 1793") the year in which the tale is set, Brown invites us to consider its events in a historical light. It is, of course, the year of the notorious yellow fever plague recounted in the novel's most famous sequence. Perhaps more importantly, though, it is also, as noted earlier, the year the French Revolution, already spinning toward carnage, drew America into its vortex: "a year utterly without parallel," says one historian, "in the history of this country." [20] In *Arthur Mervyn* the fever becomes coincident with the revolution, the year in which the tale is set wedding the two and conjuring up a panorama of social strife that Brown need not even allude to explicitly. Here, as in *Ormond,* the fact that Philadelphia was particularly identified with both the literal and figurative fever unifies the symbol further. "Factional debate over the French Revolution and its aftermath," Robert S. Levine notes, "was especially intense in Philadelphia, Brown's hometown, for as the leading immigration center it served as a refuge for those fleeing the revolutions of France and St. Domingue." [21]

Brown refrains, though, from overexploiting this connection in *Arthur Mervyn.* The overtones are present, but never shrill; nothing like the elaborate political allegory of *Ormond* recurs. Instead, the political context quietly informs the plague scenes without obscuring their presentation. Occasionally Brown musters a lexical ploy to sustain the symbolic overtones: Arthur, for instance, at the height of his bout with the disease, remarks, "a total revolution seemed to have been effected in my frame" (1:188). Toward the novel's end, moreover, Brown inserts the tale of Achsa Fielding's deceased husband, a Frenchman named Perrin, who, we are told, rose to prominence in the French Revolution, advocated violent measures, then was killed when his faction was deposed (2:424–26). Such explicit references are the exception, though, in this book that is concerned, as Levine points out, with a constellation of "revolutions," epistemological, psychological, and cultural as well as sociopolitical. [22] There is, however, one social anxiety that informs this novel with particular urgency. *Arthur Mervyn* is certainly one of the first books in our literary canon to register the drama of the black presence as perceived by whites and to hint, however obliquely, at the nightmare of black insurrection.

Though they are marginal characters, to be sure, blacks appear with some frequency during the novel's plague sequence. Arthur, while looking for the young man Wallace, observes a black hearse-driver with two white companions, "their countenances marked by ferocious indifference to danger or pity" (1:140), loading a coffin into the hearse and joking coarsely about the victims—even intimating that one was not yet dead when encoffined. Later Arthur encounters a gentleman, Medlicote, who tells him of the merchant Thetford's inhumane treatment of his ailing servant girl. Medlicote, in relating the story, notes that "instead of summoning a physician, to ascertain the nature of her symptoms, he [Thetford] called a negro and his cart from Bush-hill," who "lifted her into the cart," her exertions notwithstanding (1:158). Medlicote, continuing his narrative of the Thetford family, describes how Thetford and his entire household were taken ill with the fever, remarking, "Their sole attendant was a black woman; whom, by frequent visits, I endeavored, with little success, to make diligent in the performance of her duty" (1:160). Medlicote, finally, describes his own somewhat desolate and dependent situation: "I remain to moralize upon the scene, with only a faithful black, who makes my bed, prepares my coffee, and bakes my loaf. If I am sick, all that a physician can do I will do for myself, and all that a nurse can perform, I expect to be performed by Austin" (1:161).

These black servants and liverymen, rendered visible by the plague, seemingly immune to its ravages, are, with the exception of Austin, ominous figures, casual morticians carting off the dead or dying whites, or, like the Thetfords' maid, merely standing by unsolicitously as they die. Their very wellness suggests a suddenly inverted social order. Brown may not have consciously set out to mythologize racial anxiety, as Melville would later do. Nonetheless, this mute portrayal of stricken whites in the custody of blacks contains in embryo the vision Melville would present in "Benito Cereno." The understated drama of Brown's scenario might go unnoticed, though, were it not focused by the dark-skinned "apparition" that leaps, as it were, from the mirror to knock Arthur cold (1:148).

Arthur, at the height of the epidemic, is searching Thetford's former house for clues to Wallace's fate and whereabouts. He discovers not Wallace, but another dying victim. As Arthur recoils in horror, his thoughts absorbed with "the train of horrors and disasters that pursue the race of man," he notices a cabinet, its hinges broken and lid half raised, and deduces pillage. "Some casual or mercenary attendant, had not only contributed to hasten the death of the patient, but had rifled his property and fled" (1:147). As Arthur reconnoiters, a movement in the mirror catches his eye: "It was a human figure. . . . One eye, a scar upon his cheek, a tawny skin, a form grotesquely misproportioned, brawny as Hercules, and habited in livery, composed, as it were, the parts of one view" (1:148). Before Arthur can turn around, the figure strikes him in the temple, knocking him senseless. This "tawny . . . apparition" seen out of the corner of the white man's eye a half-second before it strikes suggests, however subliminally, a racial nightmare. In this episode, America's fever-stricken vision of racial vengeance, dimly hinted at in the black presence that broods elsewhere in the background, becomes implicit; the plague symbol takes on native significance.

The motif of black vengeance is forecast earlier in the Vincentio Lodi subplot. Vincentio Lodi is a stranger whom Welbeck meets and assists, whose father—a plantation owner in Guadaloupe—has recently died: "It appeared that the elder Lodi had flattered one of his slaves with the prospect of his freedom, but had, nevertheless, included this slave in the sale that he had made of his estate. Actuated by revenge, the slave assassinated Lodi in the open street" (1:92). Vincentio Lodi, meanwhile, at the time Welbeck meets him, is fatally ill with yellow fever, contracted in Guadaloupe. (This, in fact, is the first mention of yellow fever in the novel.) Brown thus loosely associates the motifs of black revenge and yellow fever from the start.

Lodi's murder by a slave in Guadaloupe conjures up a larger context of racial violence that could hardly have been lost on Brown's readership: the black insurrection that was culminating in the West Indies as *Arthur Mervyn* was being completed. This revolt, which claimed the lives of some 46,000 whites between 1791 and 1803, ended with the blacks defeating the foremost military power in the world.[23] Both the enormity of the revolt and the fear it conveyed to nearby slaveholding societies is clear from the following extract from a speech on the slave trade, delivered to the Council of the Leeward Islands in March 1798:

It was in St. Domingo, that the standard of revolt . . . gave the signal to her mass of blacks to fall upon and butcher the whites. Instantly they set at naught her 20,000 militia; bid defiance to her regular forces, and the shipping in her harbours; ravaged her fields, attacked her towns, and left her inhabitants weltering in their own blood.

. . . In the Leeward Islands, . . . it is the same trade which menaces us with the same horrors; . . . that has multiplied the lurking assassins, till they swarm wherever the planter turns his eyes. . . . Death stares him in the face, and indignities worse than death threaten to precede it.[24]

Fear of black insurrection had, of course, been brewing for the better part of the century; it was, one historian has noted, "a permanent fact of plantation life."[25] Following the American Revolution's popularization of the notion of natural rights, guilt augmented the fear that had grown among whites in proportion to the increasing slave population. When word of a major slave revolt in the West Indies traveled north during the early 1790s, it tapped a well of anxiety across the land.

A hint of this cultural anxiety (and the appropriateness of Brown's symbol) can be cautiously inferred from white Philadelphians' scapegoating of blacks during the 1793 yellow fever epidemic. Because blacks were at first thought to be immune to the plague, they were prevailed upon (by Dr. Benjamin Rush, among others) to nurse the sick and remove the dead and dying, as Brown depicts—a role they performed, in the main, with documented nobility. However, many whites accused blacks of exploiting the situation by extorting high fees for their services and pillaging the houses of the ill. Some even accused them of carrying the contagion.[26] Since Jonah's time, of course, disasters have led to scapegoating, and, given that blacks were thought to be immune, the projected resentment of whites isn't difficult to fathom. Nor ought we to doubt that infamies were committed by some nurses and conveyors, both black and white, during this period of wholesale social chaos. But whites' perception, at this particular historical moment, that the fever was being spread among them by blacks who then seized the time to pillage their houses and extort their money suggests that racial paranoia was stalking Philadelphia along with the plague.

Brown's tentative symbolic association of black revolt and yellow fever is strengthened by the role yellow fever was playing in the West Indian insurrection. Yellow fever proved to be the blacks' strongest ally against the colonialists, decimating the European troops repeatedly. During 1795–96 alone, yellow fever killed 12,000 of the 18,000 British troops on the island, while a comparable percentage of the 33,000 French veterans sent to recapture the colony in 1802 succumbed.[27] History, then, coupled black insurrection and yellow fever even more emphatically than Brown's symbolic imagination.

Brown, however, personalizes the nightmare of sudden violence and augments its irony by having Arthur glimpse the dark specter *in the mirror*. We can best appreciate Brown's intent by viewing the scene describing Arthur's assault in relation to an earlier scene, its formal counterpart. In that scene, Arthur, having entered Welbeck's service and donned Welbeck's clothes, also looks into a mirror. The self Arthur sees in that mirror is almost as shocking as the "apparition" he later glimpses. Dressed "in the French style," in a linen and muslin nankeen coat, white silk waistcoat, casimer pantaloons, and silk stockings, Arthur hardly recognizes his own form, "so well proportioned, so gallant, and so graceful" (1:51). This dashing, well proportioned, white-on-white reflection suggests Arthur's idealized self, even as the misshapen, dusky apparition in livery suggests his alter ego—poor, depraved, morally grotesque.

More significantly, though, it suggests a disparity in *America's* self-image. Arthur's fancied likeness is decidedly French, and, insofar as Arthur may be identified with America, suggests the nation's French self-image, based on, among other things, egalitarian ideals. Young America's fancied self-image, however, had to contend, from the first, with a social reality that belied her notions of equality. This contradiction between republican ideals and the practice of slaveholding—an integral part of the national schizophrenia—was to be temporized with, of course, until the Civil War and beyond. Brown, by the ironic device of contrasting mirror images, brings into relief this American paradox and the grotesque self beneath her enlightened projection, threatening to erupt violently, to shatter the glass.

The yellow fever plague, then, broadly associated with the "fever" of revolution and the threat of black revolution in particular, is ultimately linked, as Medlicote suggests, "not to infected substances imported from the east or west, but to a morbid constitution of the atmosphere" (1:161)—that is, to an *American* "constitutional defect." (Arthur, we recall, is plagued by a literal constitutional defect: "The seeds of an early and lingering death are sown in my constitution," he declares [1:135].)

Did Brown consider slavery America's "constitutional defect"? David Lee Clark notes: "Like most thoughtful men of his day, the Quakers in particular, Brown abhorred slavery and staunchly advocated its abolition. . . . Brown was among our earliest prophets to foresee that the slavery question would eventually lead to civil strife."[28] Some of Brown's nonfiction reveals an even more emphatic stance—that slavery is not only morally repugnant but suicidal, a disease capable of destroying the body politic. In *An Address to the Government . . .* (1803), Brown, in his ironic guise of "French Counsellor of State," pillories the American people as follows:

> When war [with France] becomes a topic of discourse, this people will turn their eyes to the calamities of St. Domingue, and then to their own provinces, where the same *intestine plague* exists in

a degree equally formidable, and where their utmost care is requisite to prevent the struggling mischief from bursting its bonds.

Devoted to the worst miseries, is the nation which harbours in its bosom a foreign race, brought, by fraud and rapine, from their native land; a race bereaved of all the blessings of humanity; whom a cruel servitude inspires with all the vices of brutes and all the passions of demons; whose injuries have been so great that the law of self-preservation obliges the state to deny the citizen the power of making his slave free; whose indelible distinctions of form, color, and perhaps of organization, will forever prevent them from blending with their tyrants, into one people; who foster an eternal resentment at oppression, and whose sweetest hour would be that which buried them and their lords in a common and immeasurable ruin. (my italics)

Brown aims his appeal toward America's fear of her blacks—a fear that, he suggests, is well-founded. His rhetoric, though, is as significant as his message, plague imagery reiterating the fever symbolism of *Arthur Mervyn:*

With what prudence can this nation attack a neighbor [i.e., France], who can fan at pleasure, the discontents of this *intestine enemy;* who can give union, design, and arms to its destructive efforts at revenge? Who can raise, at any moment, a Spartacus or L'Ouverture to distract the counsels, and employ the force which might otherwise annoy himself. . . .

This nation is not insensible to all these dangers. An example is before their eyes of a servile war. Their country is full of exiles from the scene of such warfare. Their travelers, their daily papers supply them with the picture, in all its circumstantial horrors. They are shaken by panics on this very account already, and no consideration would have a stronger influence on their conduct. (my italics)

Black insurrection, then, is painted as an imminent threat, a "rein, by which the fury of the States may be held at pleasure." [29] Nor, apparently, was Brown merely indulging in rhetoric—for he continues the pamphlet in what is, for all intents, his own voice. His remarks, while less inflammatory, not only confirm but consolidate the French persona's claims: "The blacks are a *bane in our vitals,* the most deadly that ever nation was infested with" (my italics). [30]

In those magazines he edited and wrote for (*The Monthly Magazine and American Review* and, later, *The Literary Magazine and American Register*), Brown published several articles reiterating moral and political concern over slavery. In one such piece, entitled "Thoughts on the Probable Termination of Negro Slavery in the United States of America," the author, after developing religious and legal arguments against slavery in America, closes by adverting to "that terror which prevails among us concerning negro insurrections."[31] In another article, entitled "On the Consequences of Abolishing the Slave Trade to the West Indian Colonies," the author (Brown?) discusses the prospect of continued slavery in the Western hemisphere as follows: "In all human probability, one of two events will speedily happen: either the fate of Santo Domingo will suddenly become the fate of all the negro settlements, or the West Indian system will remain a little longer on its present footing. The impending blow may possibly be warded off for a season. . . . In the course of a few years, the frail tenure will give way."[32]

Finally, Brown's short story "The Death of Cicero: A Fragment," though set in the Roman era, evinces further anxiety over a vengeful slave presence. In this fragment the head of the Roman state is overthrown, proscribed, hunted, and finally executed, despite the efforts of his friend and manservant, Tiro—the narrator of the piece—to hide him. The usurper's soldiers learn of Cicero's whereabouts, however, because a vengeful slave of Cicero's betrays him. Much of the story's drama lies in the issue of freedom versus servitude, and in the suggestion that the free, civilized world epitomized by Rome under Cicero is about to topple: "It was indeed true that liberty would be extinguished by Cicero's death, and then only would commence the reign of Anthony, and the servitude of mankind."[33] One of the story's buried ironies, therefore, is the fact that the "liberty" Cicero symbolizes is fundamentally compromised by slavery much as America's liberty, in Brown's time, was belied by its slaveholding policies. Cicero's oversight of the slave—he had forgotten, we are told, to dismiss him—proves fatal. (A benign and patronizing rulership, indeed, proves no better: Cicero is beheaded by one whose life he had pardoned earlier.)

Brown, then, was clearly troubled by the slave presence in America. Nor was his characterization of white America's insecurity ("They are shaken by panics on this very account."[34]) merely a projected bugaboo. As one literary historian notes, the perennial fear of slave insurrection, given substance by the St. Domingue bloodbath, "haunted the American political imagination of Brown's day."[35] One of the more obvious indications of the extent of this fear was Georgia's and South Carolina's proscription of the slave trade during the 1790s.[36] But the fear was verbalized in some very public forums as well. The voices of Brown's contemporaries ranged from cautionary to apocalyptic.

Congressman John Rutledge, Jr., speaking in response to a bill introduced into Congress on January 2, 1800, that called for abolition of the Fugitive Slave Law, said, "I thank God that most Negroes in America are enslaved; if they were not, dreadful would be the consequence." George Thatcher—by contrast, an advocate of emancipation—expressed the same anxiety, claiming in words similar to Brown's that slaves constituted "a cancer of immense magnitude" and amounted to "700,000 enemies" within the American body politic.[37] And a fatalistic Thomas Jefferson, writing to George Tucker in a letter of August 28, 1797, reacted to the West Indian uprising by concluding that "if something is not done, and soon done [to emancipate blacks], we will be the murderers of our own children. The day which begins our combustion must be near at hand; and only a single spark is wanting to make that day tomorrow."[38]

Brown, in short, spoke for many who saw slavery both as a threat to whites and a reproach to the nation's conscience. Ultimately, though, Brown's "tawny . . . apparition" signifies not only a fear of blacks, but a fear of self. Like the Indians in *Edgar Huntly,* blacks in *Arthur Mervyn,* one senses, are finally reflexive images, mute projections of the culture's fears and guilts. Hence their identification with the plague—a symbolic as well as literal visitation.

If the specter of social revolution is never more than hinted at in *Arthur Mervyn,* that of another revolution, by contrast, is explicitly set forth from the start: a revolution that, by the close of the century, was making America into a commercial conglomerate and counting house—and the City of Brotherly Love into a sort of casino. "Happily you are a stranger to mercantile anxieties and revolutions," the merchant Wortley says to the doctor Stevens (2:227). But Philadelphia's merchants, Brown would have us know, far outnumber her doctors. Norman S. Grabo describes the mood of the city prior to the advent of the 1793 plague:

The physical terrors were only part of Philadelphia's distress that summer. Before the pestilence struck, the city was in many ways feverish. Bank policies were erratic and unreliable. Merchants and businessmen were investing wildly in exotic financial schemes that burst with uncommon regularity. Prices—especially rents—skyrocketed. And businesses failed in startling numbers, with ruined bankrupts crowding the streets, the stock-piled wharves, the places of trade. It was a community demoralized, without confidence, without trust . . . . a city sick in soul and body.[39]

Brown himself, the same year part 1 of *Arthur Mervyn* was published, lamented the moral consequences of the Republic's pursuit of happiness in an article published in his *Monthly Magazine and American Review:*

The love of gain . . . in a very remarkable degree, pervades the United States. Before the Revolutionary War, this spirit was very prevalent, and much cultivated. . . . This circumstance gave a tone to public sentiment. To acquire property became the supreme and governing object; and the sordid colonial character was easily to be traced in almost every class of our citizens. Since the establishment of our independence, peculiar circumstances have served to increase instead of lessening this evil. . . . A more mercenary and speculating nation than our own hardly at this day exists.[40]

Small wonder, then, that money constitutes another aspect of Brown's yellow fever symbol, and the feverish pursuit of money a symptom of America's illness. Arthur Kimball has written convincingly about the motif of money in *Arthur Mervyn,* claiming the nation is "infected" and the chief germ is money.[41] James H. Justus, seconding the observation, finds *Arthur Mervyn* "a novel about the generative power of money," and notes: "In no other novel before the Civil War are we so assaulted by the sheer immediacy and pervasiveness of a commercial society." Justus catalogs the various money nexuses in the novel: "The deeds of these characters are marked by what gives meaning to their lives: commissions, bills of exchange, claims and deeds, banknotes, notes and bonds, sued mortgages and mortgages entered up, forgeries and robberies, patrimonies and inheritances, generous loans and imprudent debts, premiums of insurance, equitable rates of interest and hazardous securities, obdurate creditors and debtors prisons, executors' powers, competences and subsistencies, rewards and warrants of attorney."[42] His list alone indexes Brown's preoccupation with the theme.

The peculiar horror of Brown's plague, though, is that it tends to nullify the most intimate human ties: "Wives were deserted by husbands, and children by parents. . . . Men were seized by this disease in the streets; . . . they perished in the public ways" (1:128). And that is precisely how money operates on interpersonal relationships in *Arthur Mervyn*. Achsa Fielding's husband, for instance, deserts her after hearing of her father's (and therefore her) financial ruin. Philip Hadwin, uncle and legal guardian of the bereaved Eliza Hadwin, sues for the mortgage on her deceased father's estate, swearing, meanwhile, that Eliza can "whistle or starve" (2:306) for all he cares. Arthur's own father cuts him off and turns him out penniless, declaring him a financial burden. Dr. Stevens's friend Carleton is seized in the street and dragged off to prison by a merciless creditor, despite the plight his imprisonment occasions for his two dependent sisters.

Time and again in *Arthur Mervyn* fraud and greed subvert friendships, and financial considerations override trust and fellow-feeling. Welbeck takes part in a scam to defraud an insurance company. His scheme backfires, though, because the merchants he socializes with are in collusion against him. They succeed in bilking him to the tune of $30,000. Wortley, swindled by Welbeck, swears out a warrant for Arthur's arrest, despite repeated assurances from his best friend, Dr. Stevens, that Arthur is innocent. Arthur, upon voluntarily returning $40,000 to its rightful owners, discovers the beneficiaries have neglected to tell him of the $1,000 reward he is entitled to—and, in fact, do not intend to pay him. The "tissue of extortions and frauds" is omnipresent, epidemic (2:245).

Brown bolsters the link between money and the fever structurally. Debtors prison becomes a formal counterpart to the hospital at Bush-Hill to which fever victims are sent. Thus the warden of the prison Arthur's father is brought to evinces an insensitivity only slightly less outrageous than that of the hospital attendants at Bush-Hill. Here is how he breaks the news of Arthur's father's death to Arthur: "Sawny Mervyn you want, I suppose, said the keeper. . . . He came into limbo in a crazy condition, and has been a burthen on my hands ever since. After lingering along for some time, he was at last kind enough to give us the slip" (2:393). Both prison and hospital are characterized by a "noxious" and "stagnant" atmosphere and by withered, hopeless inmates as likely to die of their confinement as to recuperate or liquidate their debts.

Brown wasn't alone in deploring the social toll of America's money ethic. Philadelphia's Dr. Benjamin Rush, in "The Influence of the

American Revolution" (1789), had rued that in the years following the war, an "ardor in trade and speculation," combined with the issuance of a "fallacious . . . amount of paper money," had "deposed the moral faculty" of many citizens. Rush, anticipating Brown, termed this capitalist mentality a "disease."[43] Thomas Jefferson, speaking in the same vein on behalf of the landowner, maintained (in *Notes on the State of Virginia*) that "Corruption of morals . . . is the mark set on those, who, not looking up to heaven, to their own soil and industry, as does the husbandman, for their subsistence, depend for it on casualties of caprice and customers."[44] Brown's *Arthur Mervyn*, to be sure, would explode Jefferson's myth of agrarian virtue; but concerning the venality of commercialism, Brown and Jefferson thought alike—and did but voice the sentiments of many civic-minded republicans.[45]

Brown's fever symbol goes a step further, however, portraying money as a morbid and parlous communal obsession. One thinks of the merchant and swindler Thetford, courting death by refusing to close his business and flee the approaching plague—refusing, as it were, to acknowledge the germ that has infected his household and will shortly destroy him. One thinks of Wallace, ignoring his loved ones' pleas, remaining in town on the promise of a higher salary; of Welbeck, drawn to the plague-ridden city by the lure of hidden money; of the mercenary hospital attendants, gambling health for wealth. Seen in this context, Brown's image of the deserted marketplace resonates ironically.

Finally, *Arthur Mervyn* is an American tale because it is about revolutionary zeal co-opted by the temptations of wealth. Emory Elliott, reflecting on Arthur's unfulfilled plans to reform the city hospital and to allocate certain recovered funds to relieve the poor and hungry, notes that "Mervyn's most redeeming characteristic . . . is his revolutionary impulse"—an impulse that ends, perversely, in "self-serving reform."[46] And, indeed, in seeking appointment as "governor" of Bush-Hill hospital (1:162), Arthur recalls Stephen Girard, the French doctor who immigrated to Philadelphia in the early 1790s and carried out, with genius, courage, and success, the very reformational dream Arthur envisions for Bush-Hill.[47] Such benevolent revolutionism, a mirror image of the anarchic, insurrectionary social currents suggested elsewhere by the plague, is also clearly a part of America's potential. But Brown seems to doubt its chances for fulfillment in a society so oriented to *self*-advancement.

In the final analysis, however, *Arthur Mervyn*'s Americanness, while comprising these social, economic, and political concerns, derives from the American character. *Arthur Mervyn* both traces and questions the paradoxical and peculiarly American frame of mind whose ethic Melville both summed up and spoofed in the term "virtuous expediency." [48] The "American frame of mind," though, is something of a Rorschach blot. It has meant different things to different people at different times. Hindsight complicates matters further, inviting us to generalize or to extrapolate contemporary insights without due regard, perhaps, to the author's milieu. In short: given Brown's apparent intent to characterize America in his young protagonist, what index of the national psyche ought we to measure that characterization against?

THE JEFFERSONIAN MIND

Shortly after *Wieland* was published, Brown sent a copy to Thomas Jefferson. Jefferson's response to Brown's gift was a letter remarkable for its uncharacteristic defense of fiction: "Some of the most agreeable moments of my life have been spent in reading works of imagination which have this advantage over history that the incidents of the former may be dressed in the most interesting form, while those of the latter must be confined to fact. They cannot therefore present virtue in the best and vice in the worst forms possible, as the former may." [49] Fiction is good, Jefferson suggests—and this *is* characteristic—because it simplifies, clarifies, and dramatizes moral questions and orders the moral universe, the better to edify and improve mankind. The irony of Jefferson's remark grows when we reflect how little Brown's novels had to do with portraying virtue and vice in a clear, unambiguous light, their prefaced intentions notwithstanding.

That Brown should choose Jefferson for a reader further compounds the irony. Surely no one man so embodied the optimistic, rationalistic Enlightenment spirit that *Wieland*, with its dark intimations of depravity and inscrutability, explodes. Moreover, *Wieland* is a spiritual and metaphysical tragedy, and Jefferson, for all his catholicity, was of neither a spiritual nor metaphysical bent. It is *Arthur Mervyn*, that secular comedy of success and virtuous aspiration, that Brown should have sent to Jefferson.

Jeffersonianism provides a fertile context for viewing *Arthur Mervyn*. For Jeffersonian thought, though stemming from the European Enlightenment, represents an Americanization of the Enlightenment. Jefferson, political engineer as well as thinker, embodied certain peculiarly American contradictions latent in Enlightenment thought in a way no European thinker could. To the extent, moreover, that Jefferson embodied a national temperament, reflected cultural assumptions, and personified an outlook so representative that his name became the stamp of an era, Jefferson and Jeffersonianism merit attention. A close look at Jeffersonianism reveals contradictions in the culture that give credence to our worst doubts about Arthur. We are led to suspect that Arthur's ambiguous capacity to harmonize "virtue" and "recompense" is typical of a national tendency toward a self-justifying materialism, a Manifest Destiny, a virtuous expediency. Arthur emerges as neither unique nor anachronistic, but as an American avatar.

Daniel J. Boorstin in exploring Jeffersonianism looks beyond Jefferson's politics to the philosophical community that formed and nurtured his outlook. Situated in Philadelphia, this community—a circle of members within the American Philosophical Society—included David Rittenhouse (astronomer and mechanical genius), Dr. Benjamin Rush (physician, revolutionary, abolitionist), Benjamin Smith Barton (botanist), Joseph Priestly (chemist and revolutionary pamphleteer), Charles Wilson Peale (illustrator, revolutionary), and Thomas Paine (revolutionary, pamphleteer), as well as Jefferson himself. Over and above their republican fervor, these intellectuals were "united by the common challenge of their natural environment": catholicity, humanitarian goals, practical applications, and an avid curiosity about the world characterized their speculations. "The meaning of 'philosophy' under American conditions," writes Boorstin, included "the sheer joy of activity, of physical and social adjustment, and of material achievement."[50]

Humanitarian goals, curiosity, a yen for material achievement, an action-oriented ethic—these Jeffersonian values and traits precisely characterize Arthur Mervyn. His precipitate trip to Philadelphia in search of Wallace and his fantasized project of remaining there to reform the hospital at Bush-Hill exemplify these characteristics. But they also exemplify the shortcomings of such an ethos. First, an action-oriented approach can prove nearsighted. Arthur's hasty and unannounced journey to Philadelphia indirectly results in Mr. Hadwin's making the same trip unnecessarily, catching the fever, infecting his household, and dying. Second, the virtue of material achievement in a humanitarian cause can easily mask its opposite: self-aggrandizement. Arthur, no doubt, is sincere in wanting to right the abuses at the hospital in order to spare its patients from being victimized and brutalized as he had been. He also, no doubt, fancies himself a ranking municipal official.

A closer look at specific aspects of Jeffersonianism yields a cultural ground against which the novel repeatedly defines itself. Jeffersonians, for example, championed an agrarian ethic. Jefferson's agrarianism was rooted in "a moral and physical preference of the agricultural over the manufacturing man."[51] Agrarian life engendered morality: "Those who labor in the earth are the chosen people of God, if ever he had a chosen people, whose breasts he has made his peculiar deposit for substantial and genuine virtue. It is the focus in which he keeps alive that sacred fire, which otherwise might escape from the face of the earth."[52] The early sequences of *Arthur Mervyn* reflect this familiar grid of agrarian morality. As Arthur leaves the farm and is hoodwinked in the city, flees to the country's wholesome dairy lands, returns to the city to find amorality reigning with the plague, again leaves the city's noxious vapors for the sweet country air, one can almost hear Jefferson intoning, "The proportion which the aggregate of the other classes of citizens bears in any state to that of its husbandmen, is the proportion of its unsound to its healthy parts."[53]

This moral scheme is, of course, as simplistic as it is idealistic. Brown accepts the agrarian moral equation only to undermine it. Arthur soon encounters meanness of spirit, ignorance, greed, and brutishness (Philip Hadwin, for example) in the countryside, even as he discovers men of outstanding merit—Dr. Stevens, Estwick, Medlicote—in the city. Meanwhile the plague, Brown's symbol of moral malaise, shows little respect for agrarian dictum, infecting the country as well as the town.

Jeffersonian morality in general is reductive. "The moral sense," writes Jefferson, "is as much a part of man as his leg or arm."[54] It is a sense, like the physical senses, and can be healthy or diseased. This objectified conscience tends, as Boorstin points out, to downplay evil: "When the Jeffersonian came upon the concept of evil . . . he naturalized it into just another bodily disease: a disease, indeed, of the moral sense, but essentially no different from others. To blame a man because his moral sense was corruptible was like blaming him for susceptibility to yellow fever."[55] The coincidence of the metaphor aside, isn't this naturalization of the soul a bit simplistic?

Brown, as if taking the comparison on its own terms, symbolizes moral malaise by a yellow fever epidemic and depicts the villain Welbeck as physically deficient—he lacks a right index finger. Irony creeps in, though, as virtuous people succumb and die along with the vicious and crass. Moreover, the plague does not corrupt everyone: it brings out a rare generosity of spirit in some. Further ambiguity surfaces in those characters (Arthur, Wallace, Welbeck) who defy simple moral characterization. (All three succumb to sickness *and* recover in the course of the tale.) Meanwhile the novel poses this problem for the Jeffersonian: if moral corruption is as clear-cut as a physical disease or withered limb, why are the "sick" and the "sound" so easily confused? (At one point the corpse collectors are ready to seal Arthur up in a coffin, assuming him to be yet another fever victim—though in reality he is only suffering from a head wound.) A villain like Welbeck may, for argument's sake, be conspicuously "crippled," depraved (though he compensates with a front that deceives virtually everyone he encounters). But Arthur seems whole, both physically and morally. Are there perhaps shades of morality whose symptoms defy detection? Can the same individual be "sick" one day and "healthy" the next? Doesn't the metaphor at last lose its utility because it oversimplifies a complex issue?

This last criterion is especially relevant, since Jeffersonian morality took utility as its cornerstone. On this Jefferson was explicit: "Nature has constituted *utility* to man, the standard and test of virtue."[56] Any man confronted by an ethical dilemma, Jefferson implies, can ascertain the right course by consulting his interest. If the ambiguities of the term disturb, they ought to. Arthur's ability to calculate his interest with so sure an eye is a circumstantial argument not for, but against, his virtue.

Jefferson's outlook, to do him justice, derives from a world view that provides a consistent context for a utilitarian morality. For Jefferson, the principle of utility stemmed from the axiom that God created everything for a useful purpose. Because the Jeffersonian God was a Supreme Craftsman who wasted nothing and made no unnecessary parts, man, in choosing the *useful* course, did but align his own actions with this divine economy of nature.[57] If this utilitarian principle seems to confuse morality with self-interest, it does so in the spirit of faith. But also, one is tempted to think, in the anticipation of national purpose.

For the Jeffersonian outlook brought morality and the Divinity directly into the service of a national purpose. Referring to the Jeffersonian conception of the Deity as Master Builder, Boorstin writes: "Seeing God not through an ancient revelation or tradition, but through the particular needs of their generation, the Jeffersonians had put God in the service of their earthly, American task."[58] If God had created man for a useful purpose, the Jeffersonians returned the favor in kind. But their rationale in framing their theology and morality on practical need is significant.

A utilitarian morality follows not only from the economy of nature, but from the Jeffersonian facility for rationalizing man's (and the nation's) interest. Jefferson held that the individual's interest and society's were identical; to pursue one's own interest was to pursue the community's: "To succeed at building and material conquest," explains Boorstin, "seemed automatically to do something for one's neighbors. Conversely, to enrich one's neighbors was to improve America and to enhance a corporation in which every settler was a shareholder."[59] What disturbs, however, is the ease with which such a moral philosophy lends itself to a selfish practical interpretation. The doctrine of Manifest Destiny, for example, manifested not so much the nation's divine calling as its greed in Sunday garments. Or, as Boorstin notes in presenting a slightly different aspect of the same historical perspective: "The essential difference between the naturalism of the Age of Jefferson and the naturalism of the Age of Robber Barons was . . . less a difference in philosophies than a difference between stages in the development of the same philosophy."[60]

The criterion of interest is necessarily a questionable moral rule-of-thumb. *Arthur Mervyn* revolves around the extent to which virtue follows or forsakes interest. Arthur shows a Jeffersonian knack for marrying the two. In fact, his marriage to Achsa Fielding is a virtual wedding of principle to principal. And if the Jeffersonians "put God in the service of their earthly American task," Arthur certainly does no less. But how, finally, is one to distinguish between the "earthly" (i.e., humanitarian) task of the Jeffersonians and the "earthly" (i.e., worldly) task of amassing wealth? Arthur yearns, at one point, to use his acquired wealth to rehabilitate Clemenza Lodi; at another, to relieve Philadelphia's hungry. In the end, though, he completes neither fantasy; Arthur's wealth is finally the personal gain of a lucrative marriage.

Jefferson, like many rationalists of his time, based his understanding of the world on empirical evidence. Hard facts carried particular weight in Jeffersonian thought: " 'Fact' was the Jeffersonian word for the elements in that fixed and absolute external reality. It was 'facts' alone which were capable of 'unadulterated purity', and the Jeffersonian sought the uncontaminated fact much as the Platonist sought the pure idea—convinced that it alone gave access to the structure of creation."[61] Facts were the key to understanding the world; to assemble the facts was to solve its mysteries. Behind this faith in facts lay the assumption that the world was knowable; that if mysteries persisted, man was at fault for not having sought the explanation diligently enough.

The narrative structure of *Arthur Mervyn* deposes the integrity of facts. Facts become little more than grist for the narrator's mill, as one speaker after another delivers plausible yet contradictory versions of the same set of facts. Arthur, in part I, narrates his own history. In part 2, other speakers—Dr. Stevens, Wortley, Mrs. Althorpe—narrate episodes that intersect with portions of Arthur's narrative, often adducing identical facts but adding others, and thereby contradicting Arthur's story wholly or in part. Mrs. Althorpe, neighbor to the Mervyns, "a sensible and candid woman" (by one narrator's reckoning, at least [2:230]), gives this account of Arthur's departure from home: "Arthur took leave, one night, to possess himself of all his father's cash, mount the best horse in his meadow and elope. For a time, no one knew whither he had gone. At last, one was said to have met with him in the streets of this city, metamorphosed from a rustic lad into a fine gentleman. Nothing could be quicker than this change, for he left the country on a Saturday morning, and was seen in a French frock and silk stockings, going into Christ's Church the next day" (2:231). Except for the first sentence, Mrs. Althorpe's tale coincides with Arthur's story even to the detail of the French frock. Yet the first sentence, if true, reduces Arthur to an impostor, the general factuality of his tale notwithstanding.

As to the ultimate value of facts as arbiters of truth, Wortley's debate with Dr. Stevens concerning Arthur's character reveals not the usefulness but the uselessness of facts. Dr. Stevens recounts, then responds to, Wortley's argument:

> It cannot be denied, continued my friend [Wortley], that he [Arthur] lived with Welbeck at the time of his elopement; that they disappeared together; that they entered a boat, at Pine-Street wharf, at midnight; that this boat was discovered by the owner in the possession of a fisherman at Red-bank, who affirmed that he had found it stranded near his door, the day succeeding that on which they disappeared. Of all this, I can supply you with incontestable proof. If after this proof, you can give credit to his story, I shall think you made of very perverse and credulous materials.

The proof you mention, said I, will only enhance his credibility.
All the facts which you have stated, have been admitted by him.
They constitute an essential portion of his narrative. (2:226)

This passage reiterates what Arthur's career dramatizes: that facts do not
tell the whole story. The distraught fellow, covered with blood, seques-
tering the body is not necessarily the murderer. Virtually all evidence in
Arthur's world is inconclusive; and fortunately so, for Arthur.

Dr. Stevens, meanwhile, plays the sleuth in this moral detective
story. A man of science, he hopes, by gathering and assessing the facts,
to unravel the mystery of Arthur's character. However, in doing so he
makes plain that not just his faith in Arthur depends on Arthur's justification: "Facts? Let me know them, I beseech you. If Mervyn has deceived me, there is an end to my confidence in human nature. All limits
to dissimulation, and all distinction between vice and virtue will be
effaced. No man's word, no force of collateral evidence shall weigh with
me an hair" (2:248–49). He therefore solicits the testimony of trusted
friends and acquaintances, revolves their disclosures and counsels with
his wife. But his delving only multiplies the enigma.

Brown's investigation of the problem of extrapolating truth from fact
reveals two difficulties: one, the problem of discerning fact from fiction,
and, two, the role of subjective judgment in interpreting certified facts.
The first of these Brown dramatizes not only by juxtaposing contradictory versions of the same sequence of events, but also by developing the
theme of the deceptiveness of appearance. The melodrama of Arthur's
career, in which perverse circumstances regularly indict him, is Brown's
exhibit A. The second difficulty, though, deserves closer examination.

Brown suggests, in short, that, deceptive appearances notwithstanding, man's capacity for seeing truth is limited because the individual
will warps sensory evidence. Man sees what he wants to see, not what
is there. Wortley, for instance, doubts Arthur's words and acts, while
Dr. Stevens believes them. Both men try to judge objectively and believe they are doing so; but neither, in fact, does. Dr. Stevens, in saving
Arthur's life, invests himself in Arthur's cause; he has a personal stake in
seeing Arthur vindicated. Wortley, meanwhile, having been ruined by
Welbeck, aches with revenge—and Arthur is a convenient scapegoat.
Dr. Stevens tells Wortley, "Your sufferings have soured your humanity
and biassed your candor" (2:251). What Dr. Stevens perhaps does not
realize is that he is equally biased in Arthur's behalf: "Why are you so

much afraid to submit [Arthur's] innocence to this test?" Wortley at one point asks him (2:248).

Objective assessment, then, is virtually impossible. Every judge brings subjective intelligence to bear on any given question. How, then, can he expect to discern objective truth? Won't he instead shape the truth to his own biases? And, finally, how much more must this principle operate in thwarting *self*-assessment? For instance, evidence shows Arthur adept at accommodating objective appearances to subjective necessity. At one point during his stay with Welbeck, Arthur unexpectedly encounters Welbeck emerging at dawn from Clemenza Lodi's bedroom. Arthur concludes, to his anguish, that Welbeck is sexually involved with Clemenza, his "daughter." (He is, of course, both right and wrong: Clemenza is Welbeck's mistress.) Arthur brings his reasoning powers to bear on the evidence, though, and manages to purge its sexual implications:

> The lady might have been lately reduced to widowhood. The recent loss of a beloved companion would sufficiently account for her dejection, and make her present situation compatible with duty. By this new train of ideas I was somewhat comforted. I saw the folly of precipitate inferences, and the injustice of my atrocious imputations, and acquired some degree of patience in my present state of uncertainty. My heart was lightened of its wonted burthen, and I laboured to invent some harmless explication of the scene that I had witnessed the previous evening. (1:77)

Significantly, this process of rationalizing appearances becomes for Arthur its opposite—objective assessment: "These ideas [i.e., Arthur's suspicions of Welbeck's depravity] were necessarily transient. *Conclusions more conformable to appearances succeeded*" (1:76, my italics). Arthur claims, that is, to put aside preconception and judge strictly from the evidence, when in reality he makes the evidence conform to psychological necessity.

Arthur's ability and inclination to transform so obvious a truth and thereby to secure peace of mind casts indirect doubt on his career. Does he employ a similar mechanism to convince himself (and us) of his own virtue, regardless of deeds or circumstance? Has he not said, "My peace of mind depended on the favourable verdict which conscience should pass on my proceedings" (1:71)? Might not his entire narrative be an attempt "to invent some harmless explication" of his own dubious actions?

Arthur seizes the reins of narrative, we recall, at the most suspicious moment—just after Welbeck has given him $40,000 to return to the Maurices. Dr. Stevens, his doubts about Arthur finally allayed, sees Arthur, cash in hand, preparing to depart—presumably for Baltimore, where the Maurices live—and stammers several pertinent questions that suggest his doubts have returned in force. Arthur explains himself as usual, but also resolves to narrate the rest of the tale. Is he afraid, at last, to trust his presentation to another?

For Arthur an unconscious rationalizing mechanism and the self-blindness it permits is an adaptive advantage of sorts. By the novel's end, though, Arthur, on the verge of a symbolically incestuous marriage and seemingly blind to the self that has dictated this course, seems dangerously deluded rather than uniquely adapted. One senses that, were his mother still alive, Arthur could with little effort "invent some harmless explication" to justify marrying her—especially if her dowry were impressive.

In few respects does Arthur more closely embody America than in this ability to "objectively" justify a dubious but profitable course of action. Jefferson's Republican administration succeeded by consolidating government and commercial interest—Federalist aims—despite a philosophical commitment to a doctrine of states' rights and agrarian economics:

> In spite of their theory that the central government must be weak for the sake of liberty, the Republicans made it strong for the sake of America. In a few short years that lay ahead it was their fate to double the territory of the United States; to give the Constitution a generous interpretation that shocked even many a Federalist by its breadth of view; to wage war against Great Britain in the name of commerce; to reestablish the hated United States Bank; to enact a high protective tariff; to observe their Federalist opponents take their turn at defending the rights of the state; to announce that the central government was supreme in foreign affairs; and to see the Constitution upheld against the attacks of states by a son of agricultural Virginia, John Marshall, Chief Justice of the Supreme Court of the United States.[62]

How could such departures from principle be justified? With facts. Here is Jefferson explaining his purchase of the Louisiana territory, and the wide construction such an executive action placed on the Constitution: "A strict observance to the written laws is doubtless *one* of the high duties of a good citizen, but it is not the *highest*. The laws of necessity, of self-preservation, of saving our country when in danger, are of a higher obligation."[63] As to the country's danger (Spain's secret cession of Louisiana to Napoleon in 1800, when discovered, raised doubts about America's continued use of the Mississippi River as a trade route), France, by 1802, was in no position to threaten anyone in the western hemisphere; she sold the land because she feared it would otherwise be taken from her.[64] Rather, Jefferson adduces the "fact" of the nation's danger to justify the completed purchase.

Boorstin finds this propensity for creative empiricism adumbrated in Jeffersonian theology, which, he notes, ratified the "great chain of beings," but "was at once an expression of personal faith and a description of the material universe. The Jeffersonian insisted that the felt qualities of his universe were not the product of his personal belief; yet his theology had transformed every fact of natural history into a testimony of faith in the Creator." This ability to transform objective fact and so to "objectively" justify one's own biases is, of course, a fault of humanity in general, but in this respect the Jeffersonian American was perhaps especially human: "The depth of his faith made him all the more resolute not to be misled by apparent facts which might seem to show qualities in the creation which he knew to be discordant with the character of the Maker. . . . This orderly 'chain of beings' actually became the reality to be illustrated and confirmed by all particular facts."[65] Thus Jefferson and his associates conjured divine purposes for snakes, swamps, epidemics, and expansionism.

Boorstin further suggests that this propensity for rationalizing practical advantage characterizes American ideology in general:

> Puritanism, Jeffersonianism, Transcendentalism, and Pragmatism have all testified to man's inability to turn his back on philosophy. Yet, each in its different fashion, these American movements have ended in a refusal to follow philosophy where it might paralyze the hand of the artisan or conqueror. Each has found a way of assuaging man's scruples without obstructing the exploitation of the continent; each has found a means to hallow the building of a new world while implying that such building was somehow its own justification.[66]

The point is not that Arthur Mervyn, Thomas Jefferson, or America itself is a scheming hypocrite. Their own emphases on principle, however, foreshorten those departures made for the sake of expedience, and the need to "invent some harmless explication" for expedient acts betrays a tendency toward self-delusion. Jeffersonianism is finally open to criticism not for what it comprised, but for what it omitted: self-scrutiny, self-definition, and self-comprehension.[67] The same criticism applies to Arthur Mervyn.

Arthur looks but does not see. His self-contemplation, though it seems at times like soul-searching, is at last a reinventing of motive and reality calculated to render that "favorable verdict" his conscience "depends" upon. Unlike Clara Wieland or Constantia Dudley, Arthur is never traumatized into self-awareness. His chronic spying suggests a comic reversal of the secret-witness motif of *Ormond:* whereas the secret witness beheld evil, but refused subsequently to acknowledge it, Arthur stares it in the face but sees nothing amiss. The Arthur who engages to marry Achsa Fielding is in this frightening respect the same Arthur who hid in Thetford's bedroom closet and listened, never realizing he would one day enact comparable intrigues.

Arthur is no crook, but he has cultivated the necessary psychological mechanisms. He shows a forger's potential. "Cured" though he is, Arthur may yet be a carrier. His potential for suave, self-justifying depravity, magnified by the extent of self-blindness Arthur demonstrates in the closing chapters, undermines the American-dream aura of the close and embodies an untoward potential in the American character. Arthur's ability to preserve the ark intact while sacking the city recalls turn-of-the-century America's budding propensity for the same. His final "ecstacy" belies a nimble self-deceit. *Arthur Mervyn* both depicts and deposes the American—and especially the Jeffersonian—ideal of virtue fulfilled in material success.

---◆❈◆---

CHAPTER SIX

EDGAR HUNTLY:

SOMNAMBULISM

VS. SELF-KNOWLEDGE

"How little cognizance have men over the actions
and motives of each other! How total is our blindness
with regard to our own performances!"

EDGAR HUNTLY in *Edgar Huntly*

"Too much light often blinds."

CHRISTOPH MARTIN WIELAND in *Musarion*

Ormond suggests that virtue is constricting, even self-threatening. *Arthur Mervyn* suggests that it need not be—that, properly modified, it can be a key to success, however dubious that success. In this ethical restructuring, however, morality becomes elastic; virtue becomes virtuosity. At worst, the result is self-deceit, self-indulgence, and compulsive self-justification. *Edgar Huntly* dramatizes this negative potential. If Arthur Mervyn is the American Dreamer, content to sleepwalk, disinclined to pinch himself and endanger the dream's outcome, Edgar Huntly is that same dreamer in the grips of nightmare, unable first to wake up—then, having left his bed, to go back to sleep again, to resist the deeds his night-walking self leads him to perform. In *Edgar Huntly,* the universal depravity dramatized in *Wieland* reasserts itself; but the transformation recurs slowly, by visible degrees.

Edgar Huntly is Brown's most deliberate dramatic exposition of irrational evil: a time-lapse film of depravity flowering. Its protagonist, Edgar, a sympathetic youth, becomes, as it were, a savage, murdering with increasing ease and compulsion. If Wieland's butchery carries off a household of five, and Ormond's awesome vengeance spree over the killing of a Cossack comrade ends in his riding off with the heads of five Turks dangling from his saddle horn, Edgar Huntly performs no less sanguinary a feat, leaving five Indians steeped in gore and a bullet hole in the shirt-sleeve of his mentor (named, like Ormond's comrade, Sarsefield). But whereas Wieland's and Ormond's savagery erupt in sudden fits or visitations, Edgar's matures almost organically. Edgar is perhaps the first example in the American novel of D. H. Lawrence's quintessential American: "hard, isolate, stoic, and a killer." [1]

Edgar Huntly, that is to say, reenacts and extends the drama at the core of *Wieland*—Clara's transformation into a potential fratricide. But it also investigates a philosophical dilemma whose mirror image we have seen in *Ormond.* Whereas *Ormond* suggests that virtue necessitates self-blindness, *Edgar Huntly* proposes the contrapositive: that self-awareness unleashes vice. If the ending of *Ormond* raises the question of whether virtue is not as insidious, in some respects, as vice, *Edgar Huntly* asks a related question: whether self-knowledge is not as great a liability as self-ignorance. Brown's symbol for both the individual and society in *Edgar Huntly* is the sleepwalker, navigating blindly, precariously entranced, *yet infinitely dangerous to awaken.* Brown dramatizes the horrors that ensue if such a sleepwalker awakens and then, like a Transylvanian doctor nailing the lid back on the vampire's casket, tries to bury the truth, to forestall further inquiry. A repudiation of self-scrutiny, *Edgar Huntly* alone, of all Brown's books, shows us not only the ghouls that inhabit our souls, but the prohibitive consequences of looking at them.

THE HUNTER AND THE HUNTED

At one point in *Edgar Huntly; or Memoirs of a Sleep-Walker,* the protagonist probes a wooden box, the handcrafted contrivance of his neighbor, Clithero Edny. "Its structure was remarkable," says Edgar; "[Its sides] were joined, not by mortise and tennon, not by nails, not by hinges, but the junction was accurate. The means by which they were made to cohere were invisible." [2] Structurally, *Edgar Huntly* represents a similar puzzle.

The tale comprises two apparently unrelated narratives that seem juxtaposed rather than joined, and whose unconventional juncture has frustrated generations of critics. The first tale begins with an unsolved murder. Edgar's close friend and prospective brother-in-law, Waldegrave, has been killed by an unknown assassin. Edgar, bent on finding the killer and avenging the crime, returns one night to the elm tree under which Waldegrave was killed and there discovers a half-naked figure digging up the earth and weeping distractedly. Edgar prepares to accost him, but the figure, apparently asleep, walks past, brushing Edgar's arm, yet neither seeing nor noticing him. Thinking he has found the guilt-ridden killer, Edgar mounts a campaign of surveillance. The sleepwalker, he discovers, is Clithero Edny, an Irish immigrant recently employed by his neighbor Inglefield. Edgar eventually compels Clithero to confess. The crime he confesses, though, is not the slaying of Waldegrave but the killing of his maternal benefactress, Mrs. Lorimer, and her degenerate brother, Arthur Wiatte, in Ireland. Clithero, it seems, killed Wiatte in self-defense, then tried to kill Mrs. Lorimer in order to spare her the pain of discovering her brother's death. The attempt on Mrs. Lorimer's life failed; but Clithero, mistaking her swoon for death, has fled to America, tortured in mind. Edgar empathizes with his grief and resolves to reclaim him.

Edgar follows Clithero into the wilderness, hoping to dissuade him from suicide. He tracks him to a remote crag, risks his life crossing the intervening chasm, and narrowly escapes being set upon by a panther. Returning to Inglefield's, Edgar pries into Clithero's trunk and digs up a box in which Clithero has secreted Mrs. Lorimer's memoirs. Edgar's pursuit of Clithero is interrupted, however, when a stranger named Wentworth—a former friend of Waldegrave—calls to claim $7,500 that he asserts he had left in trust with Waldegrave before the murder. Wentworth's story cannot be gainsaid—Waldegrave's bank account, at the time of his death, contained $7,500 that no one had been able to account for. By now, however, Edgar and his fiancée, Waldegrave's sister, have not only come to look on the money as their own but have based their marriage plans on it. Wentworth's claim, then, is a serious blow for Edgar.

At this point, the novel shifts gears radically: Edgar awakens in a cave, bruised, confused, terrified, and ravenous. (We later learn he has walked there in his sleep.) A nightmare of trial and pursuit follows. Edgar discovers a tomahawk and contemplates suicide; confronts and kills a panther and eats its reeking fibers; wanders through pitch-black passages; stumbles on a war party of Indians holding a white girl captive; escapes from the cave, killing an Indian in the process; and, finally, returns for the girl and escapes with her into the wilderness. They stop to rest at an unoccupied cabin, only to be surprised by three of the remaining warriors. The girl is injured, but Edgar manages to kill the three braves before collapsing, unconscious, atop the third corpse.

When Edgar wakes, he is alone. Unknown to him, a rescue party, led by his paternal friend Sarsefield, has taken the girl to safety, but has left him for dead. Upon waking, Edgar retires to a stream for a drink and spots yet another Indian—whom he surprises, shoots, and stabs with a bayonet. He then resumes his trek toward civilization. During the night he crosses paths with the rescue party, but mistaking them for Indians, shoots at one, who, equally confused by the dark, returns the fire. (Edgar's near-victim turns out to be Sarsefield.) Edgar escapes by plunging into an icy river. Thoroughly (though wrongly) convinced his uncle and sisters have been murdered (one of the Indians he shoots was carrying his uncle's rifle), Edgar pushes on hopelessly, and finally arrives at a neighbor's house—where, to his amazement, he discovers Sarsefield.

Clithero, meanwhile, is found mangled by Indians, but Sarsefield, though a doctor, refuses to dress his wounds. Sarsefield, we learn, was once Mrs. Lorimer's lover in Ireland. He has since become her husband, and has brought her back with him to America. He can neither forgive nor forget Clithero's crimes. Edgar, meanwhile, cannot resist notifying Clithero that his benefactress, Mrs. Lorimer, far from being dead, is living nearby. Clithero, upon learning this, sets out after her, crazed with emotion. Sarsefield intercepts Clithero, who leaps into a river to escape and presumably drowns. Mrs. Lorimer, traumatized, miscarries, and the book closes with Edgar apologizing profusely to Sarsefield, and Sarsefield castigating Edgar for his ill-fated meddling. Somewhere in the midst of this unexpected denouement we learn that Waldegrave's mysterious assassin was an Indian.

The ending of *Edgar Huntly* rankles. The anticlimactic revelation that Waldegrave was killed by an Indian makes half the book—Clithero's narrative and his relationship to Edgar—seem unnecessary and irrelevant. It even makes the book's premise—Waldegrave's mysterious assassination—seem unnecessarily misleading. More importantly, it undermines the novel's formal, dramatic, and thematic structure. Like Clithero's strange box, Brown's construct of juxtaposed narratives coheres firmly, if improbably. Brown joins Clithero's narrative to Edgar's adventures in Norwalk by an unobtrusive formal parallelism. As critics have observed, Edgar resembles Clithero in many respects.[3] John Cleman summarizes some of these similarities: "Edgar's and Clithero's careers . . . are in many ways mirror images of each other: both are forced to take one man's life, which act leads them at least to consider (in Clithero's case) taking others; both entertain benevolent ideas which lead to disasters; both are motivated also by curiosity; both have manuscripts which they are secluding; and both are afflicted by sleep-walking, which comes to represent a similar insanity."[4] Kenneth Bernard concludes an even more detailed comparison by noting that when Sarsefield and Mrs. Lorimer marry, Edgar and Clithero become, in effect, foster brothers.[5] But what does the identification suggest? that Edgar shares Clithero's self-destructive tendencies? that Edgar too is benevolent but misguided? that Edgar, like Clithero, is partly crazy?[6] These conclusions, even if true, seem insufficient.

This elaborate parallel is not all that puzzles. As Leslie Fiedler has observed, Brown invests Edgar's adventures in the Norwalk wilderness with mythic and psychosymbolic overtones.[7] Norwalk—and especially the cave—is both a precultural setting and a dream landscape, a projection of the psyche. Edgar's confused awakening in the cave, his slaying and devouring of the panther, and his repeated immersion in water and blood all suggest primordial rituals of rebirth and initiation. The Indians he kills are both real antagonists and ghosts of the unconscious— a "tribe of ugly phantoms," such as "sleep . . . summon[s] up" (158). In fact, the whole sequence, beginning with Edgar's awakening in the pit and ending with his slaying of the Indians, plays upon primordial fears: "Famine, and blindness, and death, and savage enemies," says Edgar, "never fail to be conjured up by the silence and darkness of the night" (158). Why does Brown render Edgar's experience in such mythic terms? What is Edgar initiated into? reborn as? A mature individual? Then why his final naive and ill-considered words to Clithero about Mrs. Lorimer? A civilized man? Then why the emphasis on slaughter? A sane human being? Then why the bestial initiation rites?[8]

Fiedler answers the question in part by proposing that Huntly is initiated into self-knowledge. "Brown's novel," he says, "is the account of a young man who begins by looking for guilt in others and finds it in himself." He goes on to universalize the significance of Huntly's drama: "Any man may wake to find himself at the bottom of a pit. *We are all sleepwalkers.*"[9] Fiedler stops short, though, of specifying the precise nature of the guilt Huntly discovers. Two other critics—Arthur Kimball and Kenneth Bernard—do not.

"The Indians in *Edgar Huntly,*" says Kimball, "are really foils for the savage potential of Brown's hero." Edgar, he ventures, is reborn as a savage—hence his tomahawk, his slaying and devouring of the panther, and his career of slaughter. Kimball frames Edgar's savagery within the larger context of America's violence toward the Indian: "In *Edgar Huntly,* the underlying irony is Brown's exposé of the savage potential, not of the red man, but of the white." [10] Kimball points especially to the subtle violence of the community Edgar returns to—typified first by the drunkard Selby, who drives his wife and infant from their home, and, second, by Sarsefield, the enlightened doctor and teacher—Edgar's paradigm—who refuses, out of vengefulness, to treat the wounded Clithero.

Edgar, then, *is,* in a sense, initiated into normality, sanity, and civilization, but the initiation is ironic. The closer he gets to civilization, the more we see the barbarity civilized man—Edgar included—partakes of. Certain of Edgar's statements suggest that this irony is not lost on him. After one particularly bloody murder, he exclaims, "Such are the deeds which perverse nature compels thousands of rational beings to perform and to witness" (202). His trials over, he at last confesses, "What light has burst upon my ignorance of myself and of mankind" (6). The remark suggests that his awareness, such as it is, is predicated on self-awareness.

For Edgar awakens, in the course of his exploits, to a self he did not know existed. As his capacity to kill escalates in defiance of his principles and intentions, he is mortified by self-awareness: "Disastrous and humiliating is the state of man! By his own hands is constructed the mass of misery and error in which his steps are forever involved. . . . How total is our blindness with regard to our own performances!" (278). One critic notes, "As [Edgar] is forced to go on killing in order to stay alive, he becomes . . . more and more conscience-stricken, more and more aware of a blood or bloody kinship between the Indians and himself." [11] Having collapsed on the corpse of his fourth victim, Edgar wakes to find his "disheveled locks . . . matted and steeped in that gore which had overflowed and choked up the orifice" (191). A fifth killing leaves him not only stained with another's blood, but "overpowered" by his own "perverse nature" (202), after he not only shoots his victim but mangles him with a bayonet.

The savagery of the Indians, then, is ironically matched both by Edgar's savagery and by the violence of the white community. As William Hedges points out, "there is no one in the novel who is not a potential savage, a would-be murderer of father or son, no one who has not some of 'perverse nature' in himself." [12] This justifies the mythic dimension of the tale and even explains, in part, Brown's elaborate identification of Edgar with Clithero—a confessed killer. But aspects of the story still mystify. Why does Brown devote so much time to the Clithero section? What does Waldegrave's death have to do with Edgar's adventures? Why does Edgar become a sleepwalker in the first place? What does his somnambulism mean in relation to Clithero's? Why, in short, does the first half of the book exist?

If Arthur Kimball applies and extends Fiedler's insights in explicating the second half of *Edgar Huntly,* Kenneth Bernard does as much for the first half. Bernard begins with the question of Waldegrave's death. As if taking literally Fiedler's conclusion that Edgar "begins by looking for guilt in others and finds it in himself," [13] Bernard indicts Edgar Huntly as "the murderer, real or imagined, of Waldegrave." [14] Bernard begins by noting inconsistencies between Edgar's account of the murder and his conduct following the murder. He then catalogs extensive similarities linking Edgar to Clithero—similarities that, in light of his thesis, become suddenly significant. Next he suggests a motive for Edgar's hypothetical murder of his friend. Certain letters, addressed to Edgar by Waldegrave and expressing a religious skepticism that Edgar seems to have adopted, remained in Edgar's possession at the time of the murder. Waldegrave, having eventually repudiated his skeptical stance, had wanted Edgar to destroy the letters, but Edgar had demurred. "An argument about these letters," Bernard contends, "would explain many things, like Waldegrave's 'inexplicable obstinacy' " [15]— and perhaps even his murder. (As Bernard notes, Edgar was clearly upset over the subject of the letters: a later dream in which Waldegrave appears urging him to perform some neglected duty—burn the letters, presumably—induces Edgar to sleepwalk.)

Bernard's hypothesis that Edgar might have murdered Waldegrave during an argument over these letters, while not altogether implausible, seems farfetched. There *was,* however, a simpler, more compelling motive for murder at hand: Edgar's financial exigence. As Waldegrave's closest friend, Edgar, his claims to the contrary notwithstanding, may well have known about the $7,500 Weymouth left in trust with him. In love with Mary Waldegrave but too poor to marry her—and keenly aware that Mary would not wed him while their prospects remained dim—Edgar may have yielded to an otherwise unthinkable temptation. His characterization of Mary Waldegrave is as rife with motive as his characterization of Waldegrave's death is oxymoronic:

I know the impatience with which your poverty has formerly been borne; . . . how earnestly your wishes panted after a state which might exempt you from dependence upon daily labour and on the caprices of others, and might secure to you leisure to cultivate and indulge your love of knowledge and your social and beneficent affections. . . . Thou hast honored me with thy affection; but that union, on which we rely for happiness, could not take place while both of us were poor. . . . My present condition is wholly inconsistent with marriage. As long as my exertions are insufficient to maintain us both, it would be unjustifiable to burden you with new cares and duties. Of this you are more thoroughly convinced than I am. The love of independence and ease, and impatience of drudgery are woven into your constitution. Perhaps they are carried to an erroneous extreme. . . . By giving you possession of the means of independence and leisure, by enabling us to complete a contract which poverty alone had thus long delayed, this event [Waldegrave's death] has been, at the same time, the most disastrous and propitious which could have happened. (155–56)

Moreover, if Weymouth's story is to be believed (and we are led to think it is, in all other particulars), the neighbors seem convinced the reason Mary Waldegrave is away is that she is pregnant (148). Since Edgar is her fiancé, this development would further explain the onset of a desperation great enough to allow Edgar to contemplate theft and murder. As to the apparent absence of any letters of remittance among Waldegrave's effects, Edgar's word is, of course, all we have to go by. And considering his demonstrated propensity for hiding things in his sleep (Waldegrave's letters), who is to say Weymouth's letters of remittance did not disappear in like fashion? As Edgar himself says, "Perhaps, indeed, they still lurk in some unexpected corner" (157).[16]

This cavil concerning motive aside, however, Bernard's brash reading strikes resonant chords. It receives incidental support, moreover, from Robert E. Hemenway, who cites a source for *Edgar Huntly*—an extract from the *Vienna Gazette* of June 14, 1784.[17] This extract describes the case of a woman murdered by the youth who loved her: "What renders the case truly extraordinary is, that there are good reasons for believing that the deed was perpetrated by the youth while asleep, and was entirely unknown to himself. The young woman was the object of his affection, and the journey in which she had engaged had given him the utmost anxiety for her safety." [18] Brown cites the case in a preface to a fragment he published in *The Literary Magazine and American Register.* In that fragment, the sympathetic, sleepwalking narrator (who corresponds to Edgar Huntly) is presumably the murderer—though a local lunatic in the Clithero mold complicates the puzzle. [19] If Brown had this source in mind while writing *Edgar Huntly,* he almost certainly intended to impute Waldegrave's murder to his young protagonist, the friend of Waldegrave—Edgar Huntly.

Bernard suggests that Brown originally intended to cast Edgar as Waldegrave's killer, but later opted for a more conventional ending. Bernard fails, however, to see the significance for his thesis of the second part of the tale, which he views as a slightly mitigated abortion, a "long, melodramatic anticlimax" to the Edgar-Clithero section. [20] Missing any subtler intentions on Brown's part, he characterizes the second section as a psychological success story in which Edgar "wins the battle for his mind, throws off his guilt, and is ready to enter again the normal world, which is represented by a series of adventures with a very concrete threat, Indians." [21] This tack disregards the flagrant ironies that attend Edgar's acts and those of presumably civilized men he meets on his return to the "normal" world, as well as the overarching irony of a "civilized" society engaged in displacing and eliminating natives in the same spirit with which it was displacing and eliminating panthers from the countryside.

It is ironic that Bernard sees so little merit in the second half of *Edgar Huntly.* By concentrating almost exclusively on the Clithero-Edgar section, he misses what is perhaps the strongest indirect argument in support of his thesis that Edgar killed Waldegrave: the dramatic sequence Brown constructs in the second half of the book.

As John Cleman contends, Edgar's behavior changes as he kills one Indian after another. [22] Despite motives of self-defense, concern for the welfare of others, and revenge for real or imagined personal injuries, Edgar's killings are not all equally justifiable. His killing becomes progressively more brutal, less discriminate, and less defensible as he makes his way home.

Edgar's first killing is both unavoidable and cleanly executed. Having escaped from the cave, he becomes trapped between the Indians within and the Indian without. He resolves to retreat rather than to kill, but when the Indian outside leaves his perch on the ledge and moves toward him, Edgar, no longer able to hide, kills the brave with a tomahawk. The stroke is "quick as lightning," and the Indian expires "without a groan" (173). Brown virtually covers our (and Edgar's) eyes and ears for this first slaying: the roar of the torrent drowns out all noise, while its waters bear away the corpse.

The three killings at Queen Mab's hut are bloodier and less justifiable, flight being, as Cleman points out, a clear practical alternative.[23] Edgar discovers a secret exit through the oven—an ideal escape route—but, intent on exacting revenge for crimes he now imagines to have been committed against his uncle and sisters, he hides outside the cabin instead of fleeing, and shoots the Indians as they emerge. The first gets his just deserts (he has just used a tomahawk to fracture the ribs of the girl Edgar has befriended, and is about to kill her when Edgar's bullet stops him cold).

The second Indian is less fortunate. Edgar narrates: "[His] terrific visage was stretched fearfully forth. . . . His glances . . . lighted upon me, and on the fatal instrument which was pointed at his forehead. His muscles were at once exerted to withdraw his head, and to vociferate a warning to his fellow; but his movement was too slow. The ball entered above his ear. He tumbled headlong to the ground, bereaved of sensation though not of life, and had power only to struggle and mutter" (191). Here, for the first time, Edgar glimpses the face beneath the war paint, if only for an instant, before his bullet, aimed at that face, reduces the Indian to a vegetable.

The last killing of the sequence takes place as follows: Edgar, running for cover, is grazed by the remaining Indian's bullet. He falls to the ground, but in such a way that he can watch the Indian as he emerges from cover. When the Indian comes for his scalp, Edgar shoots him in the breast. We can hardly fault Edgar for doing what he must to survive. Yet the element of trickery—stereotypically an Indian tactic—adds irony to the portrait and reveals an unexpected cunning on Edgar's part.

All these killings are, in a sense, defensible and self-defensive. But Edgar's main motive has become revenge, rather than self-preservation and civic responsibility; his modus operandi is now premeditation and duplicity, rather than avoidance of violence. Edgar's baptism in blood (not only does he suffer a face wound, but he wakes up to find his hair matted with gore from the dead Indian he has fainted on) signifies the transformation he is undergoing. Viewing the carnage he has caused, he remarks: "My anguish was mingled with astonishment. . . . The transition I had undergone was so wild and inexplicable; all that I had performed, all that I had witnessed since my egress from the pit, were so contradictory to precedent events, that I still clung to the belief that my thoughts were confused by delirium" (194).

Edgar's fifth and last killing clarifies his transformation still further. It is both gratuitous and gruesome, and mocks his recent resolution to "shun the contest with a new enemy, almost at the expense of my life" (199). Edgar, hidden from view, finds himself in a unique position to exterminate the only remaining Indian of the war party. In spite of the recent resolution, Edgar, as it were, tricks himself into shooting: "My piece was uncocked. I did not reflect that in moving the spring a sound would necessarily be produced sufficient to alarm him" (201). Edgar's first shot disables the Indian, but does not kill him. Edgar walks away, but is drawn back by the Indian's groans. He shoots again, but misses. He completes the job by bayoneting the brave, then throws himself on the ground in remorse. Finally, "prompted by some freak of fancy" (203), he stands the Indian's musket upright in the road and departs. Edgar's remorse, no doubt, is genuine. But his whimsical monument to the dead brave hints, ever so slightly, at an almost feline pride over a mutilated prey. This purported mercy-killing, despite Edgar's Clithero-like rationalizations, bears all the marks of a bushwhacking.

Technically speaking, Edgar's career of killing ends here. But a crucial postscript occurs when Edgar takes a pot-shot at his friend Sarsefield. Brown presents the incident as an accident: physically and emotionally exhausted, Edgar, on his night trek home, hears footsteps. Fearing Indians, he hides. Figures pass in the darkness, but one solitary, armed figure appears to spot him. The figure makes a movement which Edgar interprets as leveling a rifle. Edgar hastily fires his own piece, drops it, and leaps over a cliff into a river, as his unknown adversary— who, he later learns, is no Indian, but Sarsefield—returns the fire.

As with Clara Wieland's contemplated stabbing of her brother, Edgar's misconceived shot at Sarsefield, though justified by the circumstance, reverberates ominously. Having killed five men, the last, brutally and unnecessarily, Edgar finally turns a gun on his friend, mentor, and, indeed, as Edgar later notes, his virtual father. The shot at Sarsefield not only confirms Edgar's transformation into a killer, but shows how indiscriminate and uncontrollable his killing has become. Like Clithero, he has almost killed a surrogate parent.

Once we see Edgar's ironic descent into a killer as the subject of the Indian sequence, and recognize the degree to which Edgar is eventually transformed, Bernard's thesis becomes virtually inescapable. The second part of *Edgar Huntly* traces the extent to which Edgar's inhibitions against violence can be set at naught, and demonstrates his willingness and even compulsion, under certain circumstances, to kill brutally and indiscriminately. This progression of increasingly disturbing killings—and particularly Edgar's confused attempt on Sarsefield's life—points, logically, to a final revelation which would at once complete the drama of Edgar's transformation and link that drama with Waldegrave's mysterious death: the revelation that Edgar killed Waldegrave.

That revelation, had Brown not backed off from the implications of his theme, would have been even more than an ingenious resolution of a detective mystery. For, by the end of the novel, the irony with which Brown has laced his tale has had time to take effect: we see that civilization too partakes of savagery; that the impulses awakened in Edgar are latent in all; that Edgar's complicity is potentially our own. The final indictment, had Brown lodged it, would have been, in effect, a subpoena to the reader.

As it stands, we can only celebrate the scarcely less grave implications that remain, despite the book's unsatisfying conclusion. Bernard's thesis, however lopsided its emphasis, shows extraordinary intuitive understanding of Brown's novel and method. In its light, the book becomes unified on the deepest thematic as well as structural levels. Part 1—the Edgar-Clithero episode—develops the motif of Edgar's guilt indirectly and analytically through parallel narratives; part 2—Edgar's adventures with the Indians—dramatizes Edgar's savage potential, only hinted at earlier; traces its progressive realization in a series of murders that occur, both literally and figuratively, closer and closer to home; and ironically links Edgar's discovered capacity for violence to various forms of violence—domestic, civil, and ethnic—in which society partakes.

In *Edgar Huntly*, then, the detective is all but shown to be the criminal; the quester's own identity is the object of the quest.[24] As to the lesson to be learned from this reflexive murder mystery, David Stineback says: "[*Edgar Huntly*] suggests, quite simply, that we largely create the terrors of our lives—the 'precipices' of our minds—by attempting to deny their existence. We are animal, Brown seems to be saying, to the extent that we deny our animality; and we risk insanity to the extent that we reject its potential in ourselves." [25] *Edgar Huntly,* that is to say, not only dramatizes the fact that we are all potential savages; it also cautions us against denying our savage instincts. Sleepwalking is Brown's crowning metaphor for the trance of unawareness in which we exist and act—a trance made possible by our proficiency at hiding from and rationalizing motives.

But Stineback's interpretation of Brown's attitude is a bit facile. Brown does not, in fact, propose that we simply and frankly acknowledge our animality. While he clearly deplores a sleepwalking existence, he also suggests that self-confrontation entails dangerous, perhaps disastrous, consequences. The decision to know ourselves, Brown suggests, is irrevocable. Self-scrutiny, moreover, seems to unleash the terrors it discloses. The result is a sense of insoluble dilemma.

Edgar Huntly, in other words, not only identifies and dramatizes depravity but also studies the alternatives this identification poses. In this respect it is a thematic sequel to *Wieland,* which dealt with the same question frankly but inconclusively—and perhaps the nearest thing we have to a final fictional statement of Brown's discoveries. In this chapter, I will try to show the complexity of the dilemma Brown raises in *Edgar Huntly* concerning how we ought to respond to the more perverse aspects of the heart. I will examine the dubious alternatives of hiding from and waking up to our savagery, the nature of that savagery, and the consequences of accosting our sleeper-selves.

THE DARK AT THE END OF THE TUNNEL

In the opening pages of *Edgar Huntly,* Edgar returns to the tree beneath which Waldegrave was slain and finds the half-naked Clithero digging and weeping. Edgar wonders for some time whether to accost the "apparition" or not: "Methought . . . that to forbear inquiry . . . was to violate my duty to my God and to mankind. . . . But it suddenly occurred to me, For what purpose shall I prosecute this search? . . . Is it wise to undertake experiments by which nothing can be gained, and much may be lost?" (8, 15, 16). Clithero is, as we have seen, Edgar's alter ego, though we do not learn this immediately. In retrospect, then, this scene, like all Brown's opening scenes, is significant.

No more central dilemma, perhaps, is posed in *Edgar Huntly* than whether or not to accost our night-walking selves. That dilemma, however, seems a lot more inscrutable after we have completed the book. In fact, come the end, we are obliged to wonder whether the communal good is not better served by letting sleeping dogs lie and sleepwalkers walk. For Brown's is not the typical detective story, whose archetypal purpose, W. H. Auden has suggested, is to exculpate the community by inculpating the criminal.[26] *Edgar Huntly* incriminates all—Brown, for all intents, inventing and inverting the detective story. To solve this mystery, Brown seems to suggest, is to open Pandora's box. To understand his deep-seated skepticism, we must look beyond plot and drama to the realm of image, rhetoric, and symbol. These tell a truth that intensifies the dark vision of *Edgar Huntly* and perhaps accounts, however improbably and insufficiently, for the book's peculiar ending.

Self-evasion offers, in *Edgar Huntly,* a tempting alternative to self-scrutiny. Why not, for practical purposes, look away from our deep impulses and wrongdoings and concentrate, instead, on present and future duties? Clithero opts for such a solution when he leaves his crimes and country behind to become a "sober and diligent workman" in America (25). "Gladly would I bury in oblivion the transactions of my life" (36), he admits. He tries, literally as well as figuratively, to lock up and bury his past—hence the box containing Mrs. Lorimer's manuscript, which he inters beneath the elm. But Clithero is troubled. He sleepwalks regularly to the site, compulsively exhuming the chest, then burying it again. Moreover, his profession—building cabinets—suggests that his waking life is also oriented, however subliminally, toward the craft of containment. Concealing his secret seems to be a full-time occupation.

Edgar too is hiding something. For months he resists a compulsion to return to the elm where Waldegrave was assassinated. Even after discovering Clithero, he postpones accosting him on several occasions, as if afraid of the very answers he seeks. And, like Clithero, he conceals documents—letters written by Waldegrave—in a chest. Both Edgar's and Clithero's chests suggest images of the psyche, repository of dangerous truths and painful secrets.

The problem is that the secrets Edgar and Clithero conceal by day drive them from their beds at night. This, Brown suggests, is the nature of guilt—an ever-shifting cargo, continually upsetting the soul's equilibrium. Secrets escape. The boxes in which they are stored (to follow Brown's metaphor) get crushed. Or we jimmy our own airtight contrivances—the psyche behaving like a double agent, unlocking locks with one hand and holding down lids with another.[27] Self-evasion fails, in short, because we haven't, under ordinary circumstances, the psychological mechanisms to keep our skeletons in their closets.

But, Brown hastens to add, we can and do *acquire* such mechanisms—

hence the second reason why self-evasion is not a practical alternative: once we begin to acquire such mechanisms, our dexterity at concealing motives and disguising deeds becomes itself a threat, inviting whole-sale amorality. Edgar's journey from cave to cabin, in fact, explores the evolution of a rationalizing mechanism capable of justifying savagery.

Edgar's first act, upon climbing out of the pit, is to kill a panther and devour its blood and fibers. But the primitive meal is hard to digest. Edgar is "seized by pangs, whose acuteness exceeded all that I ever before experienced." These pangs, he later discovers, "were a useful effort of nature to subdue and convert to nourishment the matter I had swallowed" (167–68). The vile meal, then, satisfies his needs; his body adjusts to and incorporates the seemingly indigestible meat. So too, Brown suggests, does the psyche assimilate repulsive truths. Edgar's digestion of the panther prefigures the conversion process his psyche will engage in after each new killing. Edgar's deeds will revile him, but the gratification of his primitive appetites will depend on (as well as condition) his ability to "digest" the meal at hand.

Benevolence and retribution are the chief rationalizations the characters employ. Genuine impulses at times, they often disguise less respectable motives. Mrs. Lorimer's adoption of Clithero, for instance, exemplifies unadulterated generosity; Edgar's sympathy for Clithero stems from benevolence as well as compulsion, and his rescue of the girl held captive by the Indians is selflessly heroic. But Clithero's benevolent knife assault on his mistress's daughter (whom he mistakes for his mistress), Edgar's benevolent mutilation of his fifth Indian victim, and Sarsefield's benevolent refusal to treat the mangled Clithero dramatize the irony of a kindness that is indistinguishable from cruelty.

The rationalizations these characters employ are both subtle and outrageous. Clithero, faced with the prospect of confessing to Mrs. Lorimer that he has killed her brother, reasons: "Cannot my guilt be extenuated? Is there not a good I can do thee? . . . Can I not set bounds to the stream [of misery]? Cannot I prevent thee from returning to a consciousness which, till it ceases to exist, will not cease to be rent and mangled?" (82–83). Edgar, having shot and disabled the last Indian, argues: "To assault and to mangle the body of an enemy, already prostrate and powerless, was an act worthy of abhorrence; yet it was, in this case, prescribed by pity. . . . Having gone this far it would have been inhumane to stop short" (201–2). Sarsefield, having seen Clithero's lacerated body and listened to Edgar's recital of Clithero's confession and atonement, responds as follows to Edgar's request that he treat Clithero's wounds: "I have listened to your tale, not without compassion. What would you have me to do? To prolong his life would be merely to protract his misery" (277). Clithero's murder attempt and justification clearly suggest psychosis. Yet Edgar's and Sarsefield's words and deeds aren't very different. Benevolence, then, is both rationale and rationalization.

Another such moot rationale is revenge. Here the bounds of censure are even more obscure. Edgar, before killing his first Indian, recalls how Indians butchered his family. Who can blame him for feeling vengeful? Yet these feelings of vengeance help negate compunction and allow Edgar to kill, in turn. This mechanism becomes clear during the series of killings at Queen Mab's hut. After discovering his uncle's rifle in the possession of an Indian he has killed, Edgar imagines his household has again been set upon. This thought becomes the impetus for a premeditated killing spree in which Edgar shoots three warriors. Again, we can't quite blame him: his deduction is reasonable, though wrong. This time, however, not a real but an imagined crime prompts Edgar's vengeance. We begin to wonder to what extent the mind may fancy others' depravities to justify its own.

By the time Edgar kills his fifth victim, the self-justifying mechanism has taken the offensive. Edgar reflects,

> Why should he be suffered to live? He came hither to murder and despoil my friends; this work he has, no doubt, performed. Nay, has he not borne his part in the destruction of my uncle and my sisters? He will live only to pursue the same sanguinary trade; to drink the blood and exult in the laments of his unhappy foes, and of my own brethren. Fate has reserved him for a bloody and violent death. For how long a time soever it may be deferred, it is thus that his career will inevitably terminate.
>
> Should he be spared, he will still roam in the wilderness, and I may again be fated to encounter him. Then our mutual situation may be widely different, and the advantage I now possess may be his. (200)

Thus, reason abetting impulse, Edgar talks himself into committing an unnecessary murder.

Brown recapitulates this motif of projected intentions and rationalized revenge in the tragicomic portrait of the drunkard Selby raving against his wife. Edgar, in search of temporary asylum, enters Selby's house. Selby hears him, asks who is there, and then, as if picturing his wife advancing on him with a red-hot poker, cries: "Is't you, Peg? Damn ye, stay away, now! I tell ye, stay away, or, by God, I will cut your throat!—I will!" (His wife is, in fact, cowering in the barn, terrified of what her deranged husband might do next.) Edgar keeps quiet, but observes sardonically that the silence "was supplied by the suggestions of [Selby's] distempered fancy": "Ay . . . ye will, will ye? Well, come on, let's see who's the better at the oak stick. If I part with ye before I have bared your bones!—I'll teach ye to be always dipping in my dish, ye devil's dam ye!" (228). Selby's "distempered fancy" caricatures Edgar's own propensity for projecting outrages onto his antagonists to justify reprisal.

The ability to rationalize dubious acts, then, grows apace with the acts themselves, creating a widening spiral of wrongdoing. Practical sense, therefore, as well as abstract morality dictates the importance of self-scrutiny—since self-evasion must either fail or, by succeeding, generate and perpetuate an intolerable cycle of wrongs. But to confront the self, as Brown makes plain, is as dangerous as to ignore it.

Early in the tale, Edgar follows the sleepwalking Clithero to a cave. The route through the dark is arduous. First Clithero passes over a fence, then through a wood, then through a "most perplexing undergrowth of bushes and briers": "Sometimes considerable force was required to beat down obstacles; sometimes [the route] led into a deep glen, the sides of which were so steep as scarcely to afford a footing; sometimes into fens, from which some exertions were necessary to extricate the feet; and sometimes through rivulets, of which the water rose to the middle" (18). Clithero at last disappears into a cave; Edgar waits outside. At dawn Edgar hears a rustling sound, which he imagines is Clithero, but which turns out to be an animal—possibly the panther Edgar later encounters. This episode, ending in the virtual transformation of man into beast, prefigures Edgar's own transformation in the cave. The nature of the journey, though, suggests both the danger and difficulty of penetrating the wilderness in which the soul lies buried ("Solebury"). The dangers pictured include falling, drowning, becoming stuck, and being attacked by wild beasts—all symbolic motifs Brown will develop in due course. Brown later executes this same picture in chiaroscuro when Edgar, having heard Clithero's confession, again pursues him to a cave. In this sequence, though, Brown pictures the nature of the danger more explicitly. First, Edgar is threatened with entrapment. The tree he has felled and used to cross a gulf becomes dislodged: "I perceived that it had already swerved somewhat from its original position, that the blast had broken or loosened some of the fibers by which its roots were connected with the opposite bank, and that if the storm did not speedily abate, there was imminent danger of its being torn from the rock and precipitated in the chasm. Thus my retreat would be cut off" (123). Second, a panther appears. Edgar, unarmed, has wandered near its lair, and risks being torn to pieces. These two dangers—being trapped "beyond the gulf," unable to return, and being set upon by the "savage" whose domain has been violated—are, figuratively speaking, the dangers Edgar, as a seeker of knowledge and self-knowledge, faces.

The first of these, the danger stemming from the irreversibility of the quest and the irrevocability of knowledge, recurs when Edgar explores the cave's dark interior: "It seemed as if I were surrounded by barriers that would forever cut off my return to air and to light" (100), Edgar remarks. The motif recurs in various guises. Clithero's trunk, Edgar discovers, is operated by a secret spring that, when triggered, cannot be reset, so that once opened, the box remains opened. Brown's diction emphasizes the point: the "spring" is both a mechanism that opens the trunk, and a "springe," or trap, snaring the intruder.[28] "Trunk," meanwhile, calls to mind an earlier instance in which a "trunk"—the felled tree trunk Edgar uses to cross the gulf separating him from Clithero's retreat—threatens, by becoming dislodged, to trap Edgar, to deny him the option of withdrawing unobserved from the place he has intruded upon. (In that episode the word *spring* also appears in a related context: the panther's "spring" across the chasm all but cuts off Edgar's retreat.)[29]

The irreversibility of the quest is emphasized repeatedly during Edgar's adventures. The pit into which he sleepwalks proves almost inescapable; the cave, once entered, becomes a prison, and, once left, cannot easily be reentered; Deb's hut, once left, cannot be regained; Edgar's rifle, once cocked, must be fired; the river, once entered, can scarcely be escaped. A repetition of key words links these instances. The mechanism of Edgar's rifle—like that of Clithero's trunk—is a "spring." The "pit" Edgar is trapped in recurs as the oven "pit" in Deb's hut—another trap of sorts. The words *cavity* and *crevice,* which appear in the description of Clithero's box, also appear in reference to the cave and, later, in reference to Deb's oven—that "cavity" into which Edgar climbs.

The second danger of Edgar's quest, that represented by the panther, is clarified by Brown's characterization of the panther. Brown links the panther, both rhetorically and formalistically, with the Indians: both are "savages" and inhabit the same cave. The panther's cry, moreover, resembles a human voice. Clearly this panther is a half-human chimera, a savage alter ego—like Clithero, like the Indians. Even more than Clithero or the Indians, though, the panther dramatizes the unreasoning, brute nature of this self.

Edgar becomes identified with this brute self when he kills the panther and ingests its blood and fibers. Edgar's ensuing actions, as noted earlier, show his gradual transformation into a killer. What they do not show is why the transformation occurs. What is the nature of the urges Edgar succumbs to? Brown suggests that they are not a freak visitation, but a primal, almost physical drive. While the plot presents Edgar's killing as a rational, though extraordinary, response to unparalleled circumstances, Brown's symbolism depicts it as an irrational necessity akin to thirst; a coursing passion that brooks no control. In fact, Brown associates Edgar's violent actions with the compulsion of thirst, and his depraved self with the image of coursing water.

When Edgar, still in pursuit of Clithero, reaches the heart of the wilderness into which Clithero has disappeared, he finds water. Brown's rhetoric of timelessness imputes mythic significance to the scene: "The aboriginal inhabitants had no motives to lead them into caves like this and ponder on the verge of such a precipice. . . . Since the birth of this continent, I was probably the first who had deviated thus remotely from the customary paths of men" (103). Figuratively speaking, Edgar is treading a far hollow of the collective unconscious: "A sort of sanctity and awe environed it, owing to the . . . utter loneliness. It was probable that human feet had never before gained this recess, that human eyes had never been fixed upon these gushing waters" (103). The torrent is the focal point of this mythic landscape. Edgar watches, hypnotized— until the face of the cliff the water courses over magically becomes a human face: "My eye was fixed upon the foaming current. At length I looked upon the rocks which confined and embarrassed its course. . . . Passing from one to the other of these, my attention lighted, as if by some magical transition, on—a human countenance" (103). The face belongs, of course, to the very ghost of Edgar's subconscious, Clithero, his looks denoting "more than anarchy of thoughts and passions" (104). Edgar's search for his alter ego, then, leads him to the verge of a torrent. The symbolic kinship between Clithero and the water persists until the close of the book, when Clithero, having been captured by Sarsefield, leaps back into the water that has magically born him.

Brown develops the torrent as a symbol of an irresistible natural force throughout *Edgar Huntly*. Upon first encountering the torrent, Edgar imagines the "convulsion of nature" (103) that must have formed the chasm through which the torrent flows. Later, the image of rock yielding to water is made more explicit. Edgar, encountering the river into which he will soon plunge, remarks: "Appearances were adapted to persuade you that these rocks had formerly joined, but by some mighty effort of nature had been severed, that the stream might find way through the chasm" (214). Not even granite walls can resist the force of the torrent, Brown suggests, casting an eye in the direction of his protagonist. (Edgar later tries to hide in a protective hollow of rock in order to sleep, but his efforts are useless; the elements reach him anyway.)

Edgar's awe for the torrent gives place to attraction, and then to an insatiable craving, as his anarchic nature becomes identified with the water even more than was Clithero's. His pursuit of Clithero hampered by "torrents of rain," Edgar remarks: "Instead of lamenting the prevalence of this tempest, I now began to regard it with pleasure. It conferred new forms of sublimity and grandeur on this scene" (122). Later the joys of the sublime become the pangs of physical need: Edgar's killing and eating of the panther in the cave generate a thirst that forces him to drink his own body fluids. His subsequent killings, meanwhile, are either followed or accompanied by draughts of water, immersion in water, or both.

Edgar's first Indian killing is expressly occasioned by his need to assuage a raging thirst. The noise of the torrent, we are told, drowns out the blow of Edgar's tomahawk. Moreover, the compunction Edgar feels following the killing is overridden by the elation he feels upon slaking his thirst: "Never before had I taken the life of a human creature. On this head I had, indeed, entertained somewhat of religious scruples. . . . I didn't escape all compunction in the present instance, but the tumult of my feelings was quickly allayed. To quench my thirst was a consideration by which all others were supplanted. I approached the torrent and not only drank copiously, but laved my head, neck and arms in this delicious element. . . . Never was any delight worthy of the raptures which I then experienced" (179–80). Given Edgar's vivid recollection of his parents' death at the hands of Indians, and recalling his recent draught of panther blood—and the consequent association of blood with water—we must at least wonder whether Edgar's raptures do not derive from mixed sources; whether his killing the Indian and gratifying his thirst are not symbolically one.

Edgar's words confirm this suspicion. Relating his killings at Deb's hut, Edgar speaks first of his "thirst of vengeance" (188), then of having "*imbibed,* from the unparalleled events which had lately happened, a spirit vengeful, unrelenting, and ferocious" (192, my italics). In that episode, Edgar, having killed three Indians and fainted, wakes parched and surrounded by carnage, and "look[s] with eagerness for the traces of a spring" (198).[30] He finds one and drinks. Again Brown confounds Edgar's draught with a more horrible satiety: "The water afforded me *unspeakable* refreshment" (198, my italics), says Edgar—then, four sentences later, describes himself as "satiated and gorged with slaughter."[31] Edgar continues: "The gratification that the spring had afforded me was so great, that I was in no haste to depart" (199). By remaining instead of departing, Edgar discovers the fifth Indian's approach and, consequently, enacts his bloodiest and least defensible killing.[32]

Edgar's final shooting is virtually simultaneous with his plunge from a cliff into a river. This time Edgar submerges himself repeatedly (to elude the bullets aimed at him). The plunge, moreover, though occasioned by a real enough threat, is preceded by what can only be termed a compulsive urge. Twice prior to the actual leap, Edgar contemplates jumping into the river, despite "midwinter" temperatures and the danger of hidden rocks. That the two acts—shooting and plunging—virtually coincide suggests that, symbolically, they are aspects of the same drive; that, for Edgar, killing is, at last, an instinctual compulsion, engaged in for its own sake, irrespective of necessity and circumstance.

Beyond a point, the two dangers of self-scrutiny alluded to above— the irrevocability of self-knowledge and the risk of annihilation by the savage self—become one. Edgar's violent urges themselves, once discerned, become irrevocable; the "spring," or watercourse, once sampled, becomes a "springe." Hence the final image of Edgar's compulsive plunge into *and entrapment in* the river. He must escape its waters or die; yet to escape is, presumably, to be drawn back in.

The river episode exemplifies the dilemma at the center of the book: Edgar's felt need to immerse himself in the dark waters of his soul and his concomitant need to be free of those waters. If evading the self is both impossible and dangerous, yet confronting the self means awakening feral instincts that feed on their own indulgence, what ought Edgar (and we) to do?

Edgar's resolution of the dilemma disturbs profoundly. His decision to accost and redeem his sleepwalking self, to enter the cave and confront the animal within, is heroic. But its unforeseen result—the fact that in hunting, he becomes the hunted; in conquering, he becomes what he conquers—overpowers him. So much so that he at last disavows his enterprise altogether, begs pardon, and reembraces the morally discredited world of Sarsefield, of a civilization "blind . . . to [its] own performances" (278).

Edgar's decision, though not overtly stated, is intimated by his increasingly regressive behavior and symbolized by his final disavowal of Clithero and acceptance of Sarsefield's moral authority, ironies notwithstanding. Thus, nostalgia for earlier bliss informs Edgar's reflections as he is swept along in the river's current: "Formerly, water was not only my field of sport but my sofa and my bed. I could float on its surface, enjoying its delicious cool, almost without the slightest motion. It was an element as fitted for repose as for exercise, but now the buoyant spirit seemed to have flown. . . . My most vehement exertions were requisite to sustain me on the surface" (224). If the water that threatens to drown Edgar objectifies his dark impulses, Edgar fondly recalls a time when these subconscious terrors were no threat; when he was able, figuratively speaking, to float on their surface.

Edgar's rhetoric reveals more about this nostalgia. In saying that "water . . . was my sofa and my bed. . . . an element as fitted for repose as for exercise," Edgar expresses a longing for his former ability to *sleep* on the water. In the book's symbolic context, his words suggest nostalgia for the blissful ignorance of the sleeper, or sleepwalker, who goes about mechanically, blind to disturbing self-truths. Nor is this nostalgia a passing fancy. Following his killings, Edgar betrays "an irresistible propensity to sleep" (219). This desire for sleep scarcely disguises an even more pronounced desire for death: "My brows were heavy. . . . I concluded to seek some shelter, and resign myself . . . to sweet forgetfulness. . . . At the bottom of the rock was a rift, somewhat resembling a coffin in shape, and not much larger in dimensions. . . . Thrusting myself into this recess as far as I was able, I prepared for repose" (216–17). Edgar's recurring temptation to leap from various heights further testifies to this suicidal urge.

Having forgone blithe ignorance, then, only to watch his brute self wake and go stalking, Edgar longs for his former figurative state of sleep, if not for its final counterpart. Edgar's prospects for sleep, however, depend, both literally and figuratively, on his returning to society. During his reunion with Sarsefield, Edgar, significantly, interrupts the interview to go to bed. His decision stems, of course, from exhaustion—he has hardly slept in days. But it's also a symbolic necessity: for if Edgar is to reenter civilized society, he must do so, figuratively speaking, by closing his eyes to the truths he has discovered.

For civilization, as Brown characterizes it, is a body of literal sleepers and figurative sleepwalkers, submerging self-awareness and functioning blindly. Edgar's household apparently sleeps for weeks on end during the period of Edgar's obsessive rambles. Edgar's uncle, roused once by the sound of Edgar sleepwalking in the attic, is the only one we ever meet. Edgar's parents, we learn, were murdered in their sleep. Inglefield's household remains "wrapt in profound sleep" (118) while Edgar pries into Clithero's trunk and box. The drunkard Selby, whom Edgar intrudes on, is more asleep than awake. Even the Indians, that primitive society Edgar stumbles on in the cave, are first shown asleep in their blankets. Later, when Brown has implicated all civil society in the web of savagery afoot, this visitation of sleep makes greater sense—universal guilt necessitating, as it were, the sleep of evasion.

If Edgar signals his reentry into society by going to sleep, he completes it by repudiating Clithero (after one last attempt to reclaim him) and adopting instead the opinion held by Sarsefield, to whom he defers in a final letter: "Clithero is a maniac. This truth cannot be concealed. . . . I imagined . . . that his understanding was deluded by phantoms in the mask of virtue and duty, and not, as you have so strenuously maintained, utterly subverted. I shall not escape your censure. . . . I have erred" (290). Even more significant, though, is Edgar's closing question: "Yet who could foresee this consequence of my intelligence?" (290). Referring ostensibly to Clithero's unforeseen reaction to the news of Mrs. Lorimer's presence in America, the quotation also suggests regret over the intelligence Edgar has gained about himself. The light of knowledge has not only opened Edgar's eyes but has blinded him. He no longer wants to see or to remember. And so he repudiates the wild man and begs Sarsefield's pardon.

Edgar's renunciation, distressing as it is, is circumscribed by a still more disturbing renunciation on Brown's part. If Edgar repudiates self-knowledge, Brown, in *Edgar Huntly*, repudiates the very act of self-scrutiny that inspires his best fiction. By sending Edgar back to sleep, as it were, Brown virtually proposes that "the man unknown to himself" (as Edgar's earlier avatar was characterized in the subtitle of *Skywalk*) remain unknown to himself forever.

Brown's career attests to this renunciation. *Edgar Huntly* is his last Gothic romance. He had yet, to be sure, to finish part 2 of *Arthur Mervyn* and *Carwin, the Biloquist*. But his final two full-length fictions, *Clara Howard* and *Jane Talbot*, are parlor novels, compared to his earlier romances. And after them he abandoned novel writing altogether. Biographers conjecture that he did so because of family disapproval and lack of financial rewards.[33] Neither explanation is convincing. Brown had written for a decade with only such encouragement as close friends bestowed. Then too, the speed and intensity with which he wrote suggest an urgency and commitment not likely to be dissolved by an adverse word from a merchant brother, or even by poor sales returns. *Edgar Huntly* suggests a more fundamental motive for Brown's abandonment of fiction: that, like Edgar, Brown may have come to fear his discoveries and their possible repercussions—even to the extent that he felt obliged, in *Edgar Huntly,* to sabotage his painstakingly constructed fictional bridge to keep the beast from crossing in pursuit. Brown, that is, seems to abort his last, possibly best, Gothic romance with an improbable ending contrived to mask those implications of the tale that prove unutterable.

One such implication, alluded to earlier, is that notions of morality are relative; that, in effect, Clithero is no worse than Sarsefield. Sarsefield himself, after listening to Edgar's presentation of Clithero's case, is forced to admit: "It is true. A tale like this could never be the fruit of invention, or be invented to deceive. He has done himself injustice. His character was spotless and fair" (274). Brown compounds the irony by presenting Sarsefield's refusal to treat Clithero's wounds ("To prolong his life would be merely to protract his misery" [277]) as an echo of Clithero's fateful presumption prior to attempting Mrs. Lorimer's life: "Common ills are not without a cure less than death, but here all remedies are in vain. Consciousness itself is the malady, the pest, of which he only is cured who ceases to think."[34] Sarsefield's remark not only rationalizes criminal neglect, but tells a truth Brown, at last, feels obliged to acknowledge: that consciousness is the ultimate enemy. Brown opts, finally, to cloak our consciousness, to hide from us revelations like the exploded notion of morality implied by his tale.

So Brown reduces Clithero, a hitherto complex character, into a mere

lunatic. In doing so, he reinstates—even at the expense of credibility—
the conventional moral universe. Brown, I would suggest, sacrifices
Clithero the character to exploit Clithero the symbol of the perverse
self. (Clithero has, of course, vacillated between character and symbol throughout the tale.) It is Edgar's alter ego that Brown, with a
clumsy flourish, unmasks as anarchy incarnate, a maniac too irrational
to temporize with. Brown ends the book with Sarsefield's uncompro-
mising verdict: "Clithero is a madman, whose liberty is dangerous,
and who requires to be fettered and imprisoned as the most atrocious
criminal" (291).

We must not try to understand, reclaim, or even look upon our inner
nature, Brown seems to say; rather, we must chain it fast. This, as we
have seen earlier, implies deploying all the resources at our disposal to
repress, conceal, and disguise our irrational selves. Hence Sarsefield's
forcible apprehension of Clithero and assumption of the role of Clithero's
"jailor . . . and tyrant" (293). Hence, too, Brown's perfunctory resolution of the initial mystery of *Edgar Huntly*. For by far the novel's gravest
implication is that Edgar himself murdered Waldegrave. To appreciate the gravity of the implication, it is worth recalling the Lockean
philosophical framework against which Brown defines his fictions.

Wieland, as many critics have noted, questions Lockean sensationalist psychology. This doctrine, summed up by Clara Wieland, states
that "the will is the tool of the understanding, which must fashion its
conclusions on the notices of sense" (35). *Wieland,* by dramatizing how
grossly sensory evidence and reason can mislead and formally lodging
the question "What if the senses be depraved?," casts a pall of doubt
over Locke's optimistic theory. *Edgar Huntly* further subverts Locke's
epistemology by asking a more fundamental question—the question
that David Hume had asked: "What if the will *defies* the understanding?
What if *the will* is depraved?"

Sick or sane, Clithero broaches the possibility. He agrees that "the
pulses of life are at the command of the will" (77). This is why his
killing of Wiatte disturbs him so. Edgar later defends Clithero on the
grounds that his will was not implicated: "It must at least be said
that his will was not concerned in this transaction" (91). But Clithero,
thinking aloud about his deed, says otherwise: "Fond and short-sighted
wretch! . . . In the rashness of thy thought, thou saidst, 'Nothing is
wanting but his death to restore us to confidence and safety.' Lo! the
purchase is made" (77). Clithero's self-condemnation may be excessive.
Both his and Edgar's sleepwalking antics, however, suggest that the will

is either depraved or simply not in control. Even the more generous conclusion shatters the Lockean vision. Edgar, speaking of one of Clithero's sleepwalking exploits (and, indirectly, of his own), says: "The deed was neither prompted by the will nor noticed by the senses of him by whom it was done. Disastrous and humiliating is the state of man!" (278).

How much more disastrous and humiliating, though, if the will be depraved? If, instead of serving the understanding, it does what it wants, driving us before it, compelling us, in extreme situations, to act without conscious intent or knowledge? This is what Edgar's career of increasingly compulsive killing suggests, and what Brown's indictment of Edgar as Waldegrave's killer would have made explicit. Well might Brown have trembled, not only at the prospect, but also at the thought of publicizing such an insight—especially considering his apparent fear that simply to look upon (or read about?) evil is to unleash it. And so, although his drama points to Edgar's complicity in Waldegrave's death, Brown opts, in a spirit of enlightened neurosis, to stifle this final revelation and instead projects the deed onto that convenient and familiar scapegoat, the Indian.

This ending—like Clithero's character transformation—is hardly more satisfying than it is convincing. Some irony emerges, perhaps, from its reminder that the larger cultural drama of white-Indian hostility is related to the drama at hand. This irony, though, is dilute. In fact, one of the insidious aspects of this ending is that in it Brown employs the very mechanism his irony has exposed elsewhere. Brown, that is, may imply that the Anglo-Indian conflict stems in part, like Edgar's killings, from violent urges shared by all, but projected onto a racial other; nevertheless, by using the same tactic (i.e., blaming the Indian) to resolve his tale, he seems to condone it.[35]

It is as if Brown, faced with two responsibilities—to indict man's depraved self, but also to parry the consequences of this intelligence—tries to do both, implicating Edgar but finally indicting peripheral villains (Clithero, the Indian) for the book's crimes. Brown's sleight of hand recalls Edgar's own sleepwalking attempt to suppress dangerous information. By concealing Waldegrave's letters in the attic, Edgar, as it were, both fulfills Waldegrave's command to destroy the letters and respects his own felt duty to preserve them. Brown, like Edgar, seeks both to display and to destroy skeptical doctrines—and compromises by hiding them.

Edgar's ultimate solution to the problem of Waldgrave's letters, though, is not only to conceal them but to *edit* them: to expunge the most skeptical passages for his reader's (Mary Waldegrave's) sake. Brown's conclusion amounts to a similar redaction. He has, in effect, taken out the most damning truth—but left us the option of reading between the lines.

Edgar's exculpation ought, finally, to be considered in light of Brown's characterization of the writing act. For *Edgar Huntly* implies that the ultimate purpose of writing is not revelation but self-justification.

At the outset, Edgar bemoans the inability of words to reveal feelings and motives: "In proportion as I gain power over words, shall I lose dominion over sentiments" (5). He notes ruefully that if Mary were there in person, "that which words should fail to convey, my looks and gestures would suffice to communicate" (6). Lacking recourse to such aids, Edgar tries to bridge the gap between words and emotions by writing precipitately. However, Brown's solution goes Edgar's one better. He develops a language of symbols to supplement and inform his literal account as looks and gestures would a spoken account. That symbolism, as we have seen, tells a grim story—words proving all too powerful, rather than the reverse.

But if writing can reveal, it can also conceal. Edgar speaks of having constructed "a writing desk and cabinet, in which I had endeavoured to combine the properties of secrecy, security, and strength" (15–16). This desk-cabinet is an icon of the ambiguous uses of writing—of its capacity to reveal *and* conceal. Sarsefield's "traveling escritoire," a combination desk and drawer, repeats the image. Edgar's copying of Waldegrave's letters, which, as noted, involves both copying and editing, reemphasizes this joint purpose. So do many of the writing contexts depicted in *Edgar Huntly*. Various characters write memoirs and letters, ostensibly to clarify events and reveal purposes. More often than not, though, these documents are principally self-justifications. Mrs. Lorimer's memoirs, for instance, are a "vindication of her conduct" in committing her brother, Arthur Wiatte (120). Waldegrave's letters to Edgar are a "defence" of skeptical doctrines (132). Edgar's lengthy letter to Sarsefield is both a confession and an attempted self-exoneration—a plea of "guilty with explanation," as it were.

And Edgar's memoirs? To what extent are they a self-justification? Like *Arthur Mervyn* with its forgery motif, *Edgar Huntly* hints that writing is an artifice, a means of manipulating damning appearances. Like Arthur Mervyn, who protests too much his benevolent intent, Edgar Huntly is a narrator whose actions raise suspicions and whose narrative may be shaped, even prompted, by a need to exonerate himself. Edgar's need may well be subliminal. If he is masking guilt for Waldegrave's murder beneath his account of the Indian assassin, he may be doing so in the same state of sleep-fogged ignorance in which he stole his own letters and precipitated his fifth Indian killing.

Brown, on the other hand, seems consciously to choose to conceal his discoveries, to renounce writing as a tool for seeing and to embrace, instead, the opportunity it affords for obscuring the truths he has disinterred. He scarcely seems at pains to disguise his manipulations— not even scrupling, evidently, over the Indian assassin's improbable failure to take Waldegrave's scalp—but instead, by a kind of brute force, replaces the lid on the box he has pried open. Whether this decision reflects moral cowardice or a higher pragmatism is hard to say. It is enough, perhaps, to suggest extenuating motives in what must otherwise seem a morally flaccid ending. One can't help remarking, though, the foreboding that led Brown, at last, to reverse the premise of his work: the need to find out why the sleeper walks and the walker sleeps.

"THE PERILS OF THE WESTERN WILDERNESS"

Now a psychodrama, now a myth of initiation, *Edgar Huntly* seems both too personal and too universal to have much cultural significance. Yet Brown in his preface "To The Public" specifically asks us to accept it as an American tale:

> America has opened new views to the naturalist and politician, but has seldom furnished themes to the moral painter. That new springs of action and new motives to curiosity should operate, that the field of investigation, opened to us by our own country, should differ essentially from those which exist in Europe, may be readily conceived. The sources of amusement to the fancy and instruction to the heart, that are peculiar to ourselves, are equally numerous and inexhaustible. It is the purpose of this work to profit by some of these sources: to exhibit a series of adventures, growing out of the condition of our country, and connected with one of the most common and most wonderful diseases or affections of the human frame. (3)

No doubt because Brown in the following paragraph highlights his replacement of "puerile superstition and exploded manners, Gothic castles and chimeras" with "incidents of Indian hostility, and the perils

of the Western wilderness" (3), critics have rarely pursued the question of the romance's Americanness beyond its introduction of native
settings and props.

Brown's rhetoric, though, suggests he is concerned more with the
moral and psychological conditions of America than with its physical and historical aspects. He speaks of "furnish[ing] themes to the
moral painter"; of "springs of action" and "motives to curiosity" that
set America apart from Europe. He speaks, moreover, of "adventures,
growing out of the condition of our country, and connected with one
of the most . . . wonderful diseases or affections of the human frame"—
implying that the nations's "condition" is somehow related to Edgar's
sleepwalking affliction. Leslie Fiedler reconciles this discrepancy in part,
pointing out that Brown's replacement of the standard Gothic props and
settings amounted to a redefinition of the operative (European) myth:
"For the corrupt Inquisitor and the lustful nobleman, [Brown] has substituted the Indian, . . . projection of natural evil. . . . For the haunted
castle and the dungeon, Brown substitutes the haunted forest (in which
nothing is what it seems) and the cave, the natural pit or abyss. . . .
These are ancient, almost instinctive symbols, the *selva oscura* going
back to Dante and beyond, while the cave as a metaphor for the mysteries of the human heart is perhaps as old as literature itself." Fiedler
explains the significance of this new myth as follows: "*The change of myth
involves a profound change of meaning.* In the American gothic, that is to
say, the heathen, unredeemed wilderness and not the decaying monu-
ments of a dying class, nature and not society becomes the symbol of
evil. . . . The European gothic identified blackness with the superego
and was therefore revolutionary in its implications; the American gothic
(at least as it followed the example of Brown) identified evil with the id
and was therefore conservative at its deepest level of implication, whatever the intent of its authors."[36] Brown's concern with the American
psyche, then, might aptly be seen as a fear of its anarchic potential.

In *Arthur Mervyn,* such an anarchic national self is glimpsed in the
"tawny . . . apparition" that leaps from the mirror, as it were, to knock
Arthur out. This image, I have suggested, evokes, however tentatively,
both a real social fear as well as a mythical fear of a racial other on
whom the guilt and hostility of the native white population has been
projected. *Edgar Huntly* brings the race differential to the fore, dramatizing Edgar's actions in direct relation to the red man's and extending
this ironic comparison to the book's end. Like the tawny apparition

in *Arthur Mervyn,* the red man in *Edgar Huntly* represents both a real antagonist *and* a cultural projection, a "phantom . . . tawny and terrific" (158, 191). But whereas in *Arthur Mervyn* the ironic identity of the white protagonist and the dark antagonist is only implied (Arthur glimpses the black *in the mirror*), formal parallels in *Edgar Huntly* make this identity far more explicit. Thus Edgar proves deadly with a tomahawk, out-tricks the Indians at their own game of killing and evading, and, on one occasion, mangles and mutilates his enemy—while the Indians, in turn, wield white men's weapons (including Edgar's uncle's fusil) and, if Brown's explanation is to be believed, murder Waldegrave with Caucasian sophistication, resisting the lure of the victim's scalp. The confusion of identities is reinforced when Sarsefield recounts his search for Edgar in the following terms: "The road which we had previously designed to take, in search of my fugitive pupil, was the same by which we must trace or intercept the retreat of the savages. Thus two purposes, equally momentous, would be answered by the same means" (250). This ironic identification culminates in Edgar's physical transformation into an Indian of sorts: "My legs, neck, and bosom were bare, and *their native hue was exchanged* for the livid marks of bruises and scarification. An horrid scar upon my cheek, and my uncombed locks; hollow eyes, made ghastly by abstinence and cold, and the ruthless passions of which my mind had been the theatre, added to the musquet which I carried in my hand, would prepossess them with the notion of a maniac or ruffian" (236, emphasis added).[37] Perhaps an unconscious or belated recognition of this identity prevents Edgar, in the penultimate chapter, from shooting the brave that enters his room, unarmed and in flight (as Edgar himself had been, only hours before) from Sarsefield.

Not just Edgar's identity, as we have seen, but that of his society as well is confounded with the red man's. If, as William Hedges suggests, "the chief signs of Indian depredation are broken families and damaged or empty houses,"[38] Edgar's cousin, who, Edgar assures us, plans to evict both Edgar and his sisters upon acceding to Mr. Huntly's property, is yet another white whose behavior ironically resembles that of the Indians. Seven members of Sarsefield's search party, meanwhile, walking "in that straight and regular succession which is peculiar to the Indians" (220), pass Edgar in the woods and are, in fact, mistaken by Edgar for Indians—as he is later by them. By such ironies Brown lets us know that the red man, besides being a flesh-and-blood antagonist, is also a projection, a white in war paint.

Brown emphasizes the Indians' psychosymbolic aspect from the start. As Norman Grabo has remarked, Brown's Indians never speak.[39] They are introduced as virtual wraiths: "Solitude and sleep," Edgar remarks, on the verge of recounting his experience of waking in the cave, "are no more than the signals to summon up a tribe of ugly phantoms. Famine, and blindness, and death, and savage enemies, never fail to be conjured up by the silence and darkness of the night" (158). This "tribe of ugly phantoms," these "savage enemies" are soon incarnated in the war party camped at the mouth of the cave Edgar wakes in; we first encounter them, though, as figments. Even the cave setting in which the Indians appear enhances their mythic stature, but deemphasizes their cultural or historical identity. The cave is precultural, prehistoric, the "heart of the wilderness" (171).

These Indians, then, are phantoms of the mind first; phantoms of the culture second; and only third, Leni-Lenapes living in late-eighteenth-century Pennsylvania. Their reality, of course, is no more to be denied than that of the tomahawk Edgar finds at his feet in the cave—though, like the tomahawk, their origin mystifies. Brown acknowledges, for example, the reality of the Indians' victimization by westering whites, referring in passing to "the perpetual encroachments of the English colonists" that drove the Delawares from their native grounds (207), and, again, to "a long course of injuries and encroachments" that "had lately exasperated the Indian tribes" (173). But even the Indian's identity as an exploited population interests Brown only as it illuminates white America. As Fiedler observes: "There is some sense in Brown of the historic 'Indian problem', of the appropriation of their lands by white colonists and their futile dreams of revenge; but Queen Mab, the spokesman for their cause, though prepared for at some length, does not finally appear in the book. It is not the Indian as social victim that appeals to Brown's imagination, but the Indian as projection of natural evil and the id; his red men are therefore treated essentially as animals, living extensions of the threat of the wilderness, like the panthers with whom they are associated."[40] Cultural bogeys, these red men exist to be annihilated. The same mechanism of projection that is dramatized in Edgar's wilderness killing spree and lampooned in Selby's drunken raving operates, in short, on a social scale—as the dead Indian found just outside Selby's home grimly attests.

Of her consanguinity[41] with this savage alter ego, however, America, Brown suggests, is unaware. Hence the intimation, in the preface, that her "condition" is related to sleepwalking.[42] "We imagined ourselves at an inaccessible distance from the danger," says Edgar, in regard to the Indian incursion he discovers after waking in the cave (173). His words, seen in light of the homicides, suggest a more basic communal unawareness. The danger, Brown suggests, lies in America's midst; her counties are rife with murderous intent.

There was, of course, a parochial context for his concern. Indian warfare aside, the violent tenor of late-eighteenth-century frontier life, especially in the border settlements, needs little documenting. On the frontier, according to Crèvecoeur, one found "men . . . no better than carnivorous animals of a superior rank" who were "often in a perfect state of war" with each other. What magistrates there were in such territories, he continues, were "little better than the rest."[43] "Eye-gouging fights were common," adds one historian.[44] Even such Pennsylvania farmers and homesteaders as we encounter in *Edgar Huntly*—the second wave, as it were, of frontier settlers—were the ranks from which the Whiskey Rebellion drew its strength.

And probably no American romance of the 1790s whose theme is man's descent into savagery can be read apart from the geographically remote but politically immediate context of the French Revolution. *Edgar Huntly* is certainly no political allegory. Nevertheless, like Brown's other novels of understated topicality, *Edgar Huntly* too evokes, at its outer bourn, the sociopolitical threat that the American republic, founded on bloodletting and revolution, might similarly founder. Arthur Kimball notes, for instance, the ideological connotations carried by the term "savage" during the Federalist era: "After the Reign of Terror American Federalists associated their political opponents, the Republicans, with French Jacobins and quickly labelled their rivals 'savages.' " Richard Slotkin corroborates the point, citing Crèvecoeur and Brackenridge, both of whom likened democratic rebels to rampaging Indians.[45] Kimball concludes, "The Terror, the American Revolution, and frontier experience with the red man combined to invest the idea of 'savagism' with ironic ambiguity."[46] That Brown may have relished the ambiguity of the motif is suggested by his concurrent use of a related one. Sarsefield, recounting his discovery of Edgar's sleepwalking affliction, represents Edgar's danger as follows: "You had roved into Norwalk. . . . Your careless feet would bear you into some whirlpool or to the edge of some precipice; *some internal revolution . . . would recall you to consciousness at some perilous moment.* Surprise and fear would disable you from taking seasonable precautions, and your destruction be made sure" (249; my italics). This threat of "internal revolution," with its political overtones, amplifies the link hinted at in the preface between Edgar's sleepwalking and a larger, national "condition" at the same time that it postfigures Edgar's transformation into a savage.

Neither of these contexts, however, sufficiently illumines the novel's dramatic core. The singularity of Edgar's transformation—as opposed to, say, Theodore Wieland's—is its subtlety. Edgar becomes a killer by degrees. His killer instinct surfaces as self-defensive violence, which leads almost imperceptibly to a willingness to slaughter. Perhaps the national "condition" Brown sought to portray was America's suscepti-bility to such a gradual transformation.

Albert K. Weinberg, in his book *Manifest Destiny*, sets forth the genesis of expansionism in Revolutionary America. Our felt national mission to inaugurate and protect democracy, says Weinberg, at first precluded land-grabbing. Nevertheless, the strategists of the Revolu-tion, he notes, sought to acquire land—especially in Canada—as a buffer against dangerous neighbors. This understandable concern for security, elevated to the status of a "natural right," led us, however, to invade a friendly neighbor. It lent itself, moreover, to increasingly broader ethical interpretations and practical gambits that anticipated Manifest Destiny. Samuel Adams, writing in 1778, expressed his hope that by the war America would acquire not just Canada, but also Nova Scotia and Florida: "We shall never be upon a solid Footing till Brit-ain cedes to us what Nature designs we should have, or till we wrest it from her." During the peace negotiations in 1783, America carried such sentiments to unprecedented extremes, claiming—and getting— rights to the unconquered western country between the Alleghenies and the Mississippi.[47] By the early 1790s, when most of the national budget was being spent to suppress the Indians in the Northwest Territory, our originally defensive "natural right" to security had clearly taken the offensive, yet it had done so by degrees. It is precisely this sort of elastic morality capable of justifying increasingly blatant offenses that *Edgar Huntly* dramatizes.

"No one knows the powers that are latent in his constitution. Called forth by imminent dangers, our efforts frequently exceed our most san-guine beliefs" (167), exclaims Edgar, just before describing the surge of strength that allows him, despite pain, exhaustion, and injury, to kill a panther with a tomahawk. The latent pun on "sanguine" renders

Edgar's words doubly apposite to his own and the nation's experience. With the root of "sanguine" (*sang,* or "blood") resonating beneath the surface meaning, the passage becomes an ironic text for the drama of Edgar's descent.[48] Imminent danger forces him to kill; but his killing— the power "latent in his constitution"—soon exceeds his most sanguinary (as well as "sanguine") belief, and eventually becomes a threat to his own and others' survival. To the extent that America's defensive war for economic rights had become a revolutionary and incompletely institutionalized republicanism, and to the extent her self-defensive ploys, particularly (though not exclusively) against the Indians, were becoming an increasingly aggressive form of domestic imperialism, Brown's words apply, perhaps, with equal irony to the nation.

THE "SPRINGS OF ACTION"

These social and political overtones, however, are relatively distant echoes of a more important cultural theme sounded in *Edgar Huntly.* Brown's frontier tale investigates above all else the central moral-philosophical dilemma of the Federalist period, a dilemma underlying America's identity as well as government: the nature of humankind.

In every respect, the American of the late eighteenth century was a more independent agent than his or her predecessors. The First Great Awakening in New England had testified, as William G. McLoughlin notes, to an individualism that had displaced the older, more patriarchal social order.[49] The same individualistic mindset, strengthened by economic motives and justified by the philosophy of John Locke, had engendered the Revolution. The Revolution, in turn, had asserted individualism (the right to life, liberty, and the pursuit of happiness) on an unprecedented political scale—and elicited it, as well, from the populace. But (as Herman Melville would ask repeatedly of his mercurial Revolutionary War hero, Israel Potter) who *was* this upstart American, this individual whose agency had come to count for so much? What motivated him, and what could be expected of him? Philosophers throughout the century had been asking the same question about modern man in general, but America's presumption and sense of prospects lent it new significance.

Russel B. Nye, in sketching the philosophical background of the new nation, stresses America's felt need, in the era immediately preceding and following the Revolution, to found a "science of human nature" that would methodically explain what sort of creature man was. He records the efforts of Dr. Benjamin Rush and others to that end. But the more human nature was scrutinized, Nye notes, the more perplexing and variable it appeared, so that "The great new problem of the era after 1750 became *self*-understanding, *self*-knowledge." [50] Questions concerning the individual's moral sense, the sufficiency of reason as a guide, the role of the passions in determining human conduct became personal issues, topics for introspection (and, increasingly, subjects for novels). Such questions took on greater urgency with the founding of the Republic.

The American republic, novel though it was, was not unprecedented. An array of classical, medieval, and early modern republics had preceded ours. But all had combusted, either suddenly and spectacularly or in a succession of brush fires or their vital spark had been snuffed by tyranny. Republics were seen as "delicate polities" primed to disintegrate into either despotism or anarchy.[51] "History," as Arthur Schlesinger, Jr., summarizes, "taught the perishability of republics." [52] The Founding Fathers understood the odds against their undertaking. Men of affairs, as one historian observes, who had "seen human nature on display in the marketplace, the courtrooms, the legislative chambers," [53] they were, by and large, convinced they knew the reason for those long odds. Alexander Hamilton told the New York ratifying convention, "The tendency of things will be to depart from the republican standard. This is the real disposition of human nature." [54] James Madison wrote in *The Federalist* (#37), "The history of almost all the great councils and consultations held among mankind . . . is a history of factions, contentions and disappointments . . . which display the infirmities and depravities of the human character." [55] "The mass of men," wrote John Jay to George Washington, "are neither wise nor good." [56] John Adams concurred: "All men are men, and not angels." [57] Even Thomas Jefferson, who perhaps more than any other of the founders believed in human potential, dryly conceded that "human nature is the same on every side of the Atlantic." [58] Corrupt and self-interested, man's nature, the framers of the Constitution feared, spelled trouble for the polis.

This deduction seemed all the more inescapable (says John Patrick Diggins) when viewed in the light of classical republican theory, which relied on the citizen's capacity for "virtue"—for looking beyond his own horizons to the good of the polis. Such an idealistic motive for civic behavior, the framers objected, could never compel obedience. They sought, therefore, to base their republic on what they felt was a realistic assessment of man's nature.[59] "Whosoever would found a state, and make proper laws for the government of it," wrote John Adams, "must presume that all men are bad by nature; that they will not fail to show that natural depravity of heart whenever they have a fair opportunity."[60] The plan of the Founding Fathers, as *The Federalist* makes clear, was to use men's worst instincts, particularly their grasping self-interest, as a means of governance. The structural principle, Vernon L. Parrington adds, was to be "that of the Gothic arch—the principle of thrust and counter-thrust."[61] And so they pitted various interests, as well as the branches of government themselves, one against the other, while compelling fair play through laws and a judiciary. The resulting Constitution, harboring the spirit of such pessimists as Hobbes, Hume, and Calvin, sought to anticipate, preempt, and institutionalize the sources of dissension.

There was, however, a counter-tradition, born of the Enlightenment in France and Scotland, that viewed human nature optimistically. The French school, articulated by Rousseau and imbibed by such American writers as Thomas Paine, Philip Freneau, and Joel Barlow, held that man is essentially good, but that society and its institutions routinely corrupt his natural instincts. This countervailing spirit, which found dramatic expression in the French Revolution, also inspired the English novelists of purpose (William Godwin, Robert Bage, Mary Wollstonecraft, et al.) during the early and mid-1790s. The Scottish Common Sense philosophers, too—Francis Hutcheson, Thomas Reid, James Beattie, et al.—although socially conservative, reiterated the principle of man's goodness. These thinkers, whose ideas were widely disseminated in American universities by John Witherspoon, David Tappan, and Archibald Alexander during the early national period, when moral philosophy was considered "the most important subject required of a college student,"[62] taught that all people are born with an innate, or "common," moral sense that precedes reason. Benevolence, they held, binds society together.

The optimistic view, while scarcely in evidence at the Constitutional Convention, had nevertheless been gathering momentum on several fronts throughout the last half of the eighteenth century, as the modern concept of man as economic free agent possessed of certain inalienable rights gained ground. The new spirit was evident, for example, in the romantic celebration of "natural man" put forth by, among others,

Crèvecoeur; in the sentimentalism of Richardson, Sterne, and their American emulators; in increasingly enlightened attitudes toward childhood, child-rearing, and paternity that stressed the child's humanity and emphasized parental affection over authority;[63] in the increasing tendency for young people to choose their own marriage partners, and for their parents to countenance the decision; in the rationalistic creeds of deism, Unitarianism, and Universalism—less brooding alternatives to Calvinism—that were making noticeable, if not exactly well-worn, inroads on the country's religious landscape; and in the anti-Calvinist elements of the Second Great Awakening. (This last sphere was itself a microcosm of the issue at hand, since the Awakening was born of contradictory yearnings for reform as well as revival. Thus Timothy Dwight, the leader of the first phase of the Awakening, championed an only slightly tempered version of the Calvinism of his grandfather, Jonathan Edwards: "The truth plainly is, and ever has been: Mankind, as a body, are uniformly more or less wicked, in proportion to the means, which they possess, of wicked indulgence."[64] Dwight's successors Lyman Beecher and Nathaniel W. Taylor, on the other hand, revised the doctrine of man's total depravity and helplessness before God: mankind was "disposed toward sin," but retained some free moral agency. As Taylor explained, "Man will not do what he can do"; but Taylor's emphasis, says William McLoughlin, "was less upon 'will not' than upon 'can do.' ")[65]

The chilling turn of the French Revolution and America's own precariousness during her first two administrations forced the political aspects of this cultural debate concerning human nature uppermost. (Party alignments during the Federalist Era, indeed, embodied the larger debate: Calvinism and Federalism were generally perceived to be yoked together, as were liberal theology and Republicanism.)[66] At base, however, the questions remained moral and philosophical ones: Could human nature be trusted? schooled? perfected? contained? Was reason capable of policing man's darker impulses? Was virtue, in the classical republican sense as well as the moral sense, a quixotic or a credible ideal? Was self-constraint—and, by implication, self-government—a feasible strategy? Could humankind understand itself well enough to answer any of these questions? This is the cultural context against which Brown's fictions must finally be read, for these are the questions his works pivot on.

Each of Brown's novels meditates the nature of virtue as well as the often ambiguous motives that propel human actions, and the guises human beings adopt to hide the nature of those motives. *Edgar Huntly,* however, more than any of Brown's works, deposes virtue—especially benevolence, that "most praised of eighteenth-century virtues"[67]—and purveys a psychology of irrationality that exceeds even the terms of *Wieland.* Man, says Edgar, knows nothing of the compulsions governing the deeds he commits. And those compulsions, Brown implies, once triggered, run away with themselves, driving all else before them.

Edgar Huntly squints, as ventured earlier, toward the unmitigated skepticism of David Hume. According to Hume, man's passions, not virtue or reason, determine his conduct; reason serves merely to rationalize that conduct. Thus (to choose yet another instance of a dynamic that we have already traced at length) Edgar, seething with curiosity over Clithero's seemingly impregnable trunk, reasons that his benevolent intentions toward Clithero might be better accomplished if he were to find out more about the man. His scruples mollified by this rationale, he breaks into the trunk. Even Edgar's search for the secret spring that operates the trunk, like Brown's announced intent to seek out the "springs" of human actions ("To the Public"), recalls Hume's attempt to "discover, at least in some degree, the secret springs and principles by which the human mind is activated in its operations"—springs that may, at last, as Hume appreciates, be among the "many secret powers . . . altogether beyond our comprehension."[68] If *Edgar Huntly* amends this doctrine at all, it does so only to suggest that the very attempt to discover these secret springs may bring about more harm than good.

Hume's dark psychology led him to condone an absolutist state as the only plausible guarantor of civil society. Brown, staunch Federalist though he was by 1799,[69] would scarcely have gone that far. But there *is* something ominous about the book's closing image—that of Sarsefield's assuming the role of Clithero's "tyrant" (261)—and about Clithero's coming to greater harm because Sarsefield's tyranny isn't harsh enough. When we recall Brown's earlier portrait of Carwin's tyrant father, embodiment of an authoritarian order that invited rebellion, the apparently condign tyranny of Sarsefield takes on additional irony. *Edgar Huntly,* in short, leaves little doubt that man is essentially a lawless savage whose nature requires diligent policing. Yet, as Larzer Ziff remarks, "to view savagery as lawless is really to view democracy as ultimately unworkable."[70] This is the book's most pessimistic social corollary.

Jay Fliegelman has termed the philosophical rejection of innate depravity "the most important historical phenomenon of the eighteenth century." [71] But in Brown's America, home of the enslaved and the enlightened, the savage and the elect, the shyster and the hayseed, the rebel and the republican, the Federalist and the Republican, this debate was far from decided. *Edgar Huntly* is Brown's most unflinching attempt to unlock the mechanism of human nature and examine its propensities, to weigh in on this debate that so concerned "the condition of our country."

CHAPTER SEVEN

CHARLES BROCKDEN BROWN
AND THE AMERICAN ROMANCE

The American novel has had to find a new experience and
discover how to put that experience into art. And the process
by which it has been done was one of progressive self-discovery
for the nation. . . . But the preliminary knowledge of ourselves
out of which mature art grows is no more a sense of one's
own people and history than of one's own tensions and
inner struggles. Indeed, these are one's history
and one's sense of racial self.

MARIUS BEWLEY, *The Eccentric Design*

"Everything upon which European society had been taught to depend
for safety and stability," writes Russel B. Nye, "—church, army, aris-
tocracy, monarchy—America had jettisoned in favor of a dubious trust
in the average human being." [1] Whether that trust was justified depended, of course, on who that average human being was and on what
he or she became when empowered. *Carwin, the Biloquist* sets forth this
dilemma of identity and empowerment from its Enlightenment premises to its revolutionary implications. Carwin's plight as the son of a
tyrannical father, his forward-looking attitudes and ambitions, and his
desire to leave home enlist our sympathy, even as his biloquial experiments excite our imagination. Yet the patricide he is hinted at having
almost performed, suggestive though it is of the nation's founding impulse, horrifies, even as the power his biloquism represents frightens.
The Illuminist Ludloe illumines the subversive uses to which such a
revolutionary power might be put, either by the biloquist or one who
manipulates him: "Men, actuated by a mistaken sense of duty, might,
under this influence, be led to commission of the most flagitious, as well
as the most heroic acts" (295). And, as one of Carwin's more ill-advised
biloquial gambits makes plain (he intervenes in a robbery and accidentally causes injury to one of the victims), his power not only lends itself

to abuse but tends to produce unforeseen consequences even when used benignly.

And that is the state of Brown's world, a world that had been and was being reshaped to uncertain ends by revolutionary changes—and, particularly, as the biloquism motif suggests, by the ascent of the individual, the unfettered voice. We've considered several of these changes, only the most obvious of which were political: they include the economic revolution whose effects Brown depicted in *The Man at Home* and *Arthur Mervyn;* the moral-philosophical revolutions of rationalism, skepticism, deism, and utilitarianism whose tenets Brown probed in *Wieland, Arthur Mervyn,* and *Edgar Huntly;* the domestic heritage of Enlightenment thought—embodied, I have suggested, in the Jeffersonian world view and scrutinized in *Arthur Mervyn;* the religious revivalism that emerged both as an expression of and a reaction to the changes the Republic was undergoing, and whose debates Brown, I have suggested, gave form to in *Wieland;* and the specter of social revolution hinted at in *Arthur Mervyn. Carwin, the Biloquist* suggests, then, the extent to which the modern individual stood poised—indeed, had already begun, for better or worse—to turn an epoch on its head. But by delivering that individual, Carwin, into Ludloe's manipulative hands, it poses a worst-case scenario.

Brown's four Gothic romances show why Brown found it easy to imagine the legacy of the Enlightenment and of America in such pessimistic terms. The dialogues these fictions set up often conclude by suggesting that, however benevolent or reasonable or just or enlightened we may reckon our impulses, they are sordid at the core. Even as Carwin steals into his father's bedroom consciously intending only to play an elaborate practical joke, but, once there, behaves as if his purpose were patricide, Clara Wieland, Constantia Dudley, Arthur Mervyn, and Edgar Huntly, their virtue notwithstanding, all become implicated in crimes of mythic proportion, crimes that suggest their unawareness of the urges that govern them.

If these characters were typical Gothic villains, of course—eccentric evildoers or incarnations of the past—their deeds wouldn't matter. It's the fact that they are ordinary Americans, specimens of the "average human being" Nye alludes to, on whom the Republic depended absolutely, that makes their dramas meaningful. In Brown's Gothicism, the country boy, the well-bred young woman, the god-fearing father usurp the torchlight; the apparition leaps, not from the ancient portrait or the monastic crypt, but from the mirror.

The romances we have discussed form a tetralogy of sorts, *Wieland* dramatizing the theme of universal depravity, *Ormond* and *Arthur Mervyn* probing its validity, testing for possible exceptions, and *Edgar Huntly* redramatizing the theme with a finality that suggests the failure of examined alternatives and the futility of further discussion. Without the perspectives offered by all four books, we might be tempted to doubt whether so dark a vision were justified. As long as a determined pursuit of virtue, for instance—and fulfillment within its confines—is at least theoretically possible, then *Wieland*'s intimations of depravity can be gainsaid. *Ormond,* however, argues against this possibility—as *Arthur Mervyn* does against the prospect that some satisfactory compromise can be struck between virtue and self-indulgence. *Edgar Huntly* shows, in turn, why the box in which we file such meditations is best left unopened.

Wieland and *Edgar Huntly* alone, in fact, exhibit a closure that focuses certain cultural ironies of Brown's theme. Whereas *Wieland* begins with a civilized Christian (Wieland's father) journeying to the wilderness to convert savages, *Edgar Huntly* ends with the benevolent zealot Edgar returning from the wilderness, having become a virtual savage.[2] Both books revolve, too, the wisdom of quests and missions. *Wieland* begins in Europe with a young man (Wieland's future father) desponding over the human condition and stumbling, by chance, on the biblical injunction "Seek, and ye shall find." The young man takes up this primarily, but perhaps not exclusively, spiritual challenge, emigrating to America to pursue his quest as well as his mission to convert savages. Presumably he lapses into complacency (he postpones his mission to the Indians for fourteen years), and thereby incurs God's wrath. His consumption by fire, however, raises the outside possibility that the biblical promise has proven to be a monkey's paw; that the act of seeking that has brought him to America has led to discoveries so volatile they, as it were, ignite and consume him.[3] *Edgar Huntly* seconds that possibility. Although Edgar's is a different kind of search, its outcome likewise consumes him, destroying his seeker self. If *Wieland* holds forth the prospect of revelation, *Edgar Huntly* spurns the prospect as fatal.

Brown's romances not only unmask human nature and dramatize the dubiousness of quests to obtain and missions to convey self-knowledge; they also examine the ways in which individuals hide from self-knowledge. Brown's age, ventured Russel B. Nye, "believed in the safety of self-revelation and the danger of concealment."[4] Brown, however, counters not only that self-revelation can be as dangerous as self-ignorance, but that deep down no one really believes in it at all; that, as John Adams and Alexander Hamilton both remarked, man's reasons routinely conceal his causes.[5] *Ormond* and *Arthur Mervyn* objectify what Brown suggests is a universal tendency toward self-evasion and rationalization in various motifs—forgery, disguise, blindness, and the secret witness (who sees but doesn't acknowledge truth). Such motifs suggest our need to ignore, re-create, or paraphrase experience—to forge for ourselves, as it were, clean bills of health, despite our infected moral sense. The writing process itself is Brown's final and most ironic symbol for this paraphrasis.

The average human being, then, in whom America placed her trust wasn't Brown's idea of a mighty fortress. Yet that average individual— "asleep" or not, "infected" or not, "constitutionally defective" or not— had acceded to unprecedented power. To scrutinize him seemed incumbent—and futile; to awaken him, necessary—and rash.

The themes Brown considered in his Gothic fictions lead straight to some of those that preoccupied our most psychologically and socially attuned nineteenth-century fiction writers, many of whom, like Brown, saw themselves as creating a national fiction. Irving, Cooper, and Hawthorne, for instance, went to great lengths to root their fictions in the American historical landscape. Others—Poe and Melville—wrote tales that, while seemingly oblivious in many respects to American concerns, actually mirrored those concerns in ways as devious, sometimes, as Brown's.

The most patent link between Brown and Hawthorne is probably their shared perception of human depravity. Subtler, though, is the similarity with which both scrutinized the psychodynamics of the rationalizing process. In *The Blithedale Romance,* Hawthorne, in an experiment closely related to Brown's in *Wieland* and *Ormond,* examines the hypothetical possibility of living a principled life. Hawthorne gives his characters every chance to succeed, placing them in a community of dedicated, rational people who have severed their ties to social institutions and the past. Blithedale in some ways recalls the Wielands' isolated, Edenic community at Mettingen. Both communities include a self-deluded monomaniac (Wieland, Hollingsworth), a lovelorn, tragic heroine (Clara, Zenobia), a frustrated male who conceals his love for one of the principal females (Pleyel, Coverdale), and a devilish interloper (Carwin, Westervelt). Only with the fifth member of the community does the comparison lapse—Catherine Wieland being a virtual cipher, no match for Hawthorne's Priscilla. (For Priscilla's counterpart we must extradite Constantia Dudley, the mesmerized subject par excellence, from *Ormond*.)

Hawthorne's Transcendentalist community, however, like the Wielands' neoclassical paradise, ends in tragedy and resignation. Blithedale fails because its members, despite their best intentions, don't perceive themselves accurately. Like Brown's protagonists, they are blind to the motives that govern their conduct. The scene at Eliot's Pulpit dramatizes the self-ignorance of the various characters. This exchange shows Priscilla blind to her programmed conventionality, Zenobia blind to the way her liberal philosophy defers to sexual impulses, Hollingsworth blind to the egotism beneath his altruistic facade, and Coverdale blind to his ulterior wish for the approval of the women. Hawthorne, like Brown, uses images of disguise, masks, veils, and the theater to elaborate his vision of a world in which delusion is the overriding motif. Whereas Brown focuses specifically on the "masks" of virtue and reason, Hawthorne's every character "wears his mask"[6]—be it that of feminism (Zenobia), philanthropy (Hollingsworth), or artistic objectivity (Coverdale).

As in Brown's works, these self-evasions bode ill for the prospects of communal enterprises. If, under the best of circumstances, the individual is scarcely able to represent himself honestly, what are the chances that a representative government will honestly represent its constituents? Such self-evasions, moreover, for Hawthorne as well as Brown, incriminate the author. Both writers question whether art does not, at last, mask instead of reveal truth; whether it is not just one more medium for perpetrating illusions. Hawthorne suggests the author is a mesmerist; Brown suggests the author is a biloquist. In both metaphors, the author's power to deceive is seen as limitless; "the potency of . . . art," as terrifying.[7]

Melville too resurrects "the man unknown to himself," redramatizes the theme of self-delusion, and impugns the author as master-deceiver.[8] In *Pierre, or The Ambiguities,* the protagonist, a young poet and country gentleman named Pierre, is led by the dictates of Christian charity and fraternal duty into the incestuous embrace of his sister, Isabel. His development recalls that of Brown's own rustic penman, Arthur Mervyn, whose pursuit of virtue leads him from one incriminating situation to another, and finally into wedlock with a woman he refers to as "my dear mamma." For both authors, the irony lies in the protagonist's inability to see the impulses governing his course.

For Melville as well as for Brown and Hawthorne, this self-blindness at last becomes an inability to penetrate all reality, external or internal. Melville's protean Confidence Man, master of disguise, personifies inscrutable appearance. (He is, of course, prefigured by Brown's Carwin, Ormond, and Welbeck—all accomplished and frequent impostors. The Confidence Man feigns identities as Ormond does, and as Carwin feigns voices, playing on people's faith and gullibility for selfish ends.) All three authors depict "reality" as an artifice; Carwin's counterfeit voices, Zenobia's counterfeit flower, and most ironically, the Counterfeit Detector alluded to in *The Confidence Man,* whose purpose is to enable the owner to spot counterfeit bills—but which may itself be a hoax—suggest the skepticism to which all three authors seem driven to subscribe.

Like Brown and Hawthorne, Melville too is irked by the ease with which the prose medium can foster deceit instead of exposing it. All books are useless guides, he suggests in *Redburn.* In *Pierre,* his seamless rhetoric transcends the sentimental-domestic genre in one breath and parodies it in the next. By the end of the book we are led to suspect, along with Isabel, that "all words are arrant skirmishers"[9]—and all writers secret witnesses, concealing rather than acknowledging the truths they see.

So the artist becomes, for all three authors, a Representative Man whose illusion-making objectifies a universal tendency to falsify reality in order to live with it. If all three authors at last become unable to continue writing fiction, perhaps it is because doing so has heightened their self-consciousness to the point of paralysis; has revealed them to themselves as con men, mesmerists, biloquists—tricksters who perhaps add to, rather than dispel, the confusion, and lead their audiences further into the darkness.

Brown's fiction, I have suggested, is remarkable—even unique for its time—in its reflection of the nation's identity. Brown implies that America is too willing to sleepwalk blithely, despite contradictions that ought to have jostled her awake. If Brown, at last, comes to question the wisdom of accosting the sleepwalker, neither his basic characterization of his subject nor his underlying fear has changed, only his sense of how best to respond. Of his contemporaries, perhaps only Hugh Henry Brackenridge showed a comparable concern with the American enterprise in his fiction. Their limited similarity, though, is revealing.

Brackenridge's *Modern Chivalry,* a picaresque spoof of *Don Quixote* set in Pennsylvania, is commonly held to satirize democracy. The target of Brackenridge's satire, however, was less democracy itself than the two-fold danger democracy courted: government by incompetents, on the one hand, and aristocratic demagoguery on the other. Robert E. Spiller summarizes Brackenridge's view: "The 'rage of mere democracy' and the aristocratic urge toward domination are the Scylla and Charybdis between which a democracy must sail." [10]

Spiller's image is revealing. Brown's romances hinge repeatedly on the difficulty of maintaining balance in the face of fatal paradoxes and polarities. The dilemma Brackenridge focuses on, though—the danger of democratic versus undemocratic excess—is but one of the tensions Brown addresses. Contending polarities, in fact, are essential to Brown's myth of America—a myth that comprises not only the issue of democracy versus reaction, but also such polarities as innocence versus experience, ethics versus expedience, reason versus superstition, Enlightenment optimism versus Calvinist pessimism, nostalgia for the past versus myopic regard for the present, money versus morality, and self-idealization versus self-awareness. Such tensions lead to a fiction of ambiguity and irony; of mirror images, alter egos, doppelgängers, and racial "others"; of narrators who begin and end in what one critic has described as "the contention of the Gemini myth," with its "opposite but equally unacceptable contingencies." [11] Brown's America is a temple on a cliff, poised midway between a jealous God and an abyss. His representative American is a "man perched on a fence at midnight." [12] Clara Wieland, caught between her crazed brother and her own feverish impulses; Constantia Dudley, who parries the threat from within the family, then stabs the threat from without; Arthur Mervyn, who juggles money and morality, hoping one hand will wash the other; Edgar Huntly, caught between the sleeping savages within the cave and the waking savage without: all are tightrope walkers. The image of Edgar Huntly crossing the chasm on a felled tree trunk objectifies the predicament all Brown's protagonists face. Brown's portrayal of the American enterprise as a precarious balancing act, and of the American as an adolescent caught between a rock and a hard spot, anticipates nineteenth-century characterizations from Robin Molineux to Redburn to Huck Finn, and previews mythic scenarios in Cooper, Irving, and Poe.

James Fenimore Cooper's *The Spy: A Tale of Neutral Ground,* for instance, concerns the viability of neutrality in its broadest sense: the possibility of navigating a course between contending extremes. Harvey Birch is neither Tory nor American regular, though he passes for one and is kin to the other. His selfless ethos transcends either. Birch steers an almost impossible course between pitfalls that characterized America both in Cooper's day and in Brown's: the threat of anarchic violence (the Skinners), the allure of a sleepy complacency, and, finally—for Birch as for Arthur Mervyn, the most insidious pitfall—the lure of money. Cooper's valedictory image of his hero is that of an old man maneuvering a skiff between whirlpools.

Washington Irving's "Rip Van Winkle," like Brown's *Wieland* and *Ormond,* concerns a protagonist caught off-balance between contrary historical moments, facing the past and the present simultaneously. Left implicit in Brown's novels, the line of demarcation between past and present is explicitly defined in Irving's tale as the American Revolution. If Clara Wieland is stunned to find her next of kin suddenly become her enemy, Rip is no less stunned to find his king deposed and his townspeople hostile. Yet for both, these developments but hint of the broader inversion their once-familiar and predictable world has undergone. Both Clara and Rip find their identities called into question; they can neither explain nor exonerate themselves, nor understand the transformation that has occurred. The shift from one extreme to another has overwhelmed them, has turned their staid equilibrium into paralysis (or, in Rip's case, comic impotence).

Even Edgar Allan Poe's "The Pit and the Pendulum," though seemingly remote from national concerns, mythologizes a polarity in the American experience rendered by Brown. David Lee Clark has proposed a direct link between the cave sequence in *Edgar Huntly* and Poe's tale—a link Alan Axelrod has elaborated on.[13] But neither comparison goes far enough. Central to our early history were, of course, the alternate dangers posed by unlicensed freedom and repressive constraint. These fears, as noted earlier, can be seen in the religious and political tensions that wracked Federalist America. *Wieland* and *Ormond* objectify this twofold danger that is at once a psychological and political polarity. Constantia Dudley, for instance, withstands the threat of Ormond's libertarianism only to be trapped by the unsuspected danger of a claustrophobic virtue.

Clara Wieland, threatened alternately by the pit outside her house and the closet within, is trapped, at last, between the licentious Carwin and her brother, the closet psychotic. Poe's drama too concerns antithetical fates: one in which the victim, constrained by ropes, is threatened with death by a descending pendulum; the other in which the victim is left at liberty—to stumble in the dark, to plunge into a chasm. At last the two threats become one: the walls contract; the pit looms. The image of the pendulum highlights the alternating aspect of the peril.

Poe's tale is essentially a psychodrama. But the historical parenthesis he provides hints at a social dimension as well. Poe brackets his tale, on the one side, by the Spanish Inquisition and, on the other, by the French Revolution. Even as the French Republican army put a halt to the Inquisition in Spain in the early nineteenth century, French soldiers intervene, in Poe's story, to rescue the narrator. This, however, is no black-white opposition between evil Inquisitors and good revolutionaries. Poe begins with a Latin epigraph alluding to bloody executions committed in the Jacobin Club House in Paris.[14] His opening paragraph, moreover, includes the following passage: "The sound of the inquisitorial voices seemed merged into one indeterminate hum. It conveyed to my soul the idea of *revolution*." (The narrator is manifestly referring to a noise resembling a mill wheel revolving, but Poe's italics suggest the word has special import.) The passage suggests the indistinguishability, beyond a point, of either extreme—Inquisition or revolution—and mirrors in religio-political terms the two mutually heinous fates that menace the narrator, and that finally become one as contracting walls force him toward the pit. (Poe's first paragraph includes other images of opposites converging: black into white, angel into specter.) Even the narrator's salvation takes on an element of irony in this framework—an irony in keeping with the tone of a story in which each respite proves but a lull followed by something worse.

Poe's story, then, presents a version of the Scylla and Charybdis myth that evokes, among other things, the alternating political-cultural nightmares of repression and revolution—nightmares a republic had reason to be sensitive to. If Poe, as Clark and Axelrod imply, was inspired by the pit in *Edgar Huntly,* perhaps he also imbibed the thematic tensions—constraint versus freedom, nightmare versus reality, mania versus sanity—that Brown's novel explores.

Revolution. The word, charged as it was with contrary possibilities (social renewal vs. social suicide, Jeffersonian ideals vs. Jacobin terror), continued to haunt nineteenth-century America and the authors who depicted her. Nor, perhaps, is it surprising that shortly after midcentury both Hawthorne and Melville should have written romances (*Septimius Felton* [1861–62], *Israel Potter* [1854–55]) that took for their starting point the American Revolution. Indeed, the America of the 1850s and 1860s in many respects resembled postrevolutionary America of the 1790s. In both eras a boom-and-bust economy, regional animosity, faction, and the canker of slavery played upon the nation's nerves and cast doubts upon its ability to contain its violent impulses. And even as the failure of the French Revolution had amplified such doubts for Brown's generation, the latter generation's doubts could only have been magnified by the collapse, in 1848, of a range of democratic revolutions throughout Germany, Italy, and Austria—revolutions that tried, but failed, to reenact what the United States had accomplished.

What's striking, though, is the extent to which Hawthorne's and Melville's reflections on America's revolutionary origins and identity hark back to Brown's. All three writers suggest that America's idealized self-conception and romanticized past are at odds with reality, and that the legacy of revolution is chronic uncertainty, national anomie.

As two of his early stories suggest, Hawthorne was ambivalent about revolution in general and the American Revolution in particular. "The Gray Champion," in which a colonial mob confronts an illegitimately appointed governor and is rallied by the ghost of a departed Puritan warrior, seems to sanctify rebellion against an abusive authority. But by identifying the spectral warrior as the Roundhead regicide Colonel Goffe, Hawthorne also seems to remind the reader that the revolutionary impulse has its grotesque as well as noble aspect. That grotesque aspect is raised into sharper relief in "My Kinsman, Major Molineux," a tale set on the eve of the American Revolution. Though the prerevolutionary mob that tars and feathers Major Molineux is presumably soon to sire a glorious republic, Hawthorne imagines it as a nightriding rabble that is at best two-faced and at worst Satanic.

In *Septimius Felton*, however, one of several romances Hawthorne began toward the end of his life but failed to complete, the Revolution itself takes center stage, if only briefly. The tale's backdrop is the Battle of Concord. The protagonist, the studious and pacifistic Felton, is accosted by a lone British soldier who insists they fight. Felton kills the man in self-defense. As the Britisher lies dying, Felton ministers to his needs, hears his dying words, and receives his personal effects—

including a parchment that, Felton later learns, contains a recipe for immortality. The bond thus formed between the two youths dwarfs the political context; Felton feels the killing has made him "not a patriot, but a murderer."[15]

Had Hawthorne gone no further, his presentation would have been unconventional, but not radical. Ballasted as the tale is by more traditional views—Hawthorne remarks, for example, on the heroism and self-sacrifice the Revolution elicited from youths like Robert Hagburn, Felton's boyhood friend, and even suggests that the Revolution in some respects energized and ennobled an otherwise complacent society— *Septimius Felton* might have merely qualified the stock romantic view of the nation's birth trauma. But Hawthorne continues analyzing Felton's emotions, observing that Felton, having buried the British soldier, "wondered at the easiness with which he had acquiesced in this deed; in fact, he felt in a slight degree the effects of that taste of blood, which makes the slaying of man, like any other abuse, sometimes become a passion" (43). In so saying, Hawthorne gestures toward the universe Brown had charted, in which self-defensive violence triggers, if not masks, aggression. Even the imagery Hawthorne uses to convey this insight recalls Brown's: "Perhaps it was his Indian trait stirring in him again; at any rate, it is not delightful to observe how readily man becomes a blood-shedding animal" (43). The Revolution, then, is for Hawthorne a catalyst that, like the plague in *Arthur Mervyn* or the wilderness in *Edgar Huntly,* activates the characters, allowing us to glimpse the mainsprings of their deeds.

Of course Septimius Felton, though drawn into the Revolutionary fray, does not become a ruthless killer, as does Edgar Huntly. His encounter with the Revolution does, however, nudge him into a life of enthrallment to a revolutionary ideal—the search for immortality— that ultimately smothers, rather than enhances, his vitality. Felton's obsessive quest for an elixir of life leads him not only to forgo marriage, but to deliberately jeopardize—indeed, for all we can tell, sacrifice— his aunt's life (he experiments on her by feeding her his elixir when she becomes ill; she dies shortly thereafter). Although Hawthorne seems to abandon interest in the Revolution motif that dominates the opening pages of his tale, that motif casts a long shadow. In the middle of the romance, he introduces an image that hints as much. Felton, having been told a particularly vivid tale that intermingles the mundane and the fantastic, describes his ensuing state of mind: "It was a moment, such as I suppose all men feel . . . , when the real scene and picture of life swims, jars, shakes, seems about to be broken up and dispersed, like the picture in a smooth pond, when we disturb its smooth mirror by throwing in a stone; and though the scene soon settles itself, and looks as real as before, a haunting doubt keeps close at hand, as long as we live, asking—'Is it stable? Am I sure of it? . . . See; it trembles again, ready to dissolve' " (101). This image of chronic anxiety over a lost stability and certitude all but summons up the novel's dormant Revolutionary context. Even a relatively limited social disruption, we are led to infer, leaves a pernicious legacy.

Brown suggested the same thing in *Wieland*. The Maxwell-Stuart subplot, as noted earlier, concerns Maxwell's would-be seduction of Mrs. Stuart, who responds to Maxwell's affections, though she draws the line at committing adultery. This "revolution in her sentiments," says Clara, "was productive only of despair. Her rectitude of principle preserved her from actual guilt, but could not restore to her her ancient affection, or save her from being the prey of remorseful and impracticable wishes" (241). Mrs. Stuart's marriage—indeed, her life—is ultimately ruined by the limited "revolution" she undergoes. This cautionary tale, as we have seen, concludes a romance set in prerevolutionary, but written in postrevolutionary, America.

Melville too was concerned with the American Revolution, as grist, first, for the sort of adventure yarn that might rally the remnants of a reading public bored and scandalized by *Moby-Dick* and *Pierre, Or The Ambiguities,* but also as a glass in which to scrutinize the nation's identity. For, if *Israel Potter* is any indication, America's paradoxes had become so pronounced for Melville that the national character seemed little more than an accretion of contradictory guises. *Israel Potter* is based on the autobiography of Israel Potter, a patriot who fought in the War of Independence, but whose exploits went unsung and whose career was thwarted by captivity, poverty, and prolonged exile in England. What makes the romance especially interesting is Melville's ironic superimposition of Israel's career and America's. Israel is presented as an American avatar, his Puritan name evoking the typological mantle the colonists-cum-republicans had donned—an assertion of faith in America as the New Jerusalem that was also a presumption of divine favor, of national election. Melville cloaks his hero and narrative in this mythic mantle, entitling his chapters "Israel in the Lion's Den," "Israel's flight toward the wilderness," "Israel in Egypt," and the like, and using biblical conceits to develop Israel's story. When this rhetorical framework comes into conflict with observed reality, however, the disparity puts the nation in a troubling light.

That moment occurs in the chapters describing the epic naval battle between the *Bon Homme Richard* (captained by John Paul Jones) and the British ship *Serapis*. In previous chapters, Britain has figured as Babylon, the oppressor. But during this sequence, so indistinguishable is the violence committed by both sides that Melville, instead of portraying a victimized America/Israel beset by the British/Babylonian lion, inverts the mythological framework, likening the antagonists to mutually wicked cities of the plain and the battle to a maritime re-enactment of the destruction of Sodom and Gomorrah.[16] During this battle, Potter, who has earlier distinguished himself by his humanity (even forbearing to kill King George III, when the opportunity presents itself), displays only a shrewd ferocity, dropping a grenade into a hatchway, at one point, and killing twenty men. And this inscrutable blend of savagery and civility, dramatized most unforgettably in the character of John Paul Jones (whose sword arm is decorated with cabalistic tattoos concealed by Parisian lace), renders America's revolution in a new—or perhaps old—light.

For if the Revolution, instead of inaugurating a New Jerusalem, signified only tribal warfare in modern dress, then what of the high-minded ideals and rhetoric that accompanied it? Brown's *Ormond* dramatizes the same paradox. Not unlike John Paul Jones, Ormond is the quintessentially civil savage, a Cossack avenger-cum-rationalistic dandy whose grand ambitions and radical rhetoric sanction murder and violence. Martinette de Beauvais, meanwhile, a self-styled lover of liberty and revolutionary, has murdered friends and associates for ideological reasons. If, like Constantia, we admire her role in the American Revolution, we also recoil from her fanaticism in the French Revolution. And that (one imagines Melville saying) is precisely the point. Revolution, and the American revolutionary identity, are fatally two-sided.

If not multisided. Melville seems, at last, thoroughly bewildered in his attempts to read the national ego. His native son, Israel, spends so much time changing clothes, swapping disguises, and pretending to be someone else that we are eventually forced to wonder who he really is. " 'Who *are* you?' " asks the British officer-of-the-deck aboard the *Shuttle* (Israel, having climbed aboard prematurely during a skirmish, is pretending to be a crewman); " 'What's your name? Are you down in the ship's books, or at all in the records of nature?' " Israel buys time with an outrageous song-and-dance, but is peremptorily tagged a "ghost" and a "phantom" (139)—Melville, as it were, throwing his hands up at the riddle.

Melville's "ghost" is the comic version of America's identity quandary. Brown's "apparition" in the glass is its Gothic counterpart: an apparition that, oblivious to morality, reason, laws, and social compacts, mocks the young citizen's modish pretensions even as it strikes him down. And, possible though it is to dismiss the apparition as a paranoid fantasy on Brown's part, or one more ironic deposition of Lockean psychology (one of Locke's metaphors for the mind was a mirror), its leap from the glass into the "reality" of the tale gives it an urgency that is hard to blink away. Whatever this brawny, misshapen nightmare from the streets of America finally signifies, Brown has glimpsed him, fixed him in the same frame as his protagonist, and snapped the picture. In investigating this American animus, he creates as trenchant a fiction as any in the national literature.

NOTES

PREFACE

1. Charles Brockden Brown, "Article XXXIV," *Monthly Magazine and American Review* 3 (1800): 266.

2. See Cathy N. Davidson, *Revolution and the Word: The Rise of the Novel in America* (New York: Oxford University Press, 1987), p. 84; Bernard Rosenthal, ed., *Critical Essays on Charles Brockden Brown* (Boston: G. K. Hall, 1981), pp. 2, 18n.

CHAPTER ONE
The Condition of Our Country

1. Richard Hofstadter, *The Paranoid Style in American Politics* (New York: Knopf, 1965), p. 13.

2. Charles Brockden Brown, "Advertisement for *Skywalk*," in *The Rhapsodist and Other Uncollected Writings by Charles Brockden Brown*, ed. Harry R. Warfel (New York: Scholars Facsimiles and Reprints, 1943), p. 136.

3. Charles Brockden Brown, Letter to William Dunlap (Nov. 28, 1794), reprinted in William Dunlap's *The Life of Charles Brockden Brown: Together with Selections from the Rarest of His Printed Works, from His Original Letters, and from His Manuscripts before Unpublished*, 2 vols. (Philadelphia: James P. Parke, 1815), 2:92.

4. Charles Brockden Brown, *The Novels and Related Works of Charles Brockden Brown*, Bicentennial Edition, 6 vols., gen. ed. Sydney J. Krause (Kent, Ohio: Kent State University Press, 1977–1987), vol. 3: *Arthur Mervyn; or Memoirs of the Year 1793* (1980), 2 parts, ed. with Historical Essay by Norman S. Grabo, 1:148.

5. See, for instance, Harry R. Warfel, *Charles Brockden Brown: American Gothic Novelist* (Gainesville: University of Florida Press, 1949), pp. 7, 26–27; Donald A. Ringe, *Charles Brockden Brown* (New York: Twayne, 1966), p. 18; Ernest Marchand, Introduction to Charles Brockden Brown's *Ormond; Or The Secret Witness*, ed. Ernest Marchand (New York: Hafner, 1937), pp. x–xiii; Fred Lewis Pattee, Introduction to *Wieland, or The Transformation*, ed. Fred Lewis Pattee (New York: Hafner, 1926), pp. x, xi.

6. David Lee Clark, *Charles Brockden Brown: Pioneer Voice of America* (Durham: Duke University Press, 1952), p. 44.

7. David Lee Clark describes Brown's romances as "novels of purpose—their purpose being the dissemination of the radicalism then stirring the people of two continents" (*Pioneer Voice*, p. 192). Ernest Marchand characterizes them as an "exploitation of the liberalism of the Revolutionary epoch"—and specifically of Godwinism (Introduction to *Ormond*, pp. xiii, xxix). Harry Levin finds Brown

"completely committed to the postulates of the Enlightenment" (*The Power of Blackness* [New York: Random House, 1958; Vintage Books], p. 21). Robert E. Spiller et al. view Brown as "a liberal Utopian dreamer, resting his hopes for mankind somewhat vaguely in the rule of reason, the rejection of the incubus of Calvinism, and an appeal to benevolence in the human spirit" (*Literary History of the United States*, rev. ed. in 1 vol. [New York: Macmillan, 1955], pp. 181–82). Discussions of *Wieland*, in particular, elicit more characterizations of Brown as an exponent of enlightened reason and Godwinian values: see Warfel, *Gothic Novelist*, pp. 108–9; Lulu Rumsey Wiley, *The Sources and Influences of the Novels of Charles Brockden Brown* (New York: Vantage Press, 1950), p. 98; Lillie Deming Loshe, *Early American Novels: 1789–1830* (New York: N.p., 1907), p. 50.

8. Warner B. Berthoff first posed this view ("Adventures of the Young Man: An Approach to Charles Brockden Brown," *American Quarterly* 9 [1957]: 421–34). Recent readings by Cathy N. Davidson and Sydney J. Krause have extended the case (see Bernard Rosenthal, ed., *Critical Essays on Charles Brockden Brown* [Boston: G. K. Hall, 1981], pp. 82, 186).

9. Based on Brown's correspondence, Robert D. Arner suggests that he was in the Federalist camp by April 1799 (Sydney J. Krause, gen. ed., *The Novels and Related Works of Charles Brockden Brown*, Bicentennial Edition, 6 vols. [Kent, Ohio: Kent State University Press, 1977–1987], vol. 6: *Alcuin: A Dialogue and Memoirs of Stephen Calvert* [1987], ed. with Historical Essay by Robert D. Arner, p. 296). His fictions, however, continue to examine issues rather than to declaim, and his first published polemic dates from 1803.

10. Alan Axelrod, *Charles Brockden Brown: An American Tale* (Austin: University of Texas Press, 1983), p. 73.

11. Daniel J. Boorstin, *The Americans: The Colonial Experience* (New York: Random House, 1958; Vintage Books), pp. 63–64, 47.

12. Clark, *Pioneer Voice*, p. 13.

13. Henry F. May, *The Enlightenment in America* (New York: Oxford University Press, 1976), p. 198.

14. Cathy N. Davidson, *Revolution and the Word: The Rise of the Novel in America* (New York: Oxford University Press, 1987), p. 107.

15. Charles Brockden Brown, *An Address to the Government of the United States on the Cession of Louisiana to the French, and on the Late Breach of Treaty by the Spaniards, including the translation of a memorial, on the War of St. Domingo, and the Cession of Mississippi to France, drawn up by a Counsellor of State* (Philadelphia: John Conrad and Co., 1803), p. 35.

16. Charles Brockden Brown, *An Address to the Congress of the United States on the Utility and Justice of Restrictions upon Foreign Commerce* (Philadelphia: C. and A. Conrad, 1809), pp. 36, 37.

17. Rod W. Horton and Herbert W. Edwards, *Backgrounds of American Literary Thought*, 2d ed. (New York: Meredith Publishing Co., 1967; Appleton, Century, Crofts), pp. 92–93, 140–41.

18. Michael T. Gilmore, ed., *Early American Literature: A Collection of Critical Essays* (Englewood Cliffs, N.J.: Prentice Hall, 1980), pp. 6–7.

19. Richard Chase, *The American Novel and Its Tradition* (Garden City, N.Y.: Doubleday, 1957; Anchor Books), p. 1.

20. Donald Robinson, *Slavery in the Structure of American Politics, 1765–1820* (New York: Harcourt, Brace, Jovanovich, 1971), p. 368; Oliver Ransford, *The Slave Trade: The Story of Transatlantic Slavery* (London: John Murray, Ltd., 1971), pp. 210, 213.

21. Alexis de Tocqueville, *Democracy in America*, 2 vols., ed. Phillips Bradley (New York: Random House, 1945; Vintage Books), 1:354.

22. Murray L. Wax, *Indian Americans: Unity and Diversity* (Englewood Cliffs, N.J.: Prentice-Hall, 1971), p. 32.

23. Ibid., pp. 32–33.

24. John C. Miller, *The Federalist Era* (New York: Harper, 1960; Colophon Books), pp. 157–58.

25. Ibid., p. 241.

26. Ibid., p. 128.

27. Vernon Louis Parrington, *Main Currents in American Thought*, 2 vols. (New York: Harcourt, Brace and World, 1927; Harvest Books), vol. 1: *The Colonial Mind: 1620–1800*, p. 328.

28. Miller, *The Federalist Era*, pp. 160, 161.

29. Vernon Stauffer, "New England and the Bavarian Illuminati" (Ph.D. diss., Columbia University, 1918), p. 106.

30. Miller, *The Federalist Era*, p. 164.

31. Claude G. Bowers, *Jefferson and Hamilton: The Struggle for Democracy in America* (New York: Houghton-Mifflin, 1925), pp. 273, 284.

32. Miller, *The Federalist Era*, p. 231.

33. Parrington, *The Colonial Mind*, p. 328.

34. John Bach McMaster, *History of the People of the United States*, 8 vols. (New York: D. Appleton and Co., 1914), 2:384.

35. Stauffer, "Illuminati," p. 134.

36. Morton Borden, *Parties and Politics in the Early Republic, 1789–1815* (New York: Thomas Y. Crowell Co., 1967), p. 28.

37. Stauffer, "Illuminati," pp. 124–25.

CHAPTER TWO
Toward an American Romance

1. Charles Brockden Brown, "Advertisement for *Skywalk*," in *The Rhapsodist and Other Uncollected Writings by Charles Brockden Brown*, ed. Harry R. Warfel (New York: Scholars Facsimiles and Reprints, 1943), p. 136.

2. Emory Elliott, "Narrative Unity and Moral Resolution in *Arthur Mervyn*," in

Critical Essays on Charles Brockden Brown, ed. Bernard Rosenthal (Boston: G. K. Hall, 1981), p. 142.

3. "To I. E. Rosenberg," Charles Brockden Brown, *The Novels and Related Works of Charles Brockden Brown,* Bicentennial Edition, 6 vols., gen. ed. Sydney J. Krause (Kent, Ohio: Kent State University Press, 1977–1987), vol. 2: *Ormond; or The Secret Witness* (1982), ed. with Historical Essay by Russel B. Nye, p. 3.

4. Ibid., vol. 6: *Alcuin, A Dialogue and Memoirs of Stephen Calvert* (1987), ed. with Historical Essay by Robert D. Arner, p. 7.

5. William Dunlap, *The Life of Charles Brockden Brown: Together with Selections from the Rarest of His Printed Works, from His Original Letters, and from His Manuscripts before Unpublished,* 2 vols. (Philadelphia: James P. Parke, 1815), 2:92.

6. Charles Brockden Brown, "The Difference between History and Romance," *Monthly Magazine and American Review* (April 1800): 251, 253.

7. David Lee Clark, *Charles Brockden Brown: Pioneer Voice of America* (Durham: Duke University Press, 1952), p. 160.

8. Charles Brockden Brown, *The Novels and Related Works of Charles Brockden Brown,* Bicentennial Edition, 6 vols., gen. ed. Sydney J. Krause (Kent, Ohio: Kent State University Press, 1977–1987), vol. 4: *Edgar Huntly; or Memoirs of a Sleep-Walker* (1984), with Historical Essay by Sydney J. Krause, pp. 363–65. Krause, in an extended footnote, traces the fate of *Skywalk* based on diary entries of William Dunlap and Elihu Smith, who read the work in manuscript during the spring of 1798.

9. Russel B. Nye calls it a series of essays, but "not a novel" (Bicentennial *Ormond,* pp. 302, 303). Norman S. Grabo calls it "a series of . . . loosely organized sketches and essays" (Historical Essay, *The Novels and Related Works of Charles Brockden Brown,* Bicentennial Edition, 6 vols., gen. ed. Sydney J. Krause [Kent, Ohio: Kent State University Press, 1977–1987]), vol. 3: *Arthur Mervyn,* p. 451).

10. Clark, *Pioneer Voice,* p. 161; Harry R. Warfel, *Charles Brockden Brown: American Gothic Novelist* (Gainesville: University of Florida Press, 1949), p. 93.

11. Brown, *The Rhapsodist,* p. 69. All future references to *The Man at Home* will be included within parentheses in the text.

12. The narrator speaks, for instance, of "a revolution in . . . character and fortune" (47); of "the momentous revolutions in human life" (56); and of a "revolution [in his condition]" (45).

13. Robert S. Levine, "Arthur Mervyn's Revolutions," *Studies in American Fiction* 12(1984): 146.

14. Robert E. Spiller, *The Cycle of American Literature* (New York: Macmillan, 1955; Mentor Books), p. ix.

15. Charles Brockden Brown, *Wieland, or The Transformation, together with Memoirs of Carwin, the Biloquist,* ed. Fred Lewis Pattee (New York: Hafner, 1926), p. xlii–xliv.

16. David Lyttle, "The Case against Carwin," *Nineteenth Century Fiction* 26

(1971): 264. Lyttle—rightly, I believe—finds this bedroom episode to be "the most memorable scene in *Carwin,*" the "only dramatically coherent part of the entire narrative." Besides proposing a biographical context for the scene (Brown, he notes, had rebelled against his own father by forsaking law), Lyttle alleges a direct relationship between *Memoirs of Carwin, the Biloquist* and *Wieland:* "Carwin's adventures after he leaves his father's house . . . are in substance the preparation for his successful and violent revenge against the surrogate father figure in *Wieland*" (264).

17. Jay Fliegelman, *Prodigals and Pilgrims: The American Revolution against Patriarchal Authority, 1750–1800* (New York: Cambridge University Press, 1982), pp. 1–5, 13, 116–18, 168, passim.

18. William G. McLoughlin, *Revivals, Awakenings, and Reform* (Chicago: University of Chicago Press, 1978), p. 47.

19. Admittedly the motif is more complex than I'm making it sound here. Biloquism isn't only an act of self-assertion. It's also an act of self-effacement—a kind of secret speaking up. This power allows Carwin to be both godlike and childlike. The motif becomes considerably more complex in *Wieland,* where the notion of throwing one's voice and speaking in voices carries psychological, historical, and aesthetic connotations. But even as the Carwin of the fragment isn't the complex character the Carwin of *Wieland* is, neither is the biloquism motif of *Carwin* as complex as the same motif in *Wieland.* In the *Carwin* fragment, biloquism, I would contend, *is* essentially a magnified, self-conscious (i.e., fetishized) form of speech.

CHAPTER THREE
Wieland: Domestic Depravity and
the Extraordinary Silence

1. Charles Brockden Brown, *The Novels and Related Works of Charles Brockden Brown,* Bicentennial Edition, 6 vols., gen. ed. Sydney J. Krause (Kent, Ohio: Kent State University Press, 1977–1987), vol. 1: *Wieland, or The Transformation: An American Tale; Memoirs of Carwin the Biloquist* (1977), ed. with Historical Essay by Alexander Cowie, p. 36. All future references to *Wieland* will be based on the Bicentennial Edition and included in parentheses within the text.

2. Cowie, Historical Essay to Bicentennial *Wieland,* pp. 319, 323. Shirley Samuels proposes that another analogue for *Wieland* may be the *Narrative for William Beadle,* which also recounts a murder-suicide episode of the late Revolutionary War period ("*Wieland:* Alien and Infidel," *Early American Literature* 25 [1990]: 58).

3. Larzer Ziff, "A Reading of *Wieland,*" *PMLA* 77 (1962): 54, 52.

4. Scott Garrow and John Cleman have perhaps come closest, highlighting Clara's stated fear that she too might become prey to the forces that have transformed her brother. Garrow fails, however, to adequately trace such a transforma-

tion and identifies it, somewhat disappointingly, as merely a "lapse into senseless depression and irrational action motivated by fear," while Cleman too timidly concludes that "the question of [Clara's] innocence is not clear-cut." (Scott Garrow, "Character Transformation in *Wieland*," *Southern Quarterly* 4 [1966]: 316; John Cleman, "Ambiguous Evil: A Study of Villains and Heroes in Charles Brockden Brown's Major Novels," *Early American Literature* 10 [1975]: 207.) Cynthia S. Jordan, meanwhile, who has presented the most detailed reading of Clara's dark side, sees no transformation in Clara's behavior—only chronic untrustworthiness. Jordan argues that Clara may actually have killed her brother, so suspect is her narrative. ("On Rereading *Wieland:* 'The Folly of Precipitate Conclusions,' " *Early American Literature* 16 [1981]: 154–74.)

   5. Edwin S. Fussell, "*Wieland:* A Literary and Historical Reading," *Early American Literature* 18 (1983–84): 174, 181.

   6. Leslie A. Fiedler, *Love and Death in the American Novel* (London: Paladin, 1960), p. 142.

   7. David Brion Davis, *Homicide in American Fiction, 1798–1860* (Ithaca, N.Y.: Cornell University Press, 1957), p. 89.

   8. Charles Brockden Brown, review of *The Foresters: An American Tale,* by Jeremy Belknap, *Monthly Magazine and American Review* 2 (1799): 432; letter to Joseph Bringhurst, May 30, 1792, quoted by Norman S. Grabo, Historical Essay to *Arthur Mervyn,* in *The Novels and Related Works of Charles Brockden Brown,* Bicentennial Edition, 6 vols., gen. ed. Sydney J. Krause (Kent, Ohio: Kent State University Press, 1977–1987), 3: 463.

   9. Roberta F. Weldon explores the relationship between *Wieland* and Cicero's *Pro Cluentio* in her article "Charles Brockden Brown's *Wieland:* A Family Tragedy," *Studies in American Fiction* 12 (1984): 2–3.

   10. Roberta F. Weldon, in characterizing the Wieland family as a microcosm of American individuality and insularity, proposes that "in the failure of this family it is possible to see a failure of the national experiment" ("A Family Tragedy," p. 8). Cynthia S. Jordan, stressing the extent to which *Wieland* renders all narrative endings—especially happy ones—suspect, concludes, "Brown's message to a young nation, nurtured from its infancy on stories promising its own happy ending . . . has only too recently begun to be heard." (Jordan, "On Rereading *Wieland,*" p. 171.) Alan Axelrod finds that the complex tension of opposites Brown's novels generate—a tension he associates with the frontier experience— makes them "American tales." (*Charles Brockden Brown: An American Tale* [Austin: University of Texas Press, 1983], pp. 28, 35.) Robert S. Levine, Jay Fliegelman, and Shirley Samuels forge stronger links between Brown's works and the national context. Levine, scrutinizing Brown's Illuminati motif in light of contemporaneous American fears, astutely observes that "the image of an unsuspecting America under assault is at the symbolic core of all of Brown's major fiction." ("Villainy and the Fear of Conspiracy in Charles Brockden Brown's *Ormond,*" *Early American*

Literature 15 [1980]: 138.) Levine, moreover, discovers in Clara Wieland's mental revolutions intimations of the political instabilities of the time. ("Arthur Mervyn's Revolutions," *Studies in American Fiction* 12 [1984]: 147.) Jay Fliegelman, in examining *Wieland,* likewise finds that "Brown's novel of authority misrepresented and authority imagined is a terrifying post–French Revolutionary account of the fallibility of the human mind, and, by extension, of democracy itself." (*Prodigals and Pilgrims: The American Revolution against Patriarchal Authority, 1750–1800* [New York: Cambridge University Press, 1982], p. 239.) Shirley Samuels notes that "the novel does not universally assign guilt to Carwin as the alien intruder, and indeed often questions whether we should instead blame, as the narrator, Clara, sometimes believes we should, the interior of the home itself." ("Wieland: Alien and Infidel," p. 52.) Samuels also documents the extent to which political and religious extremism were perceived in the 1790s as species of harlotry that put the Republic at risk of dissolution.

11. Fussell, "A Literary and Historical Reading," pp. 171–86, especially p. 184.

12. Davis, *Homicide,* p. 50.

13. Edmund Burke, *Reflections on the Revolution in France* (Garden City, N.Y.: Doubleday, 1973; Anchor Books), p. 77.

14. John Patrick Diggins, *The Lost Soul of American Politics: Virtue, Self-Interest, and the Foundations of Liberalism* (New York: Basic Books, 1984), p. 96.

15. John C. Miller, *The Federalist Era* (New York: Harper, 1960; Colophon Books), p. 233; Morton Borden, *Parties and Politics in the Early Republic, 1789–1815* (New York: Thomas Y. Crowell, 1967), p. 28.

16. Carl Nelson, "The Novels of Charles Brockden Brown: Irony and Illusion" (Ph.D. diss., State University of New York at Binghamton, 1970), p. 75.

17. Carwin's most frequently thrown command, "Hold, hold!" is only one of several echoes of *Macbeth* in *Wieland.* One of the ironic implications of this likeness may be that Brown's sleepwalking leading lady becomes a counterpart to Lady Macbeth.

18. William G. McLoughlin, *Revivals, Awakenings, and Reform* (Chicago: University of Chicago Press, 1978), p. 97. Jay Fliegelman also links these two social events, *Prodigals and Pilgrims,* p. 157.

19. Sam Adams's phrase—see McLoughlin, *Revivals,* p. 97.

20. Thomas Paine, "Common Sense," *The Thomas Paine Reader,* ed. Michael Foot and Isaac Kramnick (New York: Viking Penguin, 1987), pp. 65, 113.

21. Alan Heimert, *Religion and the American Mind* (Cambridge: Harvard University Press, 1966), p. 535.

22. Concerning the political origins of the Second Great Awakening, see especially Heimert, *Religion and the American Mind,* p. 534; Russel B. Nye, *The Cultural Life of the New Nation* (New York: Harper and Row, 1960; Harper Torchbooks), p. 213; and Perry Miller, *The Life of the Mind in America* (New York: Harcourt Brace Jovanovich, 1965), p. 4. (Miller cautions against overemphasizing the Great Re-

vival's political element, but nonetheless credits it prominently.) As to the dating of the Great Revival, a few historians—notably Donald G. Mathews ("The Second Great Awakening as an Organizing Process, 1780–1830: An Hypothesis," *American Quarterly* 21 [1969]: 23–43) and John B. Boles (*The Great Revival: 1787–1805* [Lexington: University Press of Kentucky, 1972]) hold that it began as early as the 1780s (though Boles refers mainly to its southern manifestation); generally, though, historians date it from the years just prior to 1800. See McLoughlin, Miller, Heimert, Nye, Winthrop S. Hudson (*The Great Tradition of the American Churches* [New York: Harper and Row, 1953]), and William Warren Sweet (*Religion in the Development of American Culture* [New York: Scribners, 1952]).

23. Boles, *The Great Revival*, p. 174.

24. McLoughlin, *Revivals*, pp. 104, 98–99.

25. Mathews, "Organizing Process," p. 33.

26. McLoughlin, *Revivals*, pp. 99–100, 110.

27. Nye, *The Cultural Life of the New Nation*, pp. 207–8.

28. Paul Himmel Eller, "Revivalism and the German Churches in Pennsylvania, 1783–1816" (Ph.D. diss., University of Chicago, 1933), p. 213; Nye, *The Cultural Life of the New Nation*, p. 213. McLoughlin has shown that the Jeffersonian intellectuals, many of whom were Unitarians, were also, in their turn, perceived as an elite by Jackson's constituency in the "burned-over" districts (*Revivals*, p. 115).

29. Eller, "Revivalism in Pennsylvania," p. 213; Nye, *The Cultural Life of the New Nation*, pp. 220–21; McLoughlin, *Revivals*, p. 139; Miller, *The Life of the Mind*, p. 30.

30. Nye, *The Cultural Life of the New Nation*, pp. 228, 226.

31. McLoughlin, *Revivals*, p. 12.

32. Ibid., p. 2.

33. Ibid., p. 14.

34. Fussell, "A Literary and Historical Reading," pp. 176–77, 181.

35. Fliegelman, *Prodigals and Pilgrims*, p. 239.

36. Thomas Paine, *The Age of Reason, Part One*, reprinted in *The Thomas Paine Reader*, p. 400.

37. John G. Frank, "The Wieland Family in Charles Brockden Brown's *Wieland*," *Monatshifte* 42 (1950): 349.

38. Nye, *The Cultural Life of the New Nation*, p. 207.

39. Ibid.

40. Norman S. Grabo, *The Coincidental Art of Charles Brockden Brown* (Chapel Hill: University of North Carolina Press, 1981), p. 9.

41. Quaker Henry Fell, for example, in a letter to his wife Margaret (February 19, 1657), wrote, "The Lord's word was a fire and a hammer in me" (Swarthmore Hall Collection of Quaker Manuscripts). See also George Barrell Cheever's "The Fire and the Hammer of God's Word Against Slavery," a speech given at the American Abolition Society in New York City (1858), and Orson Parker's *The Fire*

and the Hammer: Revivals and How to Promote Them (Boston: James H. Earle, 1877).

42. Frank, "The Wieland Family," p. 353.

43. William Bouwsma, *John Calvin: A Sixteenth-Century Portrait* (New York: Oxford University Press, 1988), pp. 45, 46, 48.

44. McLoughlin, *Revivals,* p. 66.

45. Sweet, *Religion in American Culture,* p. 53.

46. Nye, *The Cultural Life of the New Nation,* p. 204.

47. Heimert, *Religion and the American Mind,* p. 131.

48. Nye, *The Cultural Life of the New Nation,* p. 212.

49. Richard Hofstadter, *America at 1750: A Social Portrait* (New York: Knopf, 1971), p. xvi.

50. William Dunlap, *The Life of Charles Brockden Brown: Together with Selections from the Rarest of His Printed Works, from His Original Letters, and from His Manuscripts before Unpublished,* 2 vols. (Philadelphia: James P. Parke, 1815), 1:71.

51. Bernard Rosenthal, intro. to *Critical Essays on Charles Brockden Brown,* ed. Bernard Rosenthal (Boston: G. K. Hall, 1981), pp. 11, 2.

52. Ibid., p. 12.

53. David Lee Clark, *Charles Brockden Brown: Pioneer Voice of America* (Durham: Duke University Press, 1952), pp. 168–69.

54. See Chapter 6.

55. Charles Brockden Brown, *The Novels and Related Works of Charles Brockden Brown,* Bicentennial Edition, 6 vols., gen. ed. Sydney J. Krause (Kent, Ohio: Kent State University Press, 1977–1987), vol. 4: *Edgar Huntly; or Memoirs of a Sleep-Walker* (1984), with Historical Essay by Sydney J. Krause, p. 162.

56. Clark, *Pioneer Voice,* p. 161.

57. Sacvan Bercovitch, *The Puritan Origins of the American Self* (New Haven: Yale University Press, 1975), p. 36, passim; *The American Jeremiad* (Madison: University of Wisconsin Press, 1978), pp. 69–73.

58. McLoughlin, *Revivals,* p. 105.

59. Warfel, *Gothic Novelist,* p. 11.

60. Clark, *Pioneer Voice,* p. 8.

CHAPTER FOUR
Ormond: Fever in the Land

1. Charles Brockden Brown, *The Novels and Related Works of Charles Brockden Brown,* Bicentennial Edition, 6 vols., gen. ed. Sydney J. Krause (Kent, Ohio: Kent State University Press, 1977–1987), vol. 2: *Ormond; or The Secret Witness* (1982), ed. with Historical Essay by Russel B. Nye, p. 285. All future references to *Ormond* will be based on this edition and included in parentheses within the text.

2. David Lee Clark praises its "unity of impression" (*Charles Brockden Brown: Pioneer Voice of America* [Durham: Duke University Press, 1952], p. 173); Warner B.

Berthoff finds it "the weakest of Brown's major novels," formalistically ("The Literary Career of Charles Brockden Brown" [Ph.D. diss., Harvard University, 1954], p. 142); Ernest Marchand finds Ormond "the most fully and consistently developed" of Brown's characters (Introduction to *Ormond; Or The Secret Witness* [New York: Hafner, 1962], p. xxix); William L. Hedges finds Ormond's character "grossly aborted" ("Charles Brockden Brown and the Culture of Contradictions," *Early American Literature* 9 [1974]: 116).

3. Marchand and Lillie Deming Loshe praise its "realism" (Introduction to *Ormond*, pp. xvii–xxix; *Early American Novels, 1789–1830* [New York: N.p., 1907], p. 44); Berthoff praises its "symbolism" ("Literary Career," p. 143); Richard Chase its "melodrama" (*The American Novel and Its Tradition* [Garden City, N.Y.: Doubleday, 1957; Anchor Books], p. 30); and Kenneth Bernard its "tragedy" ("The Novels of Charles Brockden Brown: Studies in Meaning" [Ph.D. diss., Columbia University, 1962], p. 171).

4. Paul C. Rodgers, Jr. shows just how moot in his summary of critical responses ("Brown's *Ormond*: The Fruits of Improvisation," *American Quarterly* 26 [1974]: 4–22).

5. Hedges, "Culture of Contradictions," p. 118.

6. In the first camp are Samuel Martin Vilas (*Charles Brockden Brown: A Study of Early American Fiction* [Burlington, Vt.: Free Press, 1904], p. 28) and Clark. Warfel's view that *Ormond* is a critique of rationalism and a plea for the corrective of religion (*Charles Brockden Brown: American Gothic Novelist* [Gainesville: University of Florida Press, 1949], pp. 131, 136) is only a slightly inflected version of the same line. Paul Witherington's "Narrative Technique in the Novels of Charles Brockden Brown" (Ph.D. diss., University of Texas, 1964), p. 140, is another rehash of the novel as edifying morality play. In the second camp are Ernest Marchand, whose detailed introduction to the Hafner edition of the book dotes on Brown's interest in the marvelous, his fascination with the Illuminati, etc.; Donald A. Ringe, for whom the book conveys the need for a practical education for women (*Charles Brockden Brown* [New York: Twayne, 1966], pp. 50, 53); Sydney J. Krause, who values the novel as an elaboration of the Richardsonian seduction motif ("*Ormond*: Seduction in a New Key," *American Literature* 44 [1973]: 570–71); William L. Hedges, who depicts it as an abortive debate on the validity of marriage ("Culture of Contradictions," p. 117); Michael Davitt Bell, who considers Ormond primarily as an avatar of the artist as "master of duplicity" (" 'The Double-Tongued Deceiver': Sincerity and Duplicity in the Novels of Charles Brockden Brown," *Early American Literature* 9 [1974]: 149); and Robert R. Hare ("Charles Brockden Brown's *Ormond*: The Influence of Rousseau, Godwin, and Mary Wollstonecraft" [Ph.D. diss., University of Maryland, 1967], pp. 178, 213).

7. Bernard stresses Ormond's fall from power at the hands of an "unworthy" rival ("Studies in Meaning," pp. 171–72). James R. Russo argues that Constantia is actually a conniving murderer ("The Tangled Web of Deception and Impos-

ture in Charles Brockden Brown's *Ormond,*" *Early American Literature* 14 [1979]: 205–27). Rodgers contends that Brown, harried by a printer's deadline, had "no controlling . . . end in view" ("Fruits of Improvisation," pp. 7, 21). Robert E. Hemenway prefigures this position ("The Novels of Charles Brockden Brown: A Critical Study" [Ph.D. diss., Kent State University, 1966], p. 178).

8. Paul Witherington, "Charles Brockden Brown: A Bibliographical Essay," *Early American Literature* 9 (1974): 183.

9. Berthoff, "Literary Career," pp. 143, 146, 163.

10. Ibid., p. 163.

11. Hemenway, "A Critical Study," pp. 75–77. The *Wieland* outline formed the basis for Hemenway's 1966 dissertation.

12. Both Hawthorne and Melville would be similarly frustrated by the limits of allegory, and would turn instead to the possibilities afforded by symbolism.

13. Anne Dalke, "Original Vice: The Political Implications of Incest in the Early American Novel," *Early American Literature* 23 (1988): 188.

14. Leslie Fiedler has noted that "geography in the United States is mythological," and that American writers have always used it thus (*The Return of the Vanishing American* [New York: Stein and Day, 1969], p. 16). Brown is no exception. Once a childhood preoccupation, geography becomes in his novels the agent of a symbolic purpose. In *Jane Talbot* geography is an explicit metaphor, the heroine finding it an apt emblem for that process of interior analysis that she (like Brown) delights in: "I have always found great pleasure in dissecting, as it were, my heart; uncovering . . . its many folds, and laying it before you, as a country is shewn on a map" (Charles Brockden Brown, *The Novels and Related Works of Charles Brockden Brown,* Bicentennial Edition, 6 vols., gen. ed. Sydney J. Krause [Kent, Ohio: Kent State University Press, 1977–1987], vol. 5: *Clara Howard; In a Series of Letters with Jane Talbot: A Novel* [1986], ed. with Historical Essay by Donald A. Ringe, p. 255). Geography for Brown, then, is never mere geography; nor is it an accident, perhaps, that *Ormond,* his psychodrama of revolution, is set in Philadelphia.

15. Clark, *Pioneer Voice,* p. 161.

16. Vernon Louis Parrington, *Main Currents in American Thought,* 2 vols. (New York: Harcourt, Brace, World, 1927; Harvest Books), vol. 1: *The Colonial Mind: 1620–1800,* p. 205.

17. Benjamin Rush, *The Selected Writings of Benjamin Rush,* ed. Dagobert D. Runes (New York: Philosophical Library, 1947), p. 407.

18. Edmund Burke, *Reflections on the Revolution in France* (Garden City, N.Y.: Doubleday, 1973; Anchor Books), p. 76.

19. Charles Downer Hazen, *Contemporary American Opinion of the French Revolution* (Baltimore: Johns Hopkins University Press, 1897), p. 295.

20. Alexander Hamilton, James Madison, John Jay, *The Federalist Papers,* ed. Roy P. Fairfield (Garden City, N.Y.: Doubleday, 1961), Numbers 10, 14, 16, 34, 37: pp. 16, 23, 24, 41, 90, 103.

21. Timothy Dwight, "The Duty of Americans in the Present Crisis" (New Haven: Thomas and Samuel Green, 1798), pp. 13, 21.

22. See, most recently, Alan Axelrod, *Charles Brockden Brown: An American Tale* (Austin: University of Texas Press, 1983), p. 118.

23. Throughout the plague sequence, Constantia willfully insists on going where the plague is—sometimes despite her father's prohibition. Thus she sets out to visit Mathews, their landlord, in disobedience to her father's command, and Mary Whiston, despite her father's despairing plea.

24. Ringe, *Charles Brockden Brown*, p. 55; Warfel, *Gothic Novelist*, p. 131.

25. Rodgers, "The Fruits of Improvisation," p. 21; Hedges, "Culture of Contradictions," p. 118.

26. See Brown's "Adini" fragment (William Dunlap, *The Life of Charles Brockden Brown: Together with Selections from the Rarest of His Printed Works, from His Original Letters, and from His Manuscripts before Unpublished,* 2 vols. [Philadelphia: James P. Parke, 1815], 2:153).

27. I don't mean to suggest that Constantia should have received Ormond's affections, much less let him have his way with her, or that her virtue, like her reason, hasn't stood her in good stead—only that it is a sort of iron door sealing out options as well as villains.

28. The house in which the final encounter occurs is developed, rather heavy-handedly, as a metaphor for Constantia herself, and virgin vulnerability in general. (It is characterized, for instance, by its "chastity of ornament" [265].) The house, however, is constructed "of stone, . . . snow-white," and of "cement uncommonly tenacious"—images more suggestive of cold sterility and impregnability.

29. Robert S. Levine, "Villainy and the Fear of Conspiracy in Charles Brockden Brown's *Ormond,*" *Early American Literature* 15(1980): 126; Richard Hofstadter, *The Paranoid Style in American Politics* (New York: Knopf, 1965), p. 10.

30. Rodgers, "Fruits of Improvisation," pp. 9–10.

31. John Robison, *Proofs of a Conspiracy against All the Religions and Governments of Europe, Carried on in the Secret Meetings of Free Masons, Illuminati, and Reading Societies* (New York: George Forman, 1798), pp. 15, 159.

32. Dwight, "The Duty of Americans," pp. 13, 14, 24.

33. Vernon Stauffer, "New England and the Bavarian Illuminati" (Ph.D. diss., Columbia University, 1918), pp. 238, 252, 253.

34. Warfel, *Gothic Novelist*, p. 98. Robert S. Levine adduces further circumstantial evidence suggesting that Brown must have known of Morse's and Dwight's ideas, and probably Robison's as well. See "Villainy," p. 139n.

35. Stauffer, "Illuminati," pp. 124, 125, 129.

36. Parrington, *The Colonial Mind*, p. 329.

37. Charles and Mary Beard, *The Rise of American Civilization* (New York: Macmillan, 1927; rev. ed., 1934), pp. 384, 386.

38. Sophia reiterates this romantic position in political-cultural terms in her

comparison of Europe and America. She finds that "in the former, all things tended to extremes, whereas in the latter, all things tended to the same level" (236). Far from preferring America's intermediacy, however, she finds that genius, virtue, and happiness are "distinguished by a sort of mediocrity here"; she bemoans the fact that in America men are "strangers to the heights of enjoyment and the depths of misery" to which Europeans are accustomed (236).

39. Robison, *Proofs of a Conspiracy,* pp. 98, 109.

40. Several variations are rung, in Brown's other novels, on this theme: the box, once opened, cannot be closed (*Edgar Huntly*); the house or room, once entered, becomes a prison (*Arthur Mervyn, Ormond, Wieland*); the pit or abyss, once glimpsed, soon engulfs (*Wieland, Edgar Huntly*).

41. As the *Oxford English Dictionary* shows, "secret" means "silent," and is particularly applicable to the Deity. (Rev. ed. [1961], s.v. "secret.")

42. We are told of the deaths of Stephen Dudley's father and Martinette's father, and learn of the sudden deaths of Monrose, Baxter, Helena's father, and Dudley himself. Sophia's father, meanwhile, is conspicuously absent from her early history, though extensive detail is accorded her mother.

43. Bell, "Sincerity and Duplicity," p. 148. See also Terence Martin, *The Instructed Vision: Scottish Common Sense Philosophy and the Origins of American Fiction* (Bloomington: Indiana University Press, 1961), pp. 61–63.

44. Bell, "Sincerity and Duplicity," p. 149.

45. Brown, "To I. E. Rosenberg," Bicentennial *Ormond,* p. 3.

CHAPTER FIVE
Arthur Mervyn: Sickness, Success,
and the Recompense of Virtue

1. Only Ben Franklin comes close. James H. Justus, in fact, has suggested that Franklin's autobiography may have been a source for *Arthur Mervyn* ("Arthur Mervyn, American," *American Literature* 42 [1970]: 306–7).

2. Charles Brockden Brown, *The Novels and Related Works of Charles Brockden Brown,* Bicentennial Edition, 6 vols., gen. ed. Sydney J. Krause (Kent, Ohio: Kent State University Press, 1977–1987), vol. 3: *Arthur Mervyn; or Memoirs of the Year 1793,* 2 parts, ed. with Historical Essay by Norman S. Grabo, 1:204. Further references to *Arthur Mervyn* will be based on this edition and will appear in parentheses within the text.

3. R. W. B. Lewis, *The American Adam* (Chicago: University of Chicago Press, 1955), p. 97.

4. Warner B. Berthoff, Introduction to *Arthur Mervyn; or Memoirs of the Year 1793,* by Charles Brockden Brown, ed. Warner B. Berthoff (New York: Holt, Rinehart and Winston, 1962), p. xvii.

5. Kenneth Bernard, "The Novels of Charles Brockden Brown: Studies in

Meaning" (Ph.D. diss., Columbia University, 1962), p. 145; Donald A. Ringe, *Charles Brockden Brown* (New York: Twayne, 1966), pp. 82–83; Patrick Brancaccio, "Studied Ambiguities: *Arthur Mervyn* and the Problem of the Unreliable Narrator," *American Literature* 42 (1970): 18–27; Carl Nelson, "The Novels of Charles Brockden Brown: Irony and Illusion" (Ph.D. diss., State University of New York at Binghamton, 1970), pp. 97, 100; William L. Hedges, "Charles Brockden Brown and the Culture of Contradictions," *Early American Literature* 9 (1974): 124–25; Justus, "Mervyn, American," pp. 303, 314; and Michael Davitt Bell, " 'The Double-Tongued Deceiver': Sincerity and Duplicity in the Novels of Charles Brockden Brown," *Early American Literature* 9 (1974): 157.

6. Hedges, "Culture of Contradictions," p. 137.

7. See Emory Elliott's "Narrative Unity and Moral Resolution in *Arthur Mervyn*," *Critical Essays on Charles Brockden Brown,* ed. Bernard Rosenthal (Boston: G. K. Hall, 1981); Robert S. Levine, "Arthur Mervyn's Revolutions," *Studies in American Fiction* 12 (1984): 145–60; Norman S. Grabo, *The Coincidental Art of Charles Brockden Brown* (Chapel Hill: University of North Carolina Press, 1981).

8. Berthoff, Introduction to *Arthur Mervyn,* p. xvii.

9. Ringe, *Charles Brockden Brown,* p. 78.

10. *Oxford English Dictionary* (rev. ed. 1961), s.v. "notoriety," "homage." The conceit "mask of virtue" is Brown's own (*Ormond,* p. 226).

11. Warner B. Berthoff, "Adventures of the Young Man: An Approach to Charles Brockden Brown," *American Quarterly* 9 (1957): 426; Nelson, "Irony and Illusion," p. 136.

12. Perhaps the term "saint" as I have used it suggests R. W. B. Lewis's *The Picaresque Saint: Representative Figures in Contemporary Fiction* (New York: Lippincott, 1959). The association is welcome, since it reiterates the modernity of *Arthur Mervyn.* (Lewis conceives of the "picaresque saint" as the embodiment of the present paradoxical age.) Lewis's emphasis, though, differs from mine: his heroes are saints in the guise of rogues, while Arthur Mervyn is at once both and neither.

13. Carl Nelson has documented Arthur's "tendency to romanticize reality," citing, among other things, Arthur's wry comparison of his own adventures to *Arabian Nights* fantasies. ("Irony and Illusion," p. 126.) If Arthur's preening virtue is the dominant chord, this romanticizing tendency is perhaps the subdominant chord in his character.

14. Charles Brockden Brown, *The Novels and Related Works of Charles Brockden Brown,* Bicentennial Edition, 6 vols., gen. ed. Sydney J. Krause (Kent, Ohio: Kent State University Press, 1977–1987), vol. 6: *Alcuin: A Dialogue and Memoirs of Stephen Calvert* (1987), ed. with Historical Essay by Robert D. Arner, p. 20.

15. Welbeck too is, of course, adept at duplicity, but he lacks Arthur's genius for wearing different masks simultaneously, and he knows himself too well to be gulled by the deceptions he practices on others. His confessions, on the contrary, reveal an inability to hide from his misdeeds.

16. Nelson, "Irony and Illusion," p. 123.

17. Berthoff, Introduction to *Arthur Mervyn*, p. xviii.

18. Just after Welbeck has given Arthur $40,000 to return to the Maurices, Dr. Stevens sees Arthur, cash in hand, preparing to depart—presumably for Baltimore, where the Maurices live—and stammers several pertinent questions that suggest his doubts have returned in force.

19. Both Arthur and Welbeck admit to moral blindness on several occasions (see 1:87, 96, 107, 115, 221). Arthur, moreover, is forever walking, stumbling, or being left alone in the dark.

20. Charles Downer Hazen, *Contemporary American Opinion of the French Revolution* (Baltimore: Johns Hopkins University Press, 1897), p. 164.

21. Robert S. Levine, "Arthur Mervyn's Revolutions," *Studies in American Fiction* 12(1984): 147.

22. Ibid., p. 149.

23. One contemporary account, "Picture of St. Domingo," *The Literary Magazine and American Register* 1 (1803–1804): 447, suggests the figure may have been as high as 52,000. I have used Oliver Ransford's more conservative figure (*The Slave Trade: The Story of Transatlantic Slavery* [London: John Murray, Ltd., 1971], p. 213).

24. "Extracts from a Speech on the Slave Trade, Spoken before the Council of the Leeward Islands, March, 1798," *The Literary Magazine and American Register* 2 (1804): 46.

25. Howard Zinn, *A People's History of the United States* (New York: Harper and Row, 1980), p. 34.

26. J. H. Powell, *Bring Out Your Dead: The Great Plague of Yellow Fever in Philadelphia* (Philadelphia: University of Pennsylvania Press, 1974), pp. 95, 99; Mathew Carey, *A Short Account of the Malignant Fever, lately prevalent in Philadelphia* (Philadelphia, 1794), p. 63.

27. David Robinson, *Slavery and the Structure of American Politics, 1765–1820* (New York: Harcourt, Brace, Jovanovich, 1971), p. 364; William H. McNeill, *Plagues and Peoples* (New York: Doubleday, 1976; Anchor Books), p. 235.

28. David Lee Clark, *Charles Brockden Brown: Pioneer Voice of America* (Durham: Duke University Press, 1952), p. 234.

29. Charles Brockden Brown, *An Address to the Government of the United States on the Cession of Louisiana to the French, and on the Late Breach of Treaty by the Spaniards, including the translation of a memorial, on the War of St. Domingo, and the Cession of Mississippi to France, drawn up by a Counsellor of State* (Philadelphia: John Conrad and Co., 1803), pp. 37, 44, 45.

30. Ibid., p. 48.

31. "H. L.," "Thoughts on the Probable Termination of Negro Slavery in the United States of America," *Monthly Magazine and American Review* 2 (1800): 84.

32. "On the Consequences of Abolishing the Slave Trade to the West Indian Colonies," *Literary Magazine and American Register* 4 (1805): 375.

33. Charles Brockden Brown, "The Death of Cicero: A Fragment," annexed to vol. 3 of *Edgar Huntly; or Memoirs of a Sleep-Walker* (Philadelphia: H. Maxwell, 1799), p. 41.

34. Brown, *Address to the Government*, p. 44.

35. Robinson, *Slavery*, p. 7. Philip S. Foner too details America's dread of a slave revolt and documents its basis in reality: *History of Black Americans* (Westport, Conn.: Greenwood Press, 1975), pp. 451–55.

36. Robinson, *Slavery*, p. 299.

37. Ibid., pp. 313–14.

38. Thomas Jefferson, *The Writings of Thomas Jefferson*, ed. Albert Ellery Bergh, 20 vols. (Washington, D.C.: Thomas Jefferson Memorial Association, 1907), 9:418.

39. Norman S. Grabo, Historical Essay, Bicentennial *Arthur Mervyn*, p. 448.

40. Charles Brockden Brown, "On the State of American Literature," *Monthly Magazine and American Review* 1 (1799): 16.

41. Arthur G. Kimball, *Rational Fictions: A Study of Charles Brockden Brown* (McMinnville, Oreg.: Linfield Research Institute, 1968), p. 176.

42. Justus, "Mervyn, American," p. 315.

43. Benjamin Rush, *The Selected Writings of Benjamin Rush*, ed. Dagobert D. Runes (New York: Philosophical Library, 1947), p. 331.

44. Jefferson, *Writings*, 3:269.

45. Michael T. Gilmore, ed., *Early American Literature: A Collection of Critical Essays* (Englewood Cliffs, N.J.: Prentice-Hall, 1980), p. 6.

46. Elliott, "Narrative Unity," pp. 153–54.

47. Powell, *Bring Out Your Dead*, p. 102.

48. Herman Melville, *The Writings of Herman Melville*, Northwestern-Newberry Edition, 15 vols., Harrison Hayford et al. gen. eds. (Evanston and Chicago, 1968–), vol. 7: *Pierre, or The Ambiguities* (1971), ed. Harrison Hayford et al., p. 214.

49. John Peden, "Thomas Jefferson and Charles Brockden Brown," *Briarcliff Quarterly* 2 (1944): 68.

50. Daniel J. Boorstin, *The Lost World of Thomas Jefferson* (New York: Holt, 1948), pp. 9, 11–12.

51. Jefferson, *Writings*, 7:463.

52. Ibid., 3:268–69.

53. Ibid., 7:463.

54. Ibid., 15:76.

55. Boorstin, *Jefferson*, pp. 148–49.

56. Jefferson, *Writings*, 14:143.

57. Boorstin, *Jefferson*, pp. 41–49, especially 41, 43, 49.

58. Ibid., p. 29.

59. Ibid., pp. 7–8.

60. Ibid., p. 243.

61. Ibid., pp. 128–29.

62. Charles A. and Mary A. Beard, *History of the United States: A Study in American Civilization* (New York: Macmillan, 1921; rev. ed., 1929), p. 225.

63. Richard Hofstadter, gen. ed., *The American Republic,* 2 vols. (Englewood Cliffs, N.J.: Prentice-Hall, 1959), vol. 1: *The American Republic to 1865,* by Richard Hofstadter, William Miller, and Daniel Aaron, p. 317.

64. History shows Napoleon hadn't a sou to spare for occupying Louisiana—he had all but lost his most important naval base in the west (St. Domingue), and found his other western holdings threatened by slave revolts. Meanwhile, Britain's unimpeachable control of the sea left France little hope of recouping her losses or resupplying her outposts. In short, France was encumbered on several fronts, and consequently posed no real threat to the United States. (See Hofstadter, *American Republic,* p. 316; Harry Carman, William G. Kimmel, Mabel G. Walker, *Historic Currents in Changing America* [Philadelphia: John G. Winston Co., 1940], p. 170.)

65. Boorstin, *Jefferson,* p. 35.

66. Ibid., p. 4.

67. Ibid., p. 8.

CHAPTER SIX
Edgar Huntly: Somnambulism vs. Self-Knowledge

1. D. H. Lawrence, *Studies in Classic American Literature* (Garden City: Doubleday, 1953; Anchor Books), p. 73.

2. Charles Brockden Brown, *The Novels and Related Works of Charles Brockden Brown,* Bicentennial Edition, 6 vols., gen. ed. Sydney J. Krause (Kent, Ohio: Kent State University Press, 1977–1987), vol. 4: *Edgar Huntly; or Memoirs of a Sleep-Walker* (1984), ed. with Historical Essay by Sydney J. Krause, p. 114. Subsequent references to *Edgar Huntly* will be based on the Bicentennial Edition and will appear in parentheses in the text.

3. Harry R. Warfel, *Charles Brockden Brown: American Gothic Novelist* (Gainesville: University of Florida Press, 1949), pp. 159–60; Donald A. Ringe, *Charles Brockden Brown* (New York: Twayne, 1966), pp. 94, 96, 106; David Stineback, Introduction to *Edgar Huntly; or Memoirs of a Sleepwalker,* by Charles Brockden Brown (New Haven: College and University Press, 1973), p. 17.

4. John Cleman, "Ambiguous Evil: A Study of Villains and Heroes in Charles Brockden Brown's Major Novels," *Early American Literature* 10 (1975): 210–11.

5. Kenneth Bernard, "The Novels of Charles Brockden Brown: Studies in Meaning" (Ph.D. diss., Columbia University, 1962), p. 94.

6. This last reading both oversimplifies Edgar's character and undermines the universality of his tale by setting him apart from the rest of humanity, much the way allegations of Clara Wieland's insanity deny the vision of universal depravity her experience seems to point to. Yes, these characters *may* simply be crazy, though neither gives that immediate impression. But to dismiss them as such is to risk enacting, as a reader, the sort of defensive rationalizing Brown's characters often

engage in: a strategy that puts disturbing insights at arm's length. See David Lee Clark, Introduction to *Edgar Huntly; or Memoirs of a Sleep-Walker*, by Charles Brockden Brown (New York: Macmillan, 1928), p. xx; Ringe, *Charles Brockden Brown*, p. 93.

7. Leslie A. Fiedler, *Love and Death in the American Novel* (London: Paladin, 1960), p. 147.

8. The answers I have suggested are those posed by Donald Ringe and Kenneth Bernard.

9. Fiedler, *Love and Death*, pp. 148–49.

10. Arthur G. Kimball, "Savages and Savagism: Brockden Brown's Dramatic Irony," *Studies in Romanticism* 6 (1967): 214, 224.

11. William L. Hedges, "Charles Brockden Brown and the Culture of Contradictions," *Early American Literature* 9 (1974): 133.

12. Ibid., p. 134.

13. Fiedler, *Love and Death*, p. 148.

14. Bernard, "Studies in Meaning," p. 103. Richard Slotkin has seconded Bernard's stance (*Regeneration through Violence* [Middletown, Conn.: Wesleyan University Press, 1973], p. 386).

15. Bernard, "Studies in Meaning," p. 98.

16. See Terry Heller's *The Delights of Terror* (Urbana: University of Illinois Press, 1987), p. 35, for a similar reading. Heller suggests that, because Huntly has benefited from Waldegrave's death, he suffers from a subconscious guilt that leads him to identify with Clithero and try to cure him.

17. Robert E. Hemenway, "The Novels of Charles Brockden Brown: A Critical Study" (Ph.D. diss., Kent State University, 1966), p. 258.

18. [Charles Brockden Brown], Preface to "Somnambulism: A Fragment," *The Literary Magazine and American Register* 3 (1805): 335.

19. This newspaper account seems to have inspired three separate attempts at fiction on Brown's part: the lost *Skywalk, or The Man Unknown to Himself; Edgar Huntly; or Memoirs of a Sleep-Walker*, which incorporated *Skywalk;* and "Somnambulism: A Fragment," in which certain key images and proper names (i.e., the tree, Inglefield, Norwood) recall *Edgar Huntly*. Did Brown write this third version because he felt he had reneged on his original purpose in *Edgar Huntly* by ascribing Waldegrave's death to an Indian, rather than to Huntly himself?

20. Bernard, "Studies in Meaning," p. 120.

21. Ibid., p. 121.

22. Cleman, "Ambiguous Evil," pp. 208–10.

23. Ibid., p. 209.

24. Dieter Schultz, "*Edgar Huntly* as Quest Romance," *American Literature* 43 (1971): 324–25.

25. Stineback, Introduction to *Edgar Huntly*, p. 22.

26. W. H. Auden, "The Guilty Vicarage," *The Dyer's Hand and Other Essays* (New York: Random House, 1948; Vintage Books, 1968), p. 158.

27. Brown is particularly perceptive in recognizing the ambiguous nature of our evasions and the part of us that relishes what the rest of us is ashamed of. Edgar's and Clithero's chests not only hide secrets; they preserve them. Neither Edgar nor Clithero wants to destroy his secrets, only to keep them out of sight. When the sleepwalking Edgar, haunted by a dream in which Waldegrave insists he fulfill some obligation (destroy Waldegrave's heretical letters), removes Waldegrave's letters and hides them in the attic, he temporizes—as Kenneth Bernard suggests—both destroying and preserving them simultaneously ("Studies in Meaning," p. 99).

28. *Oxford English Dictionary,* rev. ed. (1961), s.v. "spring." This pun on "spring" recalls the secret-witness motif in *Ormond.* By suggesting the "spring" is also a "springe," Brown denies the hero the option of secretly witnessing (as Edgar plans to do), of peering at, then secreting, the truth. The trunk-trap, moreover, mirrors Constantia's house-prison: whereas Constantia's virtue, based at least in part on willed self-blindness, is a prison she can enter and inhabit but cannot leave, Edgar's self-ignorance (also characterized as blindness) is a box that, once opened, cannot be closed—one that must be witnessed, and witnessed to, forever. Brown's pun on "spring" goes further: "spring" also signifies "watercourse"—a symbol, in *Edgar Huntly,* for the subterranean passions our actions derive from. Brown, moreover, in his preface ("To the Public"), uses the word *spring* in yet another related context: "the 'springs' of action" (3). Beyond helping to bind the book's symbolic threads, this sophisticated pun would seem, by itself, to refute the frequent contention that Brown was a slapdash craftsman. On the contrary, Brown, like his creation Clithero, was enough of a craftsman to deploy his devices unobtrusively.

29. "Trunk" also recalls, however fleetingly, the tree beneath which Waldegrave was killed. Edgar searches that trunk for clues to the assassin, even as he later searches Clithero's trunk.

30. Their literal import aside, Edgar's words also recall his unsanctioned examination of Clithero's trunk. During that episode, he "sought . . . for [a] spring" (117) that, once found, opened the trunk—but failed to assuage his curiosity. Perhaps Brown's allusive word choice is meant to suggest that in this instance too Edgar is fueling rather than assuaging his drives—a possibility supported by the murder he soon commits. Or perhaps it merely conveys the continuing irrevocability of Edgar's acts.

31. Brown's water symbol is complex: at some level, it suggests ritual cleansing as well as unconscious compulsion. Edgar's drinking and partial immersion following his first killing is perhaps more accurately seen as both an act of purification *and* the abatement of an instinctual drive. Edgar's desire, after killing the Indians at Deb's hut, to find a spring stems from a need to "wash away the blood" from his cheek (198) as well as from the promptings of thirst. Nevertheless, the main function of the symbol seems to be to identify Edgar's killing with internal urge, rather than external circumstance.

32. The words in which Edgar recounts this fifth killing testify to an urge to kill

that bypasses rational necessity. After having precipitated the killing by cocking his rifle, Edgar both lies to himself and tells the truth when he says: "I saw that forbearance was no longer in my power; but my heart sunk while I complied with what may surely be deemed an indispensable necessity" (201). The "indispensable necessity" is not external, as he would like to think, but internal.

33. David Lee Clark, *Charles Brockden Brown: Pioneer Voice of America* (Durham: Duke University Press, 1952), pp. 194–95; Warfel, *Gothic Novelist*, p. 164.

34. Cf. Brown's earlier fictions, in which the "malady" and "pest" was generally associated with passion rather than thought—though ideological and ethical imperatives (*Ormond*) partake, admittedly, of both.

35. Sydney J. Krause argues, indeed, that Brown's attitude toward the Indians was far from enlightened. Brown, he says, "concedes the shared assumption about generalized Indians" held by Benjamin Rush and many others of his time—that the Indians occupy the lowest rung of humanity. (Historical Essay to the Bicentennial *Edgar Huntly*, pp. 363–65.) Be that as it may—and his evidence, consisting of Brown's characterization of the Indians in *An Address to the Government of the United States on the Cession of Louisiana to the French; and on the Late Breach of Treaty by the Spaniards, including the translation of a memorial, on the War of St. Domingo, and the Cession of Mississippi to France, drawn up by a Counsellor of State* (Philadelphia: John Conrad and Co., 1803) and his marginalia in Constantin Volney's *View of the Climate and Soil of the United States, to which are annexed some accounts of Florida, the French colony on the Scioto, certain Canadian colonies, and the savages or natives*, trans. Charles Brockden Brown (Philadelphia: John Conrad and Co., 1804), isn't compelling. The drama and imagery of *Edgar Huntly* allow for little substantial differentiation between Indian and white, savage and civilized. Whether Brown was consciously aware of the ironies he had constructed is, of course, another question. Perhaps, indeed, he was objectively analyzing his own racism. Or maybe, as the implications of his tale dawned on him, he felt obliged to adopt a more conventional attitude.

36. Fiedler, *Love and Death*, pp. 150–51.

37. Brown, in this passage, transforms Edgar into a Clithero-like "maniac" as well as into an Indian—identifying Edgar with both his alter egos simultaneously. "Ruffian," moreover, is the term Brown uses to describe the Indian assassin who he says killed Waldegrave (281).

38. Hedges, "Culture of Contradictions," p. 133.

39. Norman Grabo, *The Coincidental Art of Charles Brockden Brown* (Chapel Hill: University of North Carolina Press, 1981), p. 68.

40. Fiedler, *Love and Death*, p. 150.

41. Brown too uses the term ironically: Edgar hopes to "claim consanguinity" with the Selbys (226). The blood relationship, though, is finally a bloody nexus.

42. We have already seen one other instance in which Brown uses the metaphor of sleep to portray the nation's condition (*An Address to the Government. . .*). A more explicit example occurs in Brown's pamphlet *The British Treaty* (Philadelphia:

N.p., 1807; reprinted, London: John Joseph Stockdale, 1808), p. vii., in which Brown, in a preface, writes: "A late event [Britain's attack on the *Chesapeake*] has roused public indignation; Americans, waking from their long dream, appear desirous of knowing their condition." Until the end of his career, then, Brown seems to have been piqued by America's apparent unawareness of self.

43. J. Hector St. John de Crèvecoeur, *Letters from an American Farmer* (New York: New American Library, 1963; Signet Classics), p. 66.

44. Russel B. Nye, *The Cultural Life of the New Nation* (New York: Harper, 1963; Harper Torchbooks), p. 220.

45. Slotkin, *Regeneration through Violence*, p. 334, 346.

46. Kimball, "Savages and Savagism," p. 219.

47. Albert K. Weinberg, *Manifest Destiny* (Baltimore: Johns Hopkins University Press, 1935; Quadrangle, 1963), pp. 18–22.

48. The word is an icon of Brown's dramatic theme: the perils of a blithe optimism ("sanguinity") that harbors a potential for violence (suggested by the root, *sang*).

49. William G. McLoughlin, *Revivals, Awakenings, and Reform* (Chicago: University of Chicago Press, 1978), p. 53.

50. Nye, *The Cultural Life of the New Nation*, pp. 23–24.

51. Bernard Bailyn, ed., *Pamphlets of the American Revolution*, 2 vols. (Cambridge, Mass.: Harvard University Press, 1965), 1:85.

52. Arthur Schlesinger, Jr., *The Cycles of American History* (New York: Houghton-Mifflin, 1987), p. 6.

53. Richard Hofstadter, *The American Political Tradition* (New York: Alfred A. Knopf, 1948; Vintage Books), p. 3.

54. Schlesinger, *Cycles*, p. 7.

55. Roy P. Fairfield, ed., *The Federalist Papers*, by Alexander Hamilton, James Madison, John Jay (Garden City, N.Y.: Doubleday, 1961), p. 103.

56. Letter to George Washington, June 27, 1786: *Great Issues in American History* 2 vols., ed. Richard Hofstadter (New York: Random House, 1958; Vintage Books), 1:81.

57. John Adams, *The Works of John Adams* 10 vols., ed. Charles Francis Adams (Boston: Little, Brown, 1856), 4:408.

58. Thomas Jefferson, *Notes on the State of Virginia* (New York: Harper and Row, 1964), p. 115.

59. John Patrick Diggins, *The Lost Soul of American Politics: Virtue, Self-Interest, and the Foundations of Liberalism* (New York: Basic Books, 1984), p. 24.

60. Adams, *Works*, p. 408.

61. Vernon Louis Parrington, *Main Currents in American Thought*, 2 vols. (New York: Harcourt, Brace and World, 1927; Harvest Books), vol. 1: *The Colonial Mind: 1620–1800*, p. 322.

62. Nye, *The Cultural Life of the New Nation*, p. 36.

63. Jay Fliegelman, *Prodigals and Pilgrims: The American Revolution against Patriarchal Authority, 1750–1800* (New York: Cambridge University Press, 1982), p. 10.

64. Timothy Dwight, *Theology Explained and Defended in a Series of Sermons,* 12th ed., 4 vols. (New York, 1846), 1:471.

65. McLoughlin, *Revivals,* p. 118.

66. Nye, *The Cultural Life of the New Nation,* p. 213.

67. Fliegelman, *Prodigals and Pilgrims,* p. 101.

68. David Hume, *An Enquiry Concerning Human Understanding,* ed. Eric Steinberg (Indianapolis: Hackett, 1977), pp. 8, 58.

69. Robert D. Arner, in the Historical Essay to the Bicentennial *Alcuin* (Charles Brockden Brown, *The Novels and Related Works of Charles Brockden Brown,* Bicentennial Edition, 6 vols., gen. ed. Sydney J. Krause [Kent, Ohio: Kent State University Press, 1977–1987], vol. 6: *Alcuin: A Dialogue and Memoirs of Stephen Calvert* [1987]), infers as much from a letter written by Brown (April 1799) three months before the publication of *Edgar Huntly.*

70. Larzer Ziff, *Literary Democracy* (New York: Penguin, 1981), pp. 7–8.

71. Fliegelman, *Prodigals and Pilgrims,* p. 129.

CHAPTER SEVEN
Charles Brockden Brown
and the American Romance

1. Russel B. Nye, *The Cultural Life of the New Nation* (New York: Harper and Row, 1960; Harper Torchbooks), p. 100.

2. One of *Edgar Huntly's* innovations is its inversion of the captivity narrative, whose archetype, Richard Slotkin has argued, is the Christian who, despite trials among the savages, retains his or her faith and civilized values intact (*Regeneration through Violence* [Middletown, Conn.: Wesleyan University Press, 1973], p. 111).

3. I am indebted to Joseph V. Ridgely for this insight.

4. Russel B. Nye, Historical Essay to *Ormond,* Charles Brockden Brown, *The Novels and Related Works of Charles Brockden Brown,* Bicentennial Edition, 6 vols., gen. ed. Sydney J. Krause (Kent, Ohio: Kent State University Press, 1977–1987), vol 2: *Ormond; or The Secret Witness* (1982), p. 322.

5. See John Patrick Diggins, *The Lost Soul of American Politics: Virtue, Self-Interest, and the Foundations of Liberalism* (New York: Basic Books, 1984), pp. 90, 92.

6. Hyatt H. Waggoner, *Hawthorne: A Critical Study* (Cambridge: Harvard University Press, 1955; rev. ed. 1963), p. 193.

7. Nathaniel Hawthorne, *The Centenary Edition of the Works of Nathaniel Hawthorne,* 20 vols., William Charvat, Roy Harvey Pearce, Claude M. Simpson, gen. eds. (Columbus, Ohio: Ohio State University Press, 1962–1988), vol. 3: *The Blithedale Romance and Fanshawe* (1964), ed. Fredson Bowers, p. 198.

8. Whether Melville read Brown we don't know for sure. It seems likely, though, in light of Hawthorne's remark, in 1846, that "no American writer enjoys a more classic reputation on this side of the water" than Brown (Alexander Cowie, Historical Essay to *Wieland*, Charles Brockden Brown, *The Novels and Related Works of Charles Brockden Brown*, Bicentennial Edition, 6 vols., gen. ed. Sydney J. Krause [Kent, Ohio: Kent State University Press, 1977–1987], vol. 1: *Wieland, or The Transformation: An American Tale; Memoirs of Carwin, the Biloquist* [1977], p. 345).

9. Herman Melville, *The Writings of Herman Melville*, Northwestern-Newberry Edition, 15 vols., Harrison Hayford, Hershel Parker, G. Thomas Tanselle, gen. eds. (Evanston and Chicago, 1968–), vol. 7: *Pierre, or The Ambiguities* (1971), ed. Harrison Hayford et al., p. 333.

10. Robert E. Spiller et al., eds., *Literary History of the United States*, rev. ed. in 1 vol. (New York: Macmillan, 1955), pp. 179, 180.

11. Carl Nelson, "The Novels of Charles Brockden Brown: Irony and Illusion" (Ph.D. diss., State University of New York at Binghamton, 1970), p. 26.

12. Brown, Bicentennial *Ormond*, p. 76.

13. David Lee Clark, Introduction to *Edgar Huntly; or Memoirs of a Sleep-Walker*, by Charles Brockden Brown (New York: Macmillan, 1928), editor's note, p. 165; Alan Axelrod, *Charles Brockden Brown: An American Tale* (Austin: University of Texas Press, 1983), pp. 9–13, 36–46.

14. Poe's epigraph reads as follows: "Impia tortorum longas hic turba furores / Sanguinis innocui, non satiata, aluit. / Sospite nunc patrie, fracto nunc funeris antro, / Mors ubi dira fuit vita salusque patent" (Quatrain composed for the gates of a market to be erected upon the site of the Jacobin Club House at Paris) (Edgar Allan Poe, *Complete Works of Edgar Allan Poe*, First Ed., 17 vols., ed. James A Harrison [New York: AMS Press, 1965], vol. 5: *Tales*, p. 67.) The translation is as follows: "Here an impious crowd of executioners nourished, / not sated, the long tumult of innocent blood. / Now, with the country safe and the burial vault broken, / life and health will flourish where the terrors of death reigned."

15. Hawthorne, *Centenary Works*, vol. 13: *The Elixir of Life Manuscripts: Septimius Felton, Septimius Norton, The Dolliver Romance* (1977), ed. Edward H. Davidson, Claude M. Simpson, L. Neal Smith, p. 268. Future references to this work will appear in parentheses in the text.

16. Melville, *Writings*, vol. 8: *Israel Potter: His Fifty Years of Exile* (1982), ed. Harrison Hayford et al., p. 130. All other references to this work will appear in parentheses within the text.

INDEX